ANDALUZ

ANDALUZ

A Food Journey through Southern Spain

written and photographed by

Fiona Dunlop

Interlink Books

An imprint of Interlink Publishing Group, Inc.
Northampton, Massachusetts

First published 2019 by

Interlink Books
An imprint of Interlink Publishing Group, Inc.
46 Crosby Street, Northampton, MA 01060
www.interlinkbooks.com

Photos courtesy Alejandro, p. 61; Hiltrud Schulz, pp. 46,
178; Luz de Candela pp. 183, 185, 187; Eslava p. 211;
Alboronia pp. 237, 245; cadizturismo.com p. 291 (top)

Library of Congress Cataloging-in-Publication data:
Names: Dunlop, Fiona, 1952– author.
Title: Andaluz : a food journey through southern Spain /
    by Fiona Dunlop.
Description: Northampton, Massachusetts : Interlink Books,
    an imprint of Interlink Publishing Group, Inc., 2019.
Identifiers: LCCN 2018031211 | ISBN 9781623719999
Subjects: LCSH: Cooking, Spanish—Andalusian style. |
    LCGFT: Cookbooks.
Classification: LCC TX723.5.S7 D86 2019 | DDC 641.59468—dc23
LC record available at https://lccn.loc.gov/2018031211

Publisher/Commissioning Editor: Michel Moushabeck
Design and Production: Pam Fontes-May
Cookbook Editor: Leyla Moushabeck
Copyeditor: Jane Bugaeva

Printed and bound in Korea

Contents

The Andalusian Kitchen
—*Then and Now*

Andalucía is the anti-fad foodie region of Spain. Far from the pioneering extravagances of the more prosperous Basques and Catalans in the north, its cooking is earthy and unpretentious. Slow cooking is routine and seasonal, while local produce remains a constant, whether farmed or foraged. We're talking soups not foams, stews not molecular gastronomy, simple not cerebral, appetite-defying abundance not minimalism.

Far away from the globalized *costas,* in the spectacular mountainous interior, such cooking is deeply entrenched in family or village traditions and threaded through with social and emotional values. Over time, communities isolated by the rugged terrain developed distinctive culinary identities, sparking off occasional gastro-rivalries. What these *andaluces* may not know or choose not to know, however, is how many ingredients from the East came to plant their seeds in the fertile West.

As Andalucía's idiosyncratic identity includes being the birthplace of tapas (the once fly-blown bars of Seville are said to be responsible), a meal can often be an impromptu flow of bar snacks sustained by drink, chat, family, and friends. This is just one aspect of an egalitarian spirit that courses through the region. Yet Andalucía does not stand still, as cooking trends from the North have now percolated down, bringing inventive combinations and slick presentation to more sophisticated bars and restaurants. Mostly though, its cooking is rooted in a sociable *cultura campesina* (peasant culture) of fresh, honest food that matches the gregarious spirit of the *andaluces* themselves. And that is *andaluz* (Andalucian), an adjective which refers to anything emanating from this vast autonomous region of southern Spain, from Almería in the east, to Granada, Jaén, Córdoba, Antequera, Malaga, Ronda, Seville, Huelva, Jerez, and Cádiz in the far west—with plenty of sierra in between.

My quest for this book was to seek out dishes that reflect Andalucía's eight centuries of Moorish presence that lasted from AD711 to 1492. For 500 years of that time, Muslim Spain (Al-Andalus) covered most of the peninsula before slowly shrinking to an emirate along the south coast centered on Granada. Within this rich cultural heritage, I searched for dishes that were either infused with the aromatic flavors of the Middle East and North Africa, that used ancient techniques, or those that at least embraced ingredients that had transited from those lands. With such a cornucopia of input, something must remain, or had it all vanished with the final expulsion of the Moors? Was it a case of culinary cleansing, leaving only a vague, subconscious heritage of aromas, colors, and tastes, as posited by the Spanish gastronomy historian, Fernando Rueda?

"What they (the *Moriscos,* or former Muslims) ate were vile things…vegetables, grains, fruits, honey, and milk; they do not drink wine nor eat meat unless it is slaughtered by them…" These words written in 1612 by Aznar Cardona, a Catholic priest, illustrate one extreme perspective, one that is possibly still shared, albeit much diluted.

So, peering into the cooking pots of restaurants, I set out to investigate what survives and, equally, how it has evolved, scooping up recipes and tips from skilled chefs and self-taught cooks, young and old, traveling from Almería to Cádiz, from desert to verdant valleys, from sierra to sea.

Exotic imports

The Phoenicians, Greeks, and later the Romans had already taught the Iberians how to grow wheat, olives, and grapevines as well as convert Mediterranean fish into the best *garum* (fermented fish sauce) in the empire. However, the Arabs brought a total revolution in the cultivation of fruit and vegetables, in their preparation, and in overall flavor. Spice was the keyword, but not only that. By implementing intricate hill terracing and irrigation channels using water wheels (in Spanish *noria*, an Arabic word), the new occupiers turned this mountainous, part-arid terrain into a veritable land of milk and honey—or rather olive oil and molasses.

Pomegranates, bitter oranges, lemons, quince, apricots, figs, watermelon, rice, chickpeas, capers, eggplants, artichokes, almonds, pine nuts, walnuts, dates, spices, saffron, sugar cane…these are just some of the edible colors, textures, and flavors that flourished in Hispania under Moorish rule. Compared with the dreary repertoire of bland meat and cereals of the Visigoths, the previous rulers, it was as if the conquerors brought gastronomic gifts from the gods, or rather from Allah.

Every word in Spanish that begins with al- is of Arabic origin, and when not a place name, most are related to food or agriculture. The even lengthier period of Sephardic (Jewish) input has not been lost either, due to the distinctive style of their cooking, even in the face of persecution by the Inquisition. Sephardic specialties such as stuffed vegetables, breaded fish, eggplant fritters, and chickpea-based stews, have survived thanks to the *marranos* (forcibly converted Jews who continued to secretly practice Judaism). Their *adafina* is thought to have been the basis of the ubiquitous *olla podrida*, a popular slow-cooked stew of Catholic Spain that segued into Gallic pot au feu, while *fritadas* (like Italian frittatas) and *empanadillas* (meat or fish pastries) add to their legacy. In fact, many Jewish and Muslim dishes fused—as both religions eschewed pork and shared a taste for punchy, complex flavors that mixed sweet with salty or were injected with a bite of vinegar.

Nothing in this soupy mix of cultures, communities, and recipes is clear-cut, leaving countless anomalies. Even before transiting west to Al-Andalus, the dishes of Syria, Persia, and Central Asia had fused in 8th and 9th century Baghdad—that rarified melting pot of Eastern cultures. An Abbasid cookbook of the 10th century by Ibn Sayyar al-Warraq, *Annals of the Caliph's Kitchen*, shows how fashionable gastronomy became there, rather like today in the West, with hot competition between chefs, cooking courses, and recipe books written by gentlemen-gourmets. Once these seeds of sophistication journeyed to Al-Andalus and fused with the Berber influence from North Africa and existing Sephardic dishes, a very exotic, very complex stew was formed.

Ziryab's gourmet table

One of the greatest influences on gastronomy came from the 9th century Baghdadi musician, Ziryab (see also p. 20) who moved to Córdoba in 822. Appalled by the primitive eating habits left by the Visigoths and Vandals, this polymath, sybarite, and aesthete set about revolutionizing palace banquets. Under his eagle eye, the typical bare wooden boards piled with a chaotic array of platters were transformed. Fitted tablecloths of tooled leather, a craft that continues in Córdoba to this day, were laid with glazed ceramic plates from potteries in Málaga and, later, Manises and Granada (Fajalauza). The heavy metal goblets used for wine were replaced with delicate crystal glasses, originally from Persia, though later manufactured locally. This latter switch actually stemmed from a *Hadith* (sacred Islamic text) that banned eating and drinking from gold or silver vessels. Allegedly Ziryab even redesigned the wooden soupspoon, the only piece of cutlery in use, producing a lighter, more streamlined version.

With an encouraging nod from the Emir and advice from dieticians, Ziryab also imposed a rational and healthy sequence of dishes, starting with salad or soup, continuing with fish, fowl, or meat and vegetables, before ending with fruits, desserts, and nuts to "close" the stomach. This ordered style of dining spread rapidly from the upper classes to merchants, Christians, Jews, agricultural workers, and eventually across Europe. It is ironic that with today's restaurant trend for multiple small plates in no fixed order, we have made a return to the "uncivilized" habits of the Visigoths. Awake restaurateurs—1200 years have passed by!

Ziryab's favorite dishes caught on fast, such as meatballs served with flatbread fried in coriander oil, and wild asparagus, which he elevated from a common weed to a refined, tangy vegetable. *Escabeches* (marinades or pickles) of vinegar with spices were another of his innovations. One of his desserts, *guirlache*, a sticky brittle of caramel, honey, sesame, and almonds, still exists, as does *ziriabi,* an eponymous Cordoban appetizer of roasted fava beans.

Chilled soups and an old cookbook

For outsiders, Andalucía is synonymous with gazpacho, that chilled vegetable soup that cools the system at high noon. So was Ziryab's imposition of soup as a first course the genesis of *sopas frias* (cold soups)? Or did they stem from the Roman legionnaires who, it is said, existed on *posca*, a cocktail of vinegary wine, garlic, salt, stale bread, and wild herbs plucked from the wayside? Of course gazpacho as we know it came much later, once tomato and peppers had cruised across the Atlantic from the New World, but it was the Moors who concocted *ajoblanco* (crushed almond, water, and garlic soup) and its denser Cordoban cousin, *mazamorra*, in which breadcrumbs

replaced almonds. With the addition of tomatoes, this evolved into today's much-loved emulsion, *salmorejo*, and the regional variant called *porra*. But what other dishes came? And what remained after the Christian "ethnic cleansing" of the culinary arts, as author Paul Richardson has put it?

It was in the 13th century, under the Almohads (Berbers from the Atlas Mountains of Morocco), that comprehensive records were compiled of *andalusi* dishes. The culinary bible or *quran* of this era is the *Anonymous Andalusian Cookbook of the 13th Century*, a seemingly exhaustive tome of more than 500 recipes ranging from syrups and pastes to medicinal dishes, rice, egg dishes, vegetables, pastries, fish, meatballs, lamb, kid goat, fowl, game, fritters, stuffed this and that, flatbreads, cookies, and desserts. Nutritional advice is woven into the recipes, some of which are so elaborate they need weeks of preparation and many helping hands.

It is a tour de force, whether written by the original *andalusi* transcribers, who compiled it from several sources, by the first translator into English in 1987, Charles Perry, or by Candida Martinelli who has recently reworked it. Reading through its archaic recipes, I lust after the sweet bread layered with dates, or honey mutton with sweet dumplings, the ginger and lavender chicken or, simply, a hen roasted in a pot at home—I'm sure it's all delicious. I would pass on the Tortoise Pie, though.

The life of plants

Botany and medicinal plants were studied in depth, too. The pharmacist Ibn al-Baitar who lived in Malaga at the turn of the 13th century compiled a compendium of 1400 plants from Spain and North Africa with their names in Berber, Arabic, and sometimes Romance beside their applications and dosages. Some fell into kitchen pots. And with the Moors' talent for agriculture, vegetables gained a new lease on life. Terracing meant that fruits and vegetables could be grown on the steep slopes of the sierra. *Huertos* (vegetable gardens) proliferated, irrigated by a system of shared water allocation via channels, or *acequias*. These are still widely used throughout Andalucía.

Proof of the meticulous attention paid to agriculture was a manuscript called the *Córdoba Calendar* (Kitab al-Anwa) dating from 961 and thought to be a compilation of texts by Arib ibn Sa'd, a high-ranking Cordoban civil servant and physician, and by Recemundus, the Christian bishop of Granada. This wide-ranging work outlines precise farming tasks month by month, describes how each edible plant should progress through the seasons, and specifies times for planting, fertilizing, and harvesting. Not only that, it includes medicinal and dietetic tips, a weather forecast system based on astronomical calculations, and a lunar and solar zodiac. It's farming meets medicine meets astronomy and astrology—all very *andalusi*, and a forerunner of biodynamic farming.

In the market gardens, beans of all sorts flourished alongside endives, spinach, chard, radishes, leeks, carrots, cauliflower, celery, onions, and garlic. No longer mere accompaniments, these all became dishes in themselves. Garlic was, nonetheless, used sparingly, often tempered by lemon juice or almond milk. Above all the eggplant, originally from Persia, was elevated to queen of the vegetables, spawning well over twenty dishes, whether chopped, fried with honey, or stuffed with apples, fish, or meat. *Alboronia*, an eggplant-based vegetable stew and the precursor of *pisto andaluz*, like ratatouille, was said to be named after its creator, Buraniyya, the daughter-in-law of an Abbasid Caliph. Nicknamed "the glutton," this happy eater was reputed to devour forty eggplants in one meal. Artichoke hearts were popular, too, cooked with walnuts or *a la montillana*, a sauce of olive oil, garlic, lemon, saffron, mint, and stock named after Montilla, an olive and grape-growing town south of Córdoba. Today's version often has some jamón tossed in.

Couscous versus *migas* and many pastas

Wheat, pulses, and legumes were widely cultivated. Chickpeas cooked with vegetables became an embryonic *cocido*, a stew still cherished by madrileños. Chickpeas alone were nonetheless regarded as a "dish of Bedouins and gluttons" (according to the 13th century cookbook), and were only to be used for their juice or ground into flour. Instead couscous, that typical grain of the Berbers made from rubbed semolina, was steam cooked to become an aristocratic side dish served at court and festivals. Fragrant, sweet versions were cooked with orange blossom water, raisins, and cinnamon.

It seems likely that couscous (originally *alcuzcuz* in Spanish) first appeared on *andalusi* tables during the Almohad period, in the 13th century, when it came from Morocco. However, it did not survive the final expulsion of the *Moriscos* in 1609, which was the last act by Spain's Catholic monarchs to obliterate Spain's Muslim past. Once considered noble and distinguished, couscous had deteriorated into a symbol of a banned identity. So out it went, with the *Moriscos*, because for upstanding Catholics this food represented Moorish resistance to assimilation. Today, slowly, it is making a timid return to more fashionable restaurants, though it has to contend with the parallel renaissance of that national passion, *migas* (fried breadcrumbs).

In eastern Andalucía this poor man's dish (*migas de harina*) is a kind of fried porridge of flour, oil, and water that is generally served with chorizo, *morcilla* (blood sausage), and roasted peppers. Elsewhere in the peninsula, simple *migas* are usually made with leftover bread and water into *migas a la pastora* (shepherd's crumbs). Whatever the method, it pops up in countless village festivals, cooked in huge paella pans as a way of feeding the proverbial 5,000. Yet it is thought that even this dish could derive from an Arab source, the basic broth, *tharid*, of old bread and animal fat traditionally consumed during Ramadan. However, the multi-faceted *tharid* could also

swell into quite a substantial meat pie, as here (from the Anonymous 13th century cookbook):

> *Arrange the beef in a circle on the dish,*
> *and near it the lamb, and on top of it*
> *the chickens, and at the highest part of*
> *the platter the pigeons and turtledoves.*
> *Add on top of it fried birds, meatballs*
> *and fried sausage, meat patties, egg*
> *yolks, olives, and chopped almonds; then*
> *sprinkle it with the necessary amount*
> *of ground almond and cinnamon.*
> *Cover with a thin bread or crepe and*
> *serve. It is a dish of kings and viziers.*

Breads were legion too, made from a wide variety of flours and other ingredients, like oats and ginger, dates and walnuts, or almonds and raisins, all baked in wood-fired brick ovens. Finally, there were noodles, *fideos* or, in Valencian and Catalan, *fideus*, that become the dish *fideuá*. This undoubtedly derives from the Arabic *fidáws*, meaning "surplus" that entailed turning surplus flour into dry pasta for storage or travel. So here we explode another foodie myth—it was not Marco Polo who was responsible for bestowing pasta on the West, but more likely the Muslims who, after adopting the technique from the Chinese, brought it to their occupied lands of Sicily and Spain in the 10th century.

In contrast to Italy, where pasta blossomed into dozens of whimsical shapes, each one suited to a particular sauce, in Spain it never evolved from the fine, short noodle available to this day in several sizes for tossing into stews and soups. Although Moroccan Berbers still serve vermicelli sprinkled with icing sugar, cinnamon, and ground almonds as an elegant alternative to couscous, in Andalucía and the Levante (Catalunya, Valencia, and Murcia) you only encounter *fideos* and their fatter cousin, *macarrones*, in seafood dishes or soups, often as substitutes for rice.

Rice, spice, all things nice

And then there was rice, *arroz* or, in Arabic, *arruzz*. This millennial-old grain from China came via Iraq to Al-Andalus in the 10th century. It was to be the most lasting of all the agricultural imports, as the vast rice fields once worked by the Moors still mirror the skies in the lagoons of the Albufera, south of Valencia, in the Pego marshlands near Alicante, in Murcia, and south of Seville. Here they grow medium and short-grain rice, as well as the magical *bomba*, an ancient grain able to absorb two or three times its volume in water, thus absorbing maximum flavor.

From this comes paella, easily Spain's most iconic and also most misrepresented dish, a moveable peasant feast of rice with rabbit, chicken, snails, and/or seafood. It is a national passion wherever the Moors once trod, inspiring heated exchanges as to its ingredients and immense skill in its preparation. Variations include the Levante's succulent *arroz de mariscos* (seafood rice), *arroz negro* (with black squid ink), *arroz a banda* (fish rice with a separate broth), or *arroz caldoso* (soupy risotto), which is more typical of Huelva and Cadiz.

Paella's most obvious feature is the golden color of its saffron-imbued grains. The Moors used saffron generously, not just for coloring, but for its distinctive flavoring. Originally from Persia, this "red gold" became a key Spanish crop, highly prized, expensive (hand plucking stamens of autumn crocuses or *crocus sativus* is laborious), and grown exclusively in La Mancha near those emblematic windmills fantasized over by Don Quixote.

In Moorish times rice was cooked in either water or goat milk usually to accompany fish, while many sweet versions were made with sugar or honey and flavored with cinnamon. And for the Moors, *harisa* was not a fiery chili sauce but actually a creamy rice compote perfumed with cinnamon that accompanied chicken or lamb.

In fact *harîsa* was a bit of a moveable feast, as it also referred to a wheat or meat pudding considered both healthy and aphrodisiac.

Of course the Arabs, kings of the spice trade with the East, brought with them dozens of other exotic seeds and aromatic plants like coriander, caraway, anise, ginger, sumac, tamarind, cumin, cinnamon, cloves, galangal, mustard, and nutmeg to flavor and perfume their dishes, together with locally grown lavender, mint, thyme, and basil. However, those who sprinkled ground pepper over their dishes were scorned by the nobles as either Berbers or Christians.

Everything changed after the *reconquista* when most of these spices were replaced by a milder piquancy from Mediterranean herbs like thyme, rosemary, oregano, parsley, and bay leaf. Basil, unlike in Italy, is rarely used and more commonly known as a mosquito deterrent. Cinnamon is the exception, still extremely present in both savory and sweet dishes, sometimes joined by cumin. Otherwise, contemporary Andalusians have ardently rejected their spice heritage; is it yet another rejection of those Moorish roots? Even cilantro disappeared, although it's ubiquitous in neighboring Portugal.

There is however a good reason for this culinary twist, because the moment Al-Andalus was eradicated from the map, Spain underwent its next gastronomic revolution— this time from the New World via Seville. In the bulging basket of American food imports came red pepper, which, once smoked and ground, produced a potent and addictive new seasoning: *pimentòn*, or paprika. This gradually came to dominate Spain's savory dishes.

Fish, meat, fowl, and pork wars

Fish, from mullet to tuna to sardines, was boiled, fried, stuffed with dough and spices, baked in salt, marinated or pickled in vinegar, stewed in tagines, or turned into fishcakes. Coriander, fennel, garlic, pepper, a hint of saffron, and lots of eggs were the typical accompaniments. However, fish later took second place to meat, the staple diet of the new fundamentalist rulers from Morocco's southern mountains, and only the poorer classes living near the coast continued to eat it, chiefly sardines.

One fish that the Moors excelled at catching was the highly-prized Bluefin tuna (*atun rojo*) that they netted using the ingenious *almadraba* technique implemented two thousands years earlier by the Phoenicians (see p. 290). This continues every year off Barbate, south of Cádiz, though much of the tuna is whisked off to Japan. Some of what remains becomes *mojama*, air-dried tuna, a gourmet tapa thought to date from the Phoenicians (*musama* in Arabic means "dry"), while the rest is voraciously consumed in countless guises throughout western Andalucía.

For special occasions the Muslims favored beef, veal, lamb, or mutton but for everyday it was chicken (sometimes an older hen, once its egg-laying was slowing), rabbit, duck, goose, pigeon, quail, partridge, starling, turtledove, and other unspecified small birds. Records from the Spanish Inquisition showed that for celebrations the Sephardim ate peacock, swallow, and thrush. The latter, *zorzal*, can still be found in some country restaurants. Even crane was swallowed up by the Moorish pot.

Kid goat landed on the table too, but, like dairy cows, female goats were saved for milk and yogurt. Meats would be marinated then stewed with dozens of spices, as well as almonds, fruit, rosewater, pomegranate molasses, milk, or vinegar. Sometimes, for extra consistency, the meat dish would be finished with a layer of eggs. Meat pies were said to be "very good on journeys." One meat preparation that flourishes today, grilled *pinchitos* of chicken or lamb, is the Spanish version of Arab-world kebabs. Ironically, a common tapa, *pincho moruno,* which literally

means "Moorish kebab." is made of pork (which is banned by Islam)—but marinated in a heady spice mixture similar to Moroccan *ras el hanout*.

Since pork was forbidden by Judaism and Islam, the countless piggy spin-offs that pack Spanish kitchens, stores, and markets today were clearly fuelled by the *reconquista*, and, subsequently, by the Inquisition. Conversion imposed not just a change in religious practices but also a change in diet. In order to prove to your neighbors and the Inquisition's pork police that you had become a true Catholic, whether converted from Judaism or Islam, you had to devour mountains of chorizo, jamón, sausages, loins, or trotters. And if smoke did not come out of your chimney on a Saturday (the Sabbath), you were strongly suspected of covert Judaism. As a result, Spain is Europe's most porcine-obsessed country, a perfect reflection of the statement by the Galician writer Julio Camba: "Spanish cooking overflows with garlic and religious prejudices."

Olives, oil, vinegar, and *escabeches*

Despite the fact that the olive tree was introduced by the Phoenicians and Greeks, the word *aceite*, oil, actually derives from the Arabic *az-zait*, since it was the Moors who perfected and expanded oil production. Though, for a few centuries after the Reconquista, lard (*manteca*) muscled in on this elixir, yet again as culinary proof of religious identity. Luckily, Spain rediscovered olive oil in the 19th century, and today one-third of Andalusian land is striped with regimented groves of some 170 million olive trees. It may be visible proof that Andalucía is the world's largest producer of olive oil but, long ago, I was amazed to learn that after export to Italy some of that oil reemerges from bottling plants labeled as "Tuscan."

Most of Spain's 250 olive varieties were documented in the 15th century and present-day Andalucía cultivates at least a dozen on a colossal scale, the most common being *picual, hojiblanca, lechin, manzanilla,* and *picudo.* Organic oil production is progressing, as is single estate, and top chefs invariably use only extra virgin olive oil. The industry spawns plenty of negatives though, as *la oliva* remains a heavily subsidized mono-culture that makes widespread use of pesticides, prevents any agricultural diversification, and imposes limited seasonal employment on the rural population.

Vinegar was widely used for preserving, pickling, and flavoring, and was mainly made from sweet grapes, sometimes with a drop of grapefruit juice for extra sourness. A common marinade for meat and fish used sour milk, vinegar, and *morrî*, a potent sauce made from fish guts that added a hit of umami. Not surprising, the Spanish word for pickling, *escabeche*, derives from the Arabic-Persian *sikbagk.* Originally this referred to meat cooked with vinegar to mask greasy or heavy flavors, or simply to preserve it, however both the word and its application evolved, and today *escabeches* are very popular for manufactured seafood conserves like mussels or mackerel. *Boquerones*, pickled anchovies, are a tapas stalwart throughout Spain, usually freshly made, high on garlic, and liberally drizzled in olive oil. Vinegar was also used to "cook" vegetables and to dress capers and olives, while the Sephardim particularly enjoyed its acidic bite in numerous dishes.

Sweet tooth

Three of the seven prescribed courses in a typical meal were sweet, whether it be fruits, pastries, cookies, or rice and/or custard puddings—ancestors of today's ubiquitous flan. Quince paste (*carne de membrillo*) is still relished with Manchego cheese, while pumpkin, dates, and figs once became candied delicacies, sometimes stuffed with pistachio, almond, or hazelnut paste. Elche, just south of Alicante, is home to Europe's only irrigated palm grove, an entrancing expanse of about 70,000 date palms developed by the Moors to feed their atavistic taste for this fruit of the desert, whether in drinks, boiled in milk, or candied. Today, however, dates are rarely found in dishes and those sold in stores are the less than fresh, boxed versions.

And of course there were cookies, candies, and cakes—mountains of them. In fact it was the world's first sugar refinery in 9th century Baghdad that spurred an incredible boom in all things sweet, since sugar was far easier, and therefore cheaper, to obtain and use than honey. In Al-Andalus the sweet tooth flourished thanks to the cultivation of sugarcane along the coast east of Málaga. Transformed into molasses or treacle (*miel de caña*) it was widely used and is still generously drizzled today, often far too much.

This did not mean that honey was abandoned, since when blended with vinegar it created that much loved sweet-sour flavor. Today the mountains of the Axarquía (northeast of Málaga) and of the Alpujarras (between Granada and Almería) are renowned for their luscious varieties of honey: chestnut, rosemary, thyme, orange blossom, and even avocado.

Almonds, nuts, eggs, flour, and sugar syrup or honey were the core ingredients of moist, powdery *alfajores, polvorones* (although today these contain lard), *mantecadas, pestiños, yemas, rosquitos, torrijas, cabello de angel* (sugared pumpkin fibers, or "angel hair"), *loukoum,* candied fruit, *turrón* (nougat) and, of course, marzipan, a trademark of Toledo that has attained addiction status. Although introduced way back in the 8th century, this sweet confection of almonds and sugar was later adopted as a typical Christian treat, and Toledo's convents continue to do a roaring trade.

Recipes for these cakes and sweets vary from town to town, festival to festival, and even convent to convent, because ironically it is the cloistered nuns who have best preserved them, baking their secret recipes behind closed doors for whoever rings the convent bell and pays. Ave Maria! Names changed too, bringing idiosyncrasies such as "bones of a saint" and "nun's sighs." Certain *confeiterias* preserve the recipes of their family business equally jealously. The sweet legacy of the Sephardim was notably *roscas*, baked doughnut-type breads or twists that were eaten for breakfast or on the Sabbath. Ironically this evolved into diverse *roscas* that pop up on Catholic saints' days, notably San Blas.

Bizarrely, few Andalusian restaurants today are hot on desserts. Invariably you are confronted with that tired old choice of rice pudding, crème caramel, or ice cream—hardly inspiring. Move up a notch to more avant-garde establishments and the imagination does start to fly, often tortuously, and in many cases that American import, the brownie, enters the fray. Luckily the home front benefits from Andalucía's long hot summers and their wealth of soft fruits—apricots, peaches, plums, figs, and grapes—are all eaten as widely today as in the past.

Liquid diet: drinks

While, strictly speaking, Muslims did not drink alcohol (another Arabic word), at certain periods of Al-Andalus it was happily imbibed, even rhapsodized over, occasionally bringing civic problems of drunkenness. It was their formidable technological skills that developed the modern still (*alambique*, from the Arabic) originally for medicinal potions. From the Middle East the alembic made its way to the Iberian peninsula, where non-Muslims soon discovered the power of distilling grape must (leftover seed, stems, and skins of pressed grapes), so creating a neutral flavored brandy: *aguardiente*.

This whimsical poem by the 11th century Sevillian poet, Abul Hasan Ali Ibn Hisn, highlights the *andalusi* fervour for alcohol:-

> *Reflection of Wine*
> Light passing through wine
> reflects on the fingers
> of the cupbearer

dyeing them red
as juniper stains
the muzzle of the antelope
(Translated from the Spanish by Cola Franzen)

Contemporary Spaniards are notoriously fond of sweetened fruit juices sold unglamorously in cartons. Centuries ago, drink-vendors would roam the streets and markets, as in any Middle Eastern or North African city, offering sweet mint tea or diluted syrups. The most popular were made from fresh roses, orange blossom, hibiscus, myrtle, mulberries, lemons, or pomegranates. Not so today, despite that legendary city Granada being named after the pomegranate. I personally find it maddening to see this magical fruit left to wither, split, and drop from neglected trees. Press them! Sprinkle their nutritious seeds! One up on syrups was *sharbat*, served at court, a luxury fruit drink transformed into sorbet by adding ice brought down from the snowy mountains on mule-back.

Grapes morphed not only into wine and vinegar, but also into *arrope* (from the Arabic *arrúb*), a syrupy concentrate of grape must that was diluted with water or eaten like jelly with added fruit. Today it is mainly used as an additive for certain sweet wines. In contrast *horchata*, a sugary, milky drink made from tiger nuts grown in the southeastern Levant region, is still ubiquitous. As for mint tea, it is very much the preserve of Moroccan-owned *teterías* (tea rooms) in Almería, Granada, or Algeciras.

In the alcoholic drinks department, contemporary *Andalucia* does Spain proud, even if it is not the high-end vintage Rioja, Ribero del Duero, or Priorat wines of the north. Instead, you have Jerez, the source of world famous sherry—*finos*, *amontillados*, *olorosos*, *palo cortados*, and *Pedro Ximénez*, as well as the lesser-known Montilla-Moriles region that produces equally intense, though unfortified wines. For centuries Málaga's hills have been renowned for their sweet dessert wines, although other, drier types are now thriving, too. However, although both Almería and Cádiz are developing excellent reds and whites, unfortunately these rarely find their way outside the provinces.

21ˢᵗ century Andalusian cuisine

Andalucia of course espouses the healthy Mediterranean diet based on olive oil, vegetables, fish, fruit, and nuts, in which slow cooking is championed and fresh, seasonal produce is the lifeblood. Yet a bubbling new regional confidence is bringing astonishing innovation and complexity to restaurant cooking. Some 15 Andalusian restaurants boast Michelin stars, from Muelle Uno (José Carlos García) in Málaga to Abantal (Julio Fernández) in Seville, Acanthum (Xanty Elias) in Huelva to Alejandro in Roquetas, all creating phenomenal, visually exquisite dishes.

Just two Andalusian chefs have monopolized international attention until now. In his hometown of Marbella, pioneering Dani García juxtaposes influences from as far afield as Peru and Asia with his Andalusian heritage, to huge applause from a glitzy, cosmopolitan clientele. In a very different vein, over near Cádiz, Ángel León, the maverick "Chef del Mar" at Aponiente is so totally enamored of the sea, its inhabitants and its science, that he'll even magic light out of plankton on a plate. Such a trajectory from fisherman's son to three-starred Michelin magician is peerless.

In 2016, the Andalusian scene advanced further when two cutting-edge restaurants opened their doors, both rapidly gaining Michelin stars: Bardal in Ronda, owned by Benito Gómez, and Noor in Córdoba, the brainchild of Paco Morales (coincidentally, these chefs are great friends).

And this, for me, is the key. Gómez, although raised in Catalunya, chose to embrace his Andalucian origins and propose a modern take on *sierra* cooking; by sourcing ingredients from local producers he reinvents traditional flavors. "It makes no sense to eat global as we have everything here, the best produce in Spain. And there is such an incredible legacy from the Moors—with the sea just 50 km [31 miles] away!" he enthuses.

Meanwhile Morales, a gifted chef who worked in top Basque establishments, returned to his hometown of Córdoba to open a singularly ambitious restaurant. Noor means "light" in Arabic, and he is certainly illuminating something unique. The concept? A rediscovery of the authentic gastronomy of Al-Andalus, eschewing all New World ingredients. Elegantly presented, his intricate dishes are suffused with the rare fragrances and flavors of 1000 years ago. As Morales tells me, "We realized how important it is to recover our roots and bring to light this history that was buried."

So the wheel turns again, proof that despite the march of history, despite wars, intolerance, and oppression, deep roots never die. Particularly those that grow again to end up on our plates—our living, eating culture.

Al-Andalus
—A Brief History

From the Phoenicians onwards, wave after wave of invaders permeated the Iberian peninsula but the Moorish conquest of AD 711 was a watershed. It was a cultural turning point that transformed the fields, the kitchen, and the diet, introduced a proto-Renaissance in intellectual thought, brought new forms of architecture and extraordinary craftsmanship, as well as eight centuries of sporadic conflict with the Christian kingdoms of the North. That meant shifting borders, conversions, mixed marriages, uprisings, even new languages, hence ambivalent identities.

According to the late British author and Hispanophile, Gerald Brenan, this constant struggle along ever-changing frontiers between Christendom and Islam actually gave Spanish culture a unique maturity and flexibility. And as the first and only Islamic state in Europe, this era has huge, still controversial resonance today, with much of its significance concentrated in Andalucía, (a region about the size of the state of Indiana), where the Moorish presence lasted the longest.

The genesis of Al-Andalus

The evocative Arabic name for Hispania (the Roman term), Al-Andalus ("land of the Vandals") referred to one of several Germanic tribes who had exploited the power vacuum left by the Romans, soon overtaken by the Visigoths. But by the late 7th century, the geo-political map was changing radically. Across the Mediterranean a new religion, Islam, was on the march from Ummayad-ruled Damascus, advancing westwards through North Africa, converting and signing up Berbers

(indigenous North Africans) on the way. In 711, an army of some 10,000 men crossed the strait and landed between Tarifa and Gibraltar. Over the next centuries, the Arab and Berber cultures were to transform the lives and diet of the seductive land they conquered; food is, after all, the first element any migrant tries to recreate from his roots.

Córdoba and the golden age of Al-Andalus

Trouncing the Visigoths, the invaders swept north until they eventually met defeat in the Cantabrian mountains, but by then they had set up their central government in the south, in Córdoba. Al-Andalus seemed like paradise on earth, blessed with soaring mountains, fertile plains, a rugged coastline lapped by the Mediterranean, and plentiful rivers. By 750, barely a century after the death of the Prophet Mohammed, the new Islamic empire stretched all the way from today's Pakistan in the east to Portugal in the west. Although the Ummayad dynasty was soon toppled by the Abbasids of Baghdad, this same geographical sweep endured, an astounding feat.

The status of Al-Andalus changed in 755 when it declared itself independent of Middle Eastern rule, making Córdoba the capital of this new emirate. After a series of bloody battles between warring Arab and Berber tribes, the victor, Abd er-Rahman I, an Ummayad from Palmyra, was declared Emir of Córdoba, and thus became the founder of what developed into a powerful, highly advanced caliphate. At that point Al-Andalus encompassed the entire peninsula except for a strip of land edging the Bay of Biscay in the north; it would take another century for the Christian reconquista to fully gather pace and seven more centuries before the entire peninsula was reconquered.

Much has been written about 9th and 10th century Córdoba and its allegedly harmonious co-habitation of Muslims, Jews, and Christians, yet it seems unlikely that there was great inter-cultural exchange. It was more a question of living side by side and of "grudging tolerance," as the historian Richard Fletcher wrote. Even among the Muslims there were inequalities, with Arabs first in the pecking order, Berbers a distant second, while Christian slaves composed another, lower social stratum. But the achievements of this nascent caliphate were momentous, symbolized by the remarkable Great Mosque, its scale and rhythmical arches echoing those of the Ummayad mosques of Damascus and Aleppo.

At that early stage in its existence, the Andalus court was so wealthy that it could afford to distribute free wheat to its citizens during droughts, and the "green revolution" of imported crops and new farming techniques soon brought massive economic and therefore social benefits. As Richard Fletcher wrote, "The net effect of…these crops was a population less exposed to famine. More eating of fruit and vegetables meant healthier people." And healthier generally meant happier, perhaps more tolerant.

External peace reigned too, despite occasional prodding from Christian armies bent on their reconquest. Taxes were efficiently collected, and intermarriages between *muladies* (Berber converts to Islam) or *Mozarab* (Christians under Moorish rule) women and higher-class Arabs sewed some seeds of social cohesion. Muslims, Jews, and Christians living in their respective *barrios* no doubt exchanged a few cooking tips, too, and countless dishes fused.

During Abd-er Rahman II's key reign in the 9th century, dozens of other socio-cultural influences from the polished Abbasids of Baghdad helped form Al-Andalus. Patio-houses, public baths, libraries, and universities multiplied, with cultural and intellectual advances further boosted in the 10th century by the astute Abd-er Rahman III, a blue-eyed son of an Arab royal and his Christian concubine. Under his watch, the utopian city of Medinat Al-Zahara took shape in the hills above Córdoba; glinting in the sun, buildings of jasper, marble, and precious metals arose amid fountains, fragrant shrubs, rustling palms, and cypress trees. But this proto-Alhambra, a last burst of creative extravagance, lasted barely sixty five years before it was trashed in the civil wars that were starting to relentlessly fragment the caliphate. By then, too, the regency of the ruthless yet efficient minister, Almanzor, had ended, a thorn in the side of the Christian forces as much as in *andalusi* society.

Ziryab, the trendsetting aesthete

To gauge social progress in Al-Andalus, we need to rewind to the 9th century. Although it is not known how many recipes existed among the manuscripts of the well-stocked libraries of Córdoba, Toledo, and Seville, what is certain is that sweeping changes in culinary style, fashion, social mores, and music can be attributed to one man: Ziryab. This nickname, meaning "blackbird," derived from the dark complexion and mellifluous voice of a particularly gifted musician, Abu Al-Hassan Ali Ibn Nafi, who came to Córdoba from Baghdad in 822.

The thirty-three-year-old prodigy of every possible refinement struck an immediate, empathetic chord with the reigning emir, Abd er-Rahman II, thanks to their shared ages and cultural tastes. Canny enough to spot the need for such an arbiter of taste to civilize the uncouth citizens of his embryonic kingdom, the ruler wasted no time in employing Ziryab. The musician was a rare beast, as not only did he introduce the *oud* instrument to court, a forerunner of the lute and the guitar, and found a music school, but he also popularized trends as diverse as toothpaste, women's beauty salons, the game of chess, and even a sharp new haircut—bangs. As a fashion fanatic, he introduced luxurious fabrics and seasonal outfits that included wearing only white in summer. Ziryab's romantic, torch-lit poetry and music soirées were soon the hottest ticket in town. Aside from all that, he had a massive influence on gastronomy (see p. 8). Ziryab remained in his adopted city until his death in 857, leaving ten children to carry the musical flame.

Fragmentation and fundamentalism

By 1031, Cordoba's heyday imploded in a miasma of disputes and territorial fragmentation into *taifas*, small princedoms with no central control. This unleashed a decadent era of "party kings" who were often freed slaves or Berbers, and it also saw the rise in power and wealth of Seville (*Ishbilya*), which became the new capital of extravagance, hedonism, and poetry.

With this lack of unified control, the path was open for fundamentalist invaders from Morocco: first the Almóravid dynasty from their vast Moroccan empire, followed a century later by the fanatical Almohads from the Atlas Mountains. They unified the *taifas*, but also instigated religious repression, bringing an end to the days of tolerance and intensifying the persecution of Jews and Christians.

Under the Almohads, Seville prospered further and by the 12th century had become Spain's largest city, its booming economy reflected in a Great Mosque and neighboring palace. In 1236, Córdoba, that former beacon of Andalusian erudition and refinement, fell to the Christian armies, at roughly the same time as Valencia and Murcia, soon followed by Jaén and Seville. The endgame was approaching.

Centuries of rule in Seville, Jérez, Cádiz, Málaga, Granada, and Almería left spectacular structures, some with such outstanding interior craftsmanship that the Mudéjar style continued under Catholic rule, when monarchs chose to live in Moorish-style palaces like Zaragoza's Aljafería, Seville's sublime Alcázar, and later, Granada's Alhambra. Odd hybrids appeared too, such as Seville cathedral's iconic Giralda, in reality a mutated minaret or, most symbolic of all, the cathedral planted at the heart of Córdoba's mosque.

Outside the cities, the Islamic occupation left an indelible mark on the rolling sierra, the plains, and along the coastline of this charmed land, from fortresses to topography. Countless Arabic names include Andalucía's most famous river, the Guadalquivir, which simply means "big river," (others include Guadalete, Guadalhorce, Guadalmedina, Guadiana) while villages with names starting with Ben (from the Arabic for "son") all denoted Berber communities. Traveling through the region today, you cannot miss castles crowning whitewashed villages and *torres moras* (Moorish watchtowers) like sentinels on remote hilltops and cliffs. Military might went hand in hand with architecture, which suffused the landscape.

The endgame: Granada

Granada, of course, scooped up top prize in the architectural stakes thanks to the glorious forms of the Alhambra ("red fort" in Arabic) silhouetted against the snow-capped Sierra Nevada. This, the last bastion of Al-Andalus, was an emirate ruled by the Nazrid dynasty that stretched from Gibraltar to Almería. However, nearly eight centuries after the Moors' arrival, it was being chipped away inexorably: Málaga fell (bloodily) in 1487, then Almería, and finally the besieged capital itself in 1492. Ferdinand and Isabella, the Catholic monarchs of a reunited Spain, imposed the new architectural forms of the Renaissance, the Spanish language, the beliefs and rituals of the Catholic church and, not least, a pork-based diet.

The legend goes that as the deposed emir, Boabdil (Mohammed XII), rode into exile with his family, he turned to look back tearfully at his lost kingdom from a mountain pass, subsequently dubbed El Suspiro del Moro, "the Moor's sigh." Behind them, the Nazrids bequeathed the pinnacle of Al-Andalus artistry, exquisite palaces, and pleasure gardens where patterns of light and shade flickered between fountains and pools, gushing water channels fed

quadrangles of heady blossoms, and interiors displayed a matchless level of craftsmanship. As the Christian armies advanced south, the Alhambra had been like a sumptuous, fragile bubble in a shrinking universe. Yet even when it popped, the Muslim presence did not disappear overnight.

After the fall

Over the following decades the Muslims, like the Jews just before them, were forced by the Inquisition to convert (so becoming *Moriscos*) or be exiled. Many "New Christians" practiced their original religion in secret while overtly enacting the rituals of "Old Christians." A large contingent followed Boabdil south to the Alpujarra mountains and thence to Fez, while others were swapped with Christians from northern Spain, a policy aimed at diluting their communities to prevent uprisings.

This did not always work, as in 1567 rebellions erupted notably in the Alpujarras, Frigiliana, and Almería, sparked by the royal ban on spoken Arabic and all *Morisco* customs. Brutal suppression and massacres followed. The final

blow came in the early 17th century when an estimated 300,000 remaining *Moriscos* were expelled from Valencia to North Africa. Like much of *andalusi* agriculture, the Valencian rice fields languished without their industrious workers and, ironically, the Inquisition lost a profitable source of fines. The Spanish economy crashed and, for a while, rice went out of fashion.

By the end of the 18th century, indigenous Islamic identity was considered to have been totally extinguished in Spain. And yet, some historians maintain that there were covert returnees who found it impossible to live outside their beloved Al-Andalus where their family had lived for generations. Thousands of *Moriscos* even evaded the roundup, helped and protected by Catholic neighbors, particularly in the Granada region. This ethnic survival has been confirmed by studies of the population that show significant proportions of both Berber and Jewish DNA throughout Spain.

Wherever the truth lies, it is certain that the cultural impact of Al-Andalus is indelible—and some of it still bubbles in the cooking pot.

Andalusia and Me

"I breathe for Málaga.... for Cádiz, for Alcalá de los Gazules, for what is intimately Andaluz." Federico García Lorca, 1924

The first time I ever saw Andalucía was back in the 1970s. As you did in that free-thinking, free-moving, post-hippie era, I set off with two fellow students in a battered 2CV to rattle all the way from Montpellier in southwest France, where we were fine tuning our French studies, south to Marrakesh—about 1200 miles (2000 km). As soon as we had cut through the dramatic Sierra Morena, the gateway to Andalucía from the monotonous plains of La Mancha, I was transfixed. Here was a wild, grandiose landscape, a universe of elemental, raw escarpments either glowing with chalky limestone or soaking up the light with flinty shale, interspersed with carpets of olive trees or lush ravines. It was magical.

Crunching gears asthmatically, our primitive car bumped around the deserted bends before we lost our way, but eventually reached Algeciras and the ferry across the Strait of Gibraltar. Andalucía's rolling sierra studded with whitewashed *fincas* and goats, its roadside *ventas*, palm trees, donkeys, fried fish, and the gut-rot red wine of the time all left an indelible mark. It felt almost as exotic as Morocco, that mythical neighbor where the haunting muezzin sent shivers down my spine as mysterious hooded figures in *djellabas* loped through the night shadows.

There we reveled in tangy tagines or sizzling lamb kebabs grilled on braziers as well as mountainous platters of couscous. Our first sampling of this grain came after a breakdown in the Rif mountains where we were warmly served a banquet by the Number One Widow of the village before bedding down on divans in her front room. Young and impressionable,

I never forgot this first taste of either Morocco or Andalucía—or was it both: Al-Andalus?

A few years later I was back, this time to a tiny village called Sorbas, near Almería, that had barely emerged from the Middle Ages let alone from Franco's rule, which had only just ended. Fresh from an energizing holiday in New York, I had come to join my French artist-boyfriend for a complete change of scene and pace, much helped by Sorbas' dramatic cliff-top site above a primeval, eroded landscape. As Almería airport was military at the time, I had taken the very basic night train down from Madrid that only left memories of a dark, empty land pinpricked with the odd light.

It was late autumn, which meant that the annual *matanza* (slaughter) was kicking off in the village. Every morning, agonizing squeals rang out as the fattened pigs met their makers—hardly romantic, but at that stage I had no idea about the resultant joys of *jamón*, *salchichón* or chorizo. While monsieur wielded his paintbrushes or cogitated in a hammock on the roof terrace, I would set off with my camera to try and record this timeless place. Inquisitive faces framed by black headscarves peered out from tiny square windows but it was the monumental karst landscape sliced by canyons and speckled with sculptural cacti that electrified me most.

In fact, this desert of Almería, more precisely Tabernas, had already been discovered by a stream of European filmmakers, soon becoming the location of choice for every spaghetti Western ever made. Not only that, Lawrence of Arabia rode his camel through the canyons, John Lennon

adopted his trademark round glasses for *How I won the War,* and just a few years before I arrived, Antonioni had filmed part of *The Passenger* with Jack Nicholson. One evening, Sorbas' eccentric bar-owner, Juan of Bar Fatima, proudly described his fifteen seconds of fame in the movie (he limps outside the bar to mumble one line to Nicholson), before regaling us with stories of an Ash Wednesday procession that brought him a far bigger role in the traditional "burial of the sardine." "And I lifted up the sardine for God!" Thus I discovered surrealism, Andalusian-style.

Gastronomy in those days was a mere afterthought, as rural Spain, in particular impoverished Andalucía, had hardly advanced since the hardships of the Civil War. Sorbas' two grocery shops were woefully basic and I was shocked to find no butter, a product of the greener north that was alien to Andalucía. Instead there was a tasteless spread called *Tulipan* that still exists

today. Of course now, better informed, I know olive oil is a healthier substitute, though back then an inferior oil was rather too ubiquitous, drenching just about any tapa at the roadside bars, and the "extra virgin" tag was more usually applied to Mary. The village shops only stocked lard or cheaper blends of oil, though no doubt there was a private network supplying the good stuff. Even vegetables were sparse in that desert area, so low-grade pasta, pork chops, and canned sardines became our culinary mainstay—hardly gastronomic.

Yet there were revelations. The postman told us all about gathering and preparing snails ("put them in a covered bucket and purge them on flour for 48 hours"), a prelude to bringing a bagful of the live gastropods to cook for us. They were tiny, but delicious, and far tastier than the larger, meatier ones I had sampled in France. Years later I was thrilled to find hundreds of the Andalusian species crawling around a huge basket in the R'cif market in Fez, destined for *ghoulal*, snail soup.

One evening we were invited by the Sorbas butcher to have dinner in his shop along with similar village dignitaries. Here, following a spread of tasty (piggy) victuals, we were rather formally presented with a huge pan filled with… goat's head soup. Little did they know about the Rolling Stones album, released a few years earlier—or perhaps they did? When encouraged to eat the goat's eyes, said to be the greatest delicacy, I demurred, but the cheeks were a treat.

Fast forward a few more years and I was making full use of my parents' vacation home by the sea in Mojácar, not that far from Sorbas, but seemingly light years away. By then Spain's *movida* (post-Franco cultural revolution) was in full swing, and life in this cosmopolitan beach community reflected it. In the 1960s, the canny local mayor of what had become a semi-abandoned hill village had offered free houses to anyone who was prepared to restore them. Soon, a stream of artists and artisans flocked there to shape a lotus-eating spirit against a backdrop of the glittering Mediterranean.

When I first lived there, older women in long black headscarves frequented the village fountain to collect drinking water and wash clothes, while others pulled donkeys laden with homegrown vegetables to the village market. One, María, always looked out for me: "Hola guapa!" she'd cry as I came to pick through her misshapen vegetables. I still remember her huge, green-tinged tomatoes, nothing like I had ever seen or tasted in Paris or London. In fact, Almería's sandy soil was where the crossbred Raf tomato originated at about that time, now a chef favorite.

This, too, was where I discovered the joy of fresh Mediterranean fish, from gleaming sardines to slippery silvery anchovies (laborious to clean but delicious dusted in flour and fried in olive oil) to the more delicate red mullet. Every afternoon at 4pm, I could set my watch to the fishing boats chugging across the horizon to Garrucha, the nearby port, while I fantasized over what piscine treasures filled their holds. Of course I was never up in time to see them leave at dawn.

Occasionally the sybaritic rhythms of Mojácar life switched to melancholy when, on a late visit to a bar, a trio of local gypsies from nearby Turre would break into searing *cante jondo*, feet tapping, knuckles rapping the counter, and hands clapping in syncopation. Luckily, robust *carajillos* (black coffee drowned in brandy) steadied our emotions, and that elliptical Andalusian chatter soon replaced this atavistic howl of deep longing. I was slowly getting used to the guttural chopping and dropping of syllables, mashing others together—a language totally foreign to any self-respecting Castillian.

As the years rolled by and Spain entered its golden EU era, attracting vast subsidies, sprawling developments, empty motorways, and rampant corruption, the old-timers gradually disappeared. A few shepherds and goatherds remained, their protégés skipping round the hillsides to nibble tufts of herbs between carob trees, aloes, and yuccas, but otherwise life focused increasingly on tourism. Luckily that brought a few positive changes to this seductive *pueblo blanco* splashed with bougainvillea. Small, foreign-owned restaurants popped up in the narrow backstreets bringing couscous and even Persian dishes, while hip bars became well-imbibed social hubs to while away the long hot nights.

Summer after summer I would cruise down from my home in Paris in an old Mercedes laden with books, notes, my laptop, and a fax machine (this was pre-Internet) to write travel guides about exotic countries I had just travelled to. Between swims, siestas, and socializing, my focus during the long, scorching, silent afternoons was on countries like Indonesia, India, Vietnam, or Mexico. In the midst of my vagrant, globetrotting existence, Andalucía had become my anchor, my home.

But by the turn of the millennium my life had changed. I moved back from Paris to London, my parents died, and the Mojácar house was sold. I felt bereft.

I continued to travel regularly all over Spain to write travel features and books, as I did to North Africa, mainly Morocco but also Tunisia and Libya, and to the Middle East, but I missed that deep connection with the land. "Es tu tierra!" (it's your land) as a local builder once said to me, holding up a fistful of soil. Once, after driving from Extremadura into Andalucía, I realized how sensorial my attachment was when I entered a village bar to be dazzled by a chaotic patchwork of patterned tiles, whiffed garlic sizzling in olive oil, heard a cheeping canary, and was instantly served a saucer of crisp fried fish with my *caña*. It was all about lightness, simple bounty, and good cheer—and it felt like home.

Finally, after scouting around villages from the Cádiz coast to the Alpujarra mountains, I settled on a country house in a little known, mountainous region between Granada and Córdoba: the Subbética. In fact, it's the geographical heart of Andalucía, although I didn't know that then. My house hugs the edge of a hamlet of olive farmers, all deeply rural in spirit, with none of the gloss that Mojácar eventually acquired. Life slows to a crawl here. My long terrace faces hills carpeted in olive trees ending at the distant snowy peaks of the Sierra Nevada, while far below in the other direction is the village of Iznájar, topped by a Moorish castle that remained a stronghold of the emirate of Granada virtually until its capitulation. The name itself derives from the Arabic *hisn ashar* meaning "happy castle." A welcoming place indeed.

Days here are calm and uncomplicated, the perfect antidote to London's fast lane. It is still a deeply macho society where men monopolize the bars and women labor at the stoves or marshal the kids, while the young are hightailing it elsewhere. Yet I can't help but love the bountiful produce at the local markets, the homemade *salchicón*, the sweet, juicy winter oranges, the luscious green olive oil, the morning fish from Málaga sold out of the back of one van, and the freshly baked bread sold out of another.

Above all, I love my neighbors who turn up with bags bulging with peppers, tomatoes, figs, walnuts, or apricots fresh from their *huertos*, I love the old boys in flat caps (mostly named Antonio) chatting on benches who nod *hola* or *buenas* as we pass by, I love the shifting shadows and darkening clefts of the sierra, the dramatic skyscapes, the vast, twinkling night skies, the autumnal clouds that drift through the valley before dissipating into clear, golden light, the swooping, screeching swifts and swallows, the purple and yellow wildflowers that cloak the groves in spring, the stirring Easter processions and zany village *ferias* and fiestas, the blistering hot days of summer when we swim in the reservoir lake of Iznájar, the frenetic energy of the olive harvest culminating in the lingering smell of wood smoke in winter when the village mills rattle away long into the night.

So this book, in search of Al-Andalus through its culinary legacy, is my ode to the entire region—its momentous past, its bewitching landscapes, and its charming, garrulous, truly egalitarian, often surreal, and ever generous-hearted people, who are masters of *alegria*, of high decibels, and of setting the taste buds alight.

TRAVEL DIARY:
As I drive east out of Almería, dazzled by the morning sun bouncing off the Mediterranean, I mentally check off all the movies that have been shot here. They are legion, since the karst and schist sierras make perfect substitutes for Arabia and the Far West or convincing backdrops for Indiana Jones...

EAST
from Almería to Granada
desert–coast–mountains

As I drive east out of Almería, dazzled by the morning sun bouncing off the Mediterranean, I mentally check off all the movies that have been shot here. They are legion, since the karst and schist sierras make perfect substitutes for Arabia and the Far West or convincing backdrops for Indiana Jones. *Banditos* ahoy! Spiking the horizon, I spot Lawrence of Arabia's perfect props, palm trees sagging with huge clusters of fresh yellow dates. Yet nobody here seems to pick them—have they forgotten how?

Almería's glory

The previous day I looked out from the massive 10th century Alcazaba (*kasbah* or fortress) over an urban mosaic of flat roofs and cube-shaped houses, a former 10th century quarter called the Barrio de la Medina and about as North African as you can get. It could be Tangier but it is Almería, a Roman port that was transformed by Al-Andalus into its lifeline with the Islamic world.

Prosperous and cosmopolitan, it became the crossroads of Yemeni settlers and traders from Egypt, Syria, France, and Italy. The economy soared due to the production of silk—made from cocoons and transported on mules from the nearby Alpujarra mountains. Then in 955, thanks to the hyperactive Caliph Abd-er Rahman III, Almería's status was crowned by this mammoth Alcazaba, very appropriate for a city whose name derived from the Arabic *Al-mariyat*, meaning "watchtower." Later, in the 11th century, as one of the most powerful *taifas* (principalities), it nurtured poets and philosophers. Integrated into the last-stand emirate of Granada, Almería fell to Catholic forces in 1489.

Immaculately restored, the extensive crenellated walls linking two hilltops make it the largest Arab fortress in Europe. Inside, life feels dreamy: jasmine and pine trees scent the air, chattering birds dive bomb pomegranate trees, palms, and oleanders, and water is channeled to tinkling fountains. Beyond, like a mirage, the sweeping bay sparkles in a heat haze.

Compared with Andalusia's other star cities, Almería seems forgotten by the outside world. Just a decade or so ago the neighborhood around the Alcazaba was an intimidating quarter of *gitanos* (gypsies) where you had to watch your back—and your car. Even today as I wander along a dirt track behind the fortress, I pass beaten-up vehicles and decrepit houses and then, alerted by a blast of flamenco music, see an ageing, pony-tailed Lothario watching me intently from a tiny doorway.

Yet central Almería is gentrifying fast. Streets of elegant, pastel-colored houses from the 19th century mining boom lead to a sleek, refurbished food market and a hub of animated taverns off the main boulevard, the Paseo de Almería. Here I investigate Nuestra Tierra Taberna, a specialist in Almerian tapas and wine, where I indulge in a *copa* of punchy, smoky *vino de la tierra* to match a superior tapa of Iberian pork cheeks in a mozárabe sauce. Afterwards I return to the first bar I ever visited in the city at the Teatro Cervantes, a fin de siècle wedding cake where tables spill onto a terrace. Today they serve hip *pintxos*; thirty five odd years ago I burned my tongue on garlicky *gambas pil pil* swimming in hot oil.

What distinguishes Almería from other Andalusian cities is the North African presence, and not just one that caters to tourists, like in Granada. A visible community lives and works here, buying meat at a Halal butcher or fish at the market. The women wear *djellabas* and the men chain-smoke outside of cafés—when they are not toiling in El Ejido, Europe's sprawling capital of hothouse vegetables. Because centuries on, these latter-day Moors constitute the exploited lifeblood of Almería's 165 square miles of plastic polytunnels. In summer, they pile into ferries to head across the sea to visit families in Nador, Melilla, Oran, or Ghazaouet. The traffic has always been two-way.

Wild Cabo de Gata

Skirting the coastline east of Almería I spot leggy pink flamingoes stalking through lagoons, then a church tower jutting high above tiny whitewashed houses and gleaming mountains of salt. This is Las Salinas del Cabo, producer of the gourmet *flor de sal*, crystallized salt flowers, and last stop on the road before the lighthouse. In the background loom the somber, volcanic hills of the Cabo de Gata Natural Park, a haunting area of wild beaches, cliffs, cacti, Moorish fortifications, a derelict gold mine, and modest fishing villages. I have explored it many a time from north of the cape, but never from this surreal southern side, and at last discover that the name Cabo de Gata derives from Phoenician Arabic for cornelians and agates, *Cabpta-Gata*. In fact the whole area is threaded with rich mineral veins discovered millennia later by French and British mining companies; I remember picking up scattered garnets on a walk years ago.

After sampling the luscious *arroces* of El Parque restaurant, I set off again. By the roadside I stop to chat with a goatherd who tells me that it has not rained in months. "I used to have two or three hundred goats," he remarks, "Now I don't even have thirty, since there's hardly any grass left." It is sad but not surprising, as Almería has

been the driest corner of Europe for decades, a symbol of ongoing desertification.

West to Granada

I could take the inland route to Granada that traverses Andalucía's desert of hallucinatory lunar landscapes where limestone cliffs are pockmarked with cave dwellings, many still inhabited and accessorized with TV antennas and burglar alarms. Instead I follow the coast, swinging round the stark hills of shale in order to reach Roquetas de Mar where I am visiting one of the province's two Michelin-starred restaurant, Alejandro.

After an avenue of palms scything through unglamorous light industry and polytunnels, I reach a pretty harbor overlooked by an over-restored Renaissance relic, the Castillo de Santa Ana. While fishermen untangle their nets, skinny cats prowl the quay in search of scraps. One man sings into his cell phone—a love song, a lullaby, or a lament?

Later, digesting Alejandro's gourmet indulgences, I continue west into a blinding sunset. As the coast road swings and dips around barren mountains it passes oceans, not of water, but of plastic roofing. At one point, due to the refractions of the setting sun, it is impossible to distinguish between the *invernaderos* and the actual sea—I feel adrift between man and nature. At last the highway forks inland, up through the shadowy hills of the Contraviesa to the Alpujarras, and I swap this synthetic landscape for rugged escarpments and mountain villages.

Las Alpujarras

Once terraced and farmed by the Berbers of Al-Andalus, the Alpujarras became the refuge for prince Boabdil and his followers after he surrendered Granada in 1492, though he soon moved on to Morocco. A few decades later the area was a stronghold for the *Morisco* rebellions, ferociously quashed. Fast forward five centuries and these

bucolic gorges and foothills of the Sierra Nevada are a haven for alternative lifestyles; some new agers live in teepees, others teach yoga or meditation, and many are foreign. A few write books, the pioneer being Gerald Brenan back in the 1920s, and more recently the ex-rock musician-cum-sheep farmer, Chris Stewart. The dawdling pace, clean air, inspiring scenery, and local personalities are clearly conducive.

I am staying at the western gateway, the spa town of Lanjarón, source of Spain's first-ever bottled mineral water. Not surprisingly, its gushing spring water was a huge draw for Berber farmers, inspiring village houses in the valley that could easily be in the Atlas Mountains. In just over 60 miles the landscape has switched from Almería's desert into this fertile enclave where avocados, custard apples, and oranges flourish, where the streets are lined with plane trees, water channels and drinking fountains.

Dozens of gourmet grocery stores sell *jamón serrano* from nearby Trévelez, a village just below peninsular Spain's highest peak, Mulhacén (named after Granada's penultimate emir). Beside the dangling legs are sausages, local honeys and jams, goat cheese, olive oil, and fig cakes as well as fruit and vegetables piled into gorgeous esparto grass or wicker baskets. Alpujarran pottery has its own style, too, with one traditional design clearly derived from a Berber tagine pot, while coarse *jarapa* rugs inject splashes of color. Farming actually peaks in bounty further east at Laujar de Andarax, which, ever since the Moors, has been famed for its cereals, vines, vegetables, olives, mulberry trees, fruit, and sheep, and today produces excellent wine. Paradise indeed.

When I walk down from the flourishing gardens of the Alcadima hotel, I can't help but shiver at the sight of a theatrical castle, now on supports, teetering on a high crag in the valley. I know the legend only too well; the last *Morisco* rebel leader threw himself off its walls rather than be taken prisoner by King Ferdinand.

Granada—ultimate expression of paradise

As I leave Lanjarón, I pass a stooped old man pulling a mule piled high with hay, no doubt the last muleteer—times are changing fast. In half an hour, the road curls northwards to reach Granada, the most emblematically Moorish of all of Andalucía's cities, with its iconic Alhambra overlooking the *vega*, the agricultural plain to the west, and the snowy peaks of the Sierra Nevada to the east.

Modern-day Granada may be a thriving university town and a worthy descendant of the scholarly College of Yusuf founded by the Nazrids, but tourism is part of the mix, so you need a good nose (or this book) to track down quality taverns and restaurants. They do exist, as do the descendants of Nazrid craftsmen who made vividly patterned ceramics and introduced marquetry (wood mosaics) and lute making, the latter evolving into today's much-coveted guitars. All three crafts flourish to this day.

But there is more than that. This mythical city possesses a strange schizophrenia, pitting the lower, mainly Catholic town full of Renaissance façades, baroque monasteries, and broad avenues against the exquisite palaces and gardens of the hilltop Alhambra and the labyrinthine Moorish quarter of the hillside opposite, the once walled Albayzín. The first is grandiose, proud, the expression of conquerors and commerce, the other delicate, secretive, sensuous—and for me, far more seductive.

It is in the steep Albayzín that you sense a lingering Moorish presence—up twists and turns of alleyways and stairways, through horseshoe arches and past *carmenes* with their walled, fragrant gardens of jasmine, honeysuckle, and plumbago, spiked by cypress trees. Although the original twenty seven mosques all disappeared beneath churches, at the very top of the hill I peep inside El Salvador to admire an impressive survivor, an Almohad courtyard of horseshoe arches. And

there is a surprise, too. Right beside the tourist lookout terrace of San Nicolás is the striking Great Mosque, completed in 2003 for Granada's burgeoning community of Muslim converts and Moroccan shopkeepers. Many of the converts live in this neighborhood beside dreadlocked travellers trailing mangy dogs and a few more gentrified inhabitants. Part noble, part humble, the Albayzín is a social conundrum, in García Lorca's words, "a tragedy of contrasts," but still exotic.

At the bottom of the hill by the Darro river I make a beeline for a modest building that actually predates most of the Alhambra: the 11th century Arab baths. As light filters through star-shaped apertures into the luminous, vaulted tiled rooms, I am struck by how much beauty was woven into a banal washhouse. Like the mosques, most *baños* were destroyed after the *reconquista* but this one miraculously survived.

In contrast, a few doors down is the imposing Renaissance Convent of Santa Catalina where nuns beaver away baking melt-in-your-mouth almond cookies and other sweets, mostly from Moorish recipes. You can buy them at a little grille, but the recipes remain a fiercely guarded secret. When I called to inquire and spoke to the sister in charge of the kitchen, I received a resolute "no!"

Up in the Alhambra another seductive story unfolds. Here you enter a magical treasure chest of craftsmanship designed to evoke paradise, where Persian influences pervade lush patios and pools frame intimate inner salons and walkways. Walls dazzle with multi-colored geometric *zelij* (mosaic tiles) while ceiling domes of intricately carved stucco *muqarnas* (honeycomb) create a kind of filigree nirvana, echoed in exquisitely inlaid wooden ceilings. Altogether they capture the sumptuous refinement of this last gasp of Moorish Spain, despite its internal feuds, (the) treachery, and (the) tragedies. Of course I have to weave through hordes of visitors from all over the world, yet artistry triumphs and on every visit I am entranced.

Later, as the light fades, I return for a night visit to the Generalife, the summer palace, to amble between towering hedges and scented shrubs and end at the dancing fountains in the Patio de las Acequias. Far below, the lights of Granada flicker, mirrored by a dome of celestial stars, while on the next hillside, framed by cypress trees, the illuminated windows of the Nazrid towers glow. It almost feels as if Boabdil, his wife Morayma, and his mother Aisha had never left.

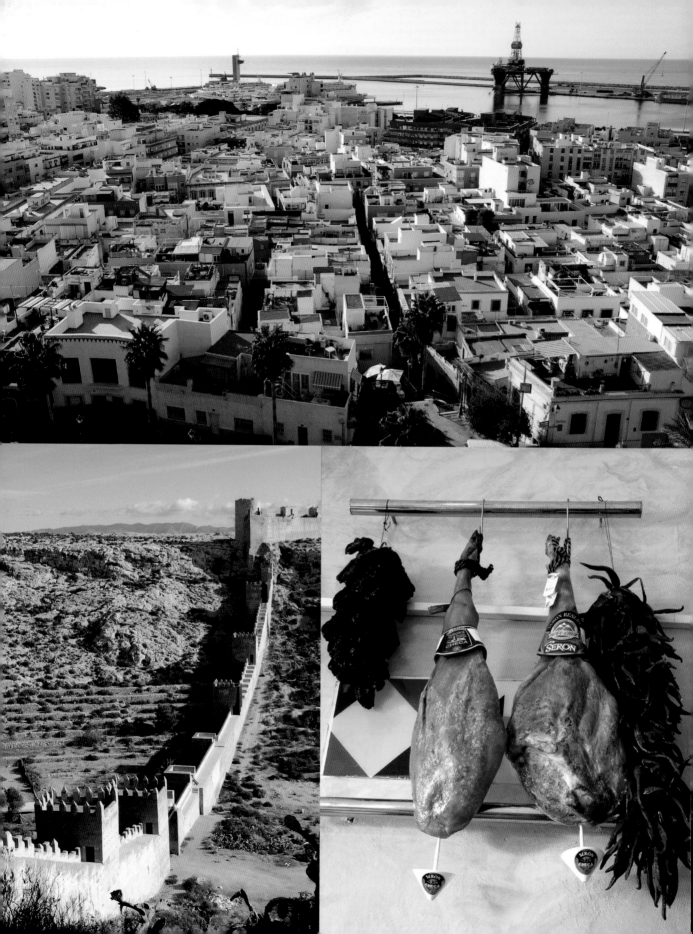

NUESTRA TIERRA TABERNA, *Almería*

Right in the heart of Almería's main cluster of tapas bars, or taverns, is this relatively young addition, its name meaning "our land." And the tapas here really are about showcasing the products of the province. The agricultural history of this arid corner of Spain has long been checkered, although everything changed in the 1970s when acres of plastic greenhouses started to proliferate. Diego Ferrón, the tavern manager, explains, "Almería is known for a survival diet due to its extensive desert." The basic dish of *migas* (fried breadcrumbs or flour), for example, has long been a staple.

Diego and his brother Moises are the third generation of bar owners in their family—catering courses through their veins. While studying for a diploma in tourism, Diego crisscrossed the entire province and, as a result, there is very little he doesn't know about local specialties. "People say we don't value what we have here, so when we opened in 2012 I wanted to use old-fashioned recipes but with a modern twist. And as Almería borders the province of Granada, there are many similarities—one being the incredible choice of free tapas." Diego's concept has clearly worked, as the bar has already moved to larger premises and is packed night after night.

Serves 4

Cod, tomato, and red pepper salad
Zaramandoña

This typical appetizer is from Tabernas, in northeastern Almería province, which has been the location for numerous blockbusters set in the desert, thanks to its stark karst landscapes. Diego maintains that *zaramandoña* is rare these days, although it is a cousin of Granada's much more common *remojón*. He suggests replacing the red pepper with green, and adding a handful of chopped black olives.

2 medium-large red bell peppers
7 oz (200 g) cod fillet
10 dry-packed sun-dried tomatoes
3 tablespoons extra virgin olive oil
1 tablespoon white wine vinegar
Salt and white pepper
3 scallions, finely chopped
2 hardboiled eggs, grated or chopped

Preheat the oven to 400°F (200°C) and roast the peppers for 20 minutes or so (or grill them on a grill pan), until the skins are scorched. Remove, peel off the charred skin, hull and deseed them, then slice into strips.

In a saucepan, cover the cod and sun-dried tomatoes in water, bring to a boil, then simmer for about 10 minutes, until the cod is cooked. Remove with a slotted spoon, flake the cod, and chop the tomatoes.

Mix the oil and vinegar to make a vinaigrette, and season with salt and pepper according to taste.

In a glass bowl, combine the peppers, cod, sundried tomatoes, and the scallions, stir in the vinaigrette, and sprinkle with the hardboiled egg. Serve immediately.

Serves 4

Pork loin in garlic sauce
Lomo al ajo cabañil

According to Diego, this is a sauce you can use with most kinds of meat but, when possible, he uses rabbit or kid goat—both are healthy, lean alternatives to pork. The recipe originates in the north of Almería province, in the sierra around Velez Rubio and Velez Blanco, home to the prehistoric Indalo cave figure that has been adopted as a protective symbol throughout the region. May this garlic sauce protect you.

3–5 tablespoons extra virgin olive oil
2 potatoes, peeled and cut into chunks
14 oz (400 g) pork loin, cut into pieces of similar size
Salt and white pepper
½ cup (125 ml) white wine
½ cup (125 ml) white wine vinegar
8 large cloves garlic, peeled and minced
1 teaspoon ground cumin
Handful of flat-leaf parsley leaves, chopped

Heat 3 tablespoons of the oive oil in a deep, wide frying pan and fry the potatoes over medium heat until tender, 10 to 15 minutes. Remove from the pan and set aside.

Tip the pork into the same pan, adding a little more oil, season with salt and pepper, and fry over medium heat for 20 to 25 minutes until nearly cooked. Stir or shake the pan occasionally to separate the pieces.

Once nearly cooked, add the wine, then the reserved potatoes. Warm them slightly, then add the vinegar. Combine, being careful not to break up the potatoes.

Add the garlic, cumin, and parsley, and simmer on low heat for a further 5 minutes until completely cooked.

Cod, potato, and garlic soup
Ajo colorão

Typical of Almerian coastal towns and villages, the pungent, fishy flavor of this "survival" soup is heightened by punchy paprika, cumin, and saffron. It can be served hot or cold—a useful characteristic. Diego serves it as a tapa in a small bowl. Serve this soup with slices of sourdough bread.

1 lb 12 oz (800 g) floury potatoes
2 large ripe tomatoes
Scant 1 tablespoon mild paprika
9 oz (250 g) cod fillet, cut into chunks
1 medium white onion
2 teaspoons ground cumin
1 teaspoon saffron
Generous ¾ cup (200 ml) extra virgin olive oil
Salt

In a large pot, cover the potatoes with water and add the tomatoes and half the paprika. Bring to a boil, lower the heat, and simmer for about 20 minutes until the potatoes are nearly cooked (test with a fork). Add the fish and continue to bubble until completely cooked, 5 to 6 minutes.

Using a slotted spoon, transfer the potatoes, tomatoes, and cod to a bowl, reserving the cooking liquid.

Tip the potato mixture and the onion into a blender, along with the remaining paprika, cumin, and saffron, and about 1 cup (250 ml) of the reserved cooking liqid. Process to a purée.

Transfer the mixture to a large bowl. Beating continuously with a fork, slowly add the olive oil in a trickle, to thicken the soup to a fluid but thick consistency. Add salt to taste.

Serve hot or chilled.

Serves 6

Pork cheeks with Mozarabic sauce
Carillada de cerdo con salsa mozarabe

This delicious meat dish is deceptive, since it looks simple, but the sweet, complex sauce contains multiple layers of flavor. It incorporates dates, which grow in abundance in this region, with raisins and wine. It works just as well with beef or lamb, though pork cheeks cooked slowly like this become meltingly soft. Serve with creamy mashed potatoes to mop up the sauce, and perhaps some carrots.

Extra virgin olive oil
2 lb 10 oz (1.2 kg) pork cheeks or tenderloin
3 onions, chopped
2 cups (9 oz/250 g) diced carrots
3 tomatoes, roughly chopped
1 cup (250 ml) red wine if using pork cheeks,
    or 2 cups (500 ml) if using tenderloin
½ cup (2 ¾ oz/75 g) black seedless raisins
4 dates, pitted and chopped
Handful of fresh thyme
½ teaspoon salt
½ teaspoon white pepper

In a large, deep pan, sauté the meat in plenty of olive oil to brown on all sides. Transfer the meat to a plate and set aside.

Add the onions and carrots to the pan, fry briefly to color, and then add the tomatoes. Cover the pan, lower the heat, and simmer for about 10 minutes to reduce to a sauce.

Return the meat to the pan, add the wine, raisins, dates, and thyme and season with the salt and pepper. Bring to a simmer, cover, and cook slowly until the meat is almost falling apart, 2 to 3 hours (tenderloin will cook faster).

Once cooked, transfer the meat to serving plates. Beat the remaining sauce with a fork to thicken. Pour some sauce over each portion of meat and serve immediately.

Serves 4 to 6

Caramel bread pudding
Pan de calatrava

This traditional pudding is like a coarsely textured crème caramel. It originated in Murcia, just north of Almería, where it used to be made with stale bread. In this recipe from Diego's aunt, Marí Carmen, the dessert has been upgraded with *magdalenas*, oval sponge cakes. You will need an 8-inch (20-cm) round cake pan or ovensafe dish and a larger dish to make a bain-marie (see note).

Oil or butter, for greasing
2 cups (500 ml) milk
1 tablespoon cinnamon
1 tablespoon vanilla extract
Thickly peeled zest of one lemon
1 cup (7 oz/200 g) sugar
3 beaten eggs
10 *magdalenas* or French madeleines, or
   7 oz (200 g) vanilla sponge cake
Whipped cream, to serve (optional)

Caramel sauce
1 cup (7 oz/200 g) sugar
2 tablespoons water
1 teaspoon lemon juice

Note: A bain-marie, or water bath, can be easily improvised. Find a baking dish that is larger than your cake pan, place the pan inside, then fill the larger dish with hot water to reach about three-quarters of the way up. The bubbling hot water in the oven will cook the pudding without drying it out.

Preheat the oven to 350°F (180°C) and grease an 8-inch (20-cm) round cake pan or ovensafe dish with oil or butter.

First, make the caramel sauce: In a small, heavy bottomed pan, combinine the sugar, water, and lemon juice. Heat over low heat, tipping the pan from side to side until the sugar dissolves (do not use a spoon). Continue for about 2 minutes, or until the mixture bubbles, caramelizes, and the edges turn golden brown. Quickly pour the caramel into the cake pan or dish, coating the base.

To make the pudding, combine the milk with the cinnamon, vanilla, and lemon zest in a small pan, and slowly bring to a boil. Remove from heat, remove the lemon zest, and add the sugar. Allow to cool a little, add the eggs, and whisk the mixture with a fork or electric hand mixer to amalgamate.

Roughly break up and scatter the *magdalenas* over the caramel in the pan, covering the surface completely, then pour the milk and egg mixture on top.

Place the mold in a bain-marie (see note) in the oven for 45 minutes or until cooked. Check that it's ready by piercing with a knife or skewer; when it comes out clean, it is done.

Allow to cool thoroughly. Easing it away from the pan with a knife, if necessary, flip the pudding upside down onto a plate. You can keep it overnight in the refrigerator but bring to room temperature before serving.

Serve as it is, or with whipped cream.

Serves 4

Cheese parcels in honey and orange reduction
Saquitos de queso con miel y naranja

"Girls love this tapa," laughs Diego—it's hardly surprising, since it combines delicious textural contrast with subtle, sweet Moorish flavors. You need to complete the final stage just minutes before eating. Add whipped cream as an extra sweet hit.

1 cup (250 ml) orange juice
Scant ½ cup (100 ml) clear honey
3 balls fresh mozzarella (each around 2½
   inches/6 cm in diameter), quartered
12 sheets filo pastry, 9 x 14 inches/
   23 x 36½ cm (or cut larger sheets to size)
2 cups (500 ml) sunflower oil
1¼ cups (5½ oz/150 g) chopped walnuts, or
   1½ cups (5½ oz/150 g) slivered almonds
2 tablespoons confectioner's sugar (optional)

First, make the reduction: in a small pot, combine the orange juice and honey and simmer over low heat, stirring occasionally, for about 30 minutes, until syrupy.

Prepare the cheese parcels by loosely wrapping each section of cheese in filo pastry, pressing the seams together. While working on assembling them, keep the pastry sheets and finished parcels moist under a damp tea-towel to avoid drying out.

In a small saucepan, heat the sunflower oil over medium heat. When it is smoking, quickly plunge the parcels into the oil for 20 seconds, or until the pastry turns golden. Using a slotted spoon, transfer to a plate lined with paper towels to absorb any excess oil.

Immediately transfer to a serving plate, drizzle with the reduction, sprinkle with nuts, and dust with confectioner's sugar, if desired. Serve immediately.

RESTAURANTE EL PARQUE, *Cabo de Gata*

El Parque feels like the last outpost of civilization in southeast Spain. It sits at the base of a serpentine road leading up to the Cabo de Gata lighthouse that commands a headland known to Greek and Phoenician sailors thousands of years ago. From here the coast swings north to demarcate Spain's largest volcanic area—wild, semi-deserted, and a protected *parque natural*.

The restaurant belongs to Manuel Barbero, 78, who gravitates between Madrid and the fishing hamlet of La Almadraba de Monteleva, right beside the salt pans of Las Salinas. Despite this remoteness, it is barely half an hour's drive from Almería.

"Es mi tierra!" (it's my land!) he exclaims when I ask him how he found the spot back in 1990. In those early days it was a typical *chiringuito* (beach bar) with walls of cane and a floor of sand. Now upgraded into a large wooden cabin with views of the sierra and the sea, it magnetizes locals, who pile in for perfectly cooked, ultra-fresh seafood and succulent *arroces*. These rice dishes are skillfully prepared by the tireless cook, María Martinez, although the recipes are Manuel's. At the front of house, another María keeps this popular institution buzzing all year round. May those Valencian inventors of paella up the coast eat their hearts out!

Serves 4 to 6

Soupy seafood rice
Arroz caldoso de marisco

Although Manuel claims these quantities are for four people, they will easily stretch to two more, depending on appetites. In such cases, increase the quantity of rice and stock a little. The local *gambon rojo* (known as *carabinero* in western Andalusia) or red shrimp, comes from the fishing port of Garrucha, just up the coast from the Cabo de Gata, but you can use jumbo shrimp. María makes her own stock using the sea bass heads and bones, although to save time, buy good quality, fresh fish stock. Use a terracotta ovensafe dish if you have one.

⅓–scant ½ cup (80–100 ml) extra virgin olive oil

4 cloves garlic, diced

2 tomatoes, chopped

1 sprig of parsley, chopped

9 oz (250 g) clams, cleaned

1½ lb (700 g) squid, cleaned and sliced in rings,
    or cuttlefish, cleaned and cut in small pieces

1¾ cups (11 oz/320 g) round-grain rice such
    as Bomba, Calasparra, or Arborio

4 medium langoustines

9 oz (250 g) jumbo shrimp in shells

1 lb (500 g) mussels

1 green bell pepper, seeded, deribbed,
    and sliced into rings

Scant ½ cup (1¾ oz/50 g) peas

About 7½ cups (1.75 liters) fish stock

5½ oz (150 g) sea bass fillet, sliced

In a large ovensafe terracotta pot or saucepan, make a *sofrito* base by cooking the oil, garlic, tomato, and parsley over medium heat, stirring often. Once it starts to color, add the clams and squid or cuttlefish. Stir from time to time to prevent anything sticking, and cook until the clams open and the squid turns golden. This will take only a few minutes.

Now tip in the rice and sauté for 3 to 4 minutes, stirring constantly. Remove from the heat.

Arrange all the shrimp and mussels on top of the rice in a radial pattern, then scatter on the green pepper and peas.

Return the pot to the heat and pour in the stock without stirring. Bring to a boil over high heat and bubble vigorously for 10 minutes, then add the sliced sea bass, inserting the chunks between the shellfish.

After 3 minutes more at a vigorous boil, reduce the heat to medium, and simmer for a further 7 minutes, keeping an eye on the stock level and adding more if it gets too dry (it should be a soupy consistency). Test the rice to check that it is cooked.

Serve immediately.

Serves 4 to 6

Seafood paella
Arroz de marisco

If possible, use a traditional paella dish to make this grand Spanish classic, otherwise a very large frying pan will do. Spain discovered rice thanks to the Moors who cultivated extensive rice fields in the lagoons near Valencia; from there, rice and risotto emigrated to Italy—a surprising fact. The rice lagoons survive and their cooked spin-offs, *arroces*, have become Spanish staples as well as a tourist cliché. Only a handful of restaurants in the province of Almería (south of the paella kings in Valencia and Murcia) can claim to have truly mastered the art of paella. Make sure you have what the Valencians call a *soccarat*, a crunchy base of rice grains stuck (but not burned) to the bottom of the pan—delicious to scrape up!

⅓–scant ½ cup (80–100 ml) extra virgin olive oil
4 cloves garlic, chopped
2 tomatoes, chopped
1 sprig parsley
9 oz (250 g) clams, cleaned
2 ¼ lb (1 kg) squid or cuttlefish, cleaned, cut into rings or pieces
1 ¾ cups (11 oz/320 g) round-grain rice such as Bomba, Calasparra, or Arborio
9 oz (250 g) *carabinero* (scarlet shrimp) or jumbo shrimp in their shells
9 oz (250 g) shrimp
9 oz (250 g) mussels, shells cleaned
4 medium crayfish
Scant ½ cup (1 ¾ oz/50 g) peas
3 ½ cups (800 ml) fish and vegetable stock
1 lemon, quartered

In a paella pan or a large frying pan, make a *sofrito* base: heat the oil over medium heat and sauté the garlic, tomato, and parsley until tender, stirring often. As soon as it starts to color, add the clams and squid. Stir from time to time so that nothing sticks, and cook until the clams open and the squid becomes golden, just a few minutes.

Tip in the rice, heat for 3 to 4 minutes, then remove from the heat. Arrange the large and small shrimp, mussels, and crayfish on top, radiating from the center, and scatter the peas in between.

Return to the heat and pour in the fish stock, distributing it evenly without stirring. Bring to a boil and let it bubble vigorously, uncovered, for about 10 minutes, then turn the heat down and simmer for another 10 minutes, until the liquid has completely absorbed.

Remove from the heat and allow to sit for a few minutes, then arrange the lemon quarters around the edges, and serve.

Serves 4

Almerian *migas* or "crumbs"
Migas Almerienses

This is a real muscle-building dish, since you need to work energetically to keep the semolina moving while it is cooking. It was originally a poor man's dish made from stale breadcrumbs or balls of flour-and-water dough. That version survives elsewhere, but the superior semolina *migas* are a local passion around here, often served in Almería's bars as a small tapa. If you can't find *morcilla* (blood sausage), use more chorizo. And if you can't find fresh, semi-cured chorizo, you can substitute dried.

⅔ cup (150 ml) olive oil
2 heads garlic, outer skin peeled, sliced crosswise
2 green bell peppers, seeded and cut into strips
3½ oz (100 g) *morcilla* (blood sausage), sliced
5½ oz (150 g) fresh Spanish chorizo, sliced
5½ oz (150 g) bacon, cut into large pieces
2 cups (500 ml) water
3 cups (1 lb/500 g) semolina
Salt
3½ oz (100 g) pitted olives, split

In a paella pan or a deep frying pan, heat the olive oil over medium heat. Place the garlic in the oil cut-side down, and fry until golden. Transfer to a plate and set aside, leaving the oil in the pan.

Sauté the green pepper in the same pan until tender and lightly browned, then transfer to the plate. In the same pan, fry the blood sausage and chorizo slices for 5 minutes or so, turning them, then add the bacon and continue to fry until crispy, about 5 minutes. Transfer to the plate, leaving any remaining oil in the pan.

Add the measured water to the pan, then stir in the semolina and a pinch of salt. Cook over medium heat for 30 to 40 minutes, using a metal spatula to push, scrape, and turn the semolina constantly, and adding more water if it thickens too much. It is ready when it has turned a golden color, has a toasty smell, tastes of bread, and has become quite elastic.

Remove from the heat and share between dishes or arrange on one large serving dish, garnishing with all the fried ingredients on top. Serve with a plate of olives on the side.

Serves 4

Lemon cake
Pastel de limón

The perfect follow-up to a pig-out paella, this light lemony flan is also quite
easy to make. Manuel suggests serving it decorated with whipped cream
or drizzled with honey and sprinkled with chopped walnuts.

1 ¼ cups (300 ml) whole milk
2 x 3 oz (85 g) packages lemon gelatine
⅔ cup (5 ¾ oz/160 g) plain yogurt
Finely grated zest and juice of 1 lemon
2 tablespoons confectioner's sugar

In a saucepan, heat the milk until hot, but not boiling,
and sprinkle in the gelatin, stirring to dilute it.

In a bowl, mix together the yogurt, lemon zest
and juice, and the confectioner's sugar. Stir well to
combine. Add the milk and continue to beat with
a fork or whisk until it becomes a smooth paste.

Pour the mixture into an 11 by 7 inch (28
by 18 cm) baking dish with shallow sides,
and chill in the refrigerator for about 3 hours
until set. Cut into slices before serving.

ALEJANDRO, *Roquetas de Mar, Almería*

Alejandro, after whom this restaurant is named, is an elusive young chef—one day in Hong Kong, the next in Mexico City, and only rarely in Roquetas where he grew up. However he is the Skype-chef, liaising from afar with his parents, Juan Sánchez Juarez and Encarnación Ruiz López, in whose hands the calm, elegant restaurant remains. Far from strangers to the job, this charming couple used to run their own restaurant nearby, Bocacho, where Alejandro honed his skills before opening his doors in 2006. Since then, his travels have lured him away, though he returns to Roquetas whenever possible.

Located right beside the fishing harbor, the restaurant makes the most of the fresh catch that arrives every morning, typically swordfish, tuna, red mullet, white shrimp, and lobsters. Alejandro's longstanding Michelin star is justified by a consistent finesse and creativity in the dishes, as well as consummate service, and it is a surprise to find such quality in this haphazardly urbanized resort of southeastern Spain. The streamlined yachts bobbing in the marina nonetheless point to some well-heeled visitors.

Encarna, Alejandro's mother, is particularly knowledgeable about Andalusian traditions, and by including couscous on the menu makes a rare nod to the Berber past.

To top it all off, every dish is light and highly nutritious.

Serves 4

Cherry and tomato gazpacho
Gazpacho de cereza y tomate

Sweet cherries are a Middle Eastern fruit thought to have originated in Anatolia and later cultivated in Al-Andalus. Not the case for the tomato, of course, that American interloper. At Alejandro, an elegant cocktail glass of this gazpacho kicks off their lengthy tasting menu. You can increase the quantities to suit a normal-size dinner, but since the gazpacho is intense and dense, you won't need large helpings. You will need to marinate it overnight.

½ small onion, chopped
½ clove garlic, chopped
1 ½ tablespoons chopped red bell pepper
1 tablespoon chopped green bell pepper
3 ½ oz (100 g) ripe Raf tomatoes or plum
 tomatoes (about 3), chopped
½ teaspoon fine salt
Generous ¾ cup (200 ml) mineral water
½ teaspoon ground cumin
1 teaspoon sherry vinegar
½ cup (2 ½ oz/70 g) cherries, pitted
1 ½ tablespoons fresh breadcrumbs
3 tablespoons extra virgin olive
 oil, plus more to garnish
Mint or basil leaves, to garnish

In a bowl, combine all the ingredients except the olive oil and herbs, stir roughly together and leave to marinate overnight.

The following day, tip the mixture into a food processor and blend to a smooth purée. Strain into a bowl and return to the blender. With the machine running, slowly add the olive oil to achieve a smooth emulsion.

Serve in small glasses, garnished with a few drops of extra virgin olive oil and the mint or basil leaves.

Marinated sardine lasagna with ajoblanco
Lasaña de sardinas marinadas con ajoblanco

Exquisite to look at and to eat, this dish is quite a tour de force to make, but will undoubtedly impress your dinner guests. The textural contrasts and delicacy take it light-years away from classic Andalusian cooking—but the sardines and *ajoblanco* are rooted in local culture. The *ajoblanco* can also be expanded into a solo appetizer—just float some seedless white grapes or melon cubes on top. Tobiko is a classic Japanese roe used in sushi and maki rolls, crunchy and smoky in taste. You will need to start a day ahead.

6 small sheets of rice paper, soaked in
   warm water for 20 seconds
2 heaped teaspoons finely chopped pistachios
1 ½ oz (42 g) tobiko (flying fish roe)
Edible flowers (optional)
1 heaped teaspoon lemon salt (crush coarse sea
   salt with lemon zest, pepper, and paprika)

Ajoblanco
¼ cup (1 oz/30 g) blanched almonds
1 ¾ tablespoons pine nuts
½ clove garlic
1 teaspoon sherry vinegar
3 tablespoons fresh breadcrumbs
3 tablespoons mineral water
2 teaspoons sunflower oil
3 tablespoons extra virgin olive oil

Marinated sardines
Scant 1 cup (225 ml) mineral water
3 teaspoons coarse sea salt
⅓ cup (80 ml) sherry vinegar
2 lb 10 oz (1.2 kg) fresh sardines,
   descaled, filleted, and rinsed
2 ½ cups (600 ml) sunflower oil

Make the ajoblanco
Combine all the ingredients in a bowl and leave to marinate overnight. The following day, tip the mixture into a food processor and blend to a smooth purée. Strain into a bowl and chill in the refrigerator.

Make the marinated sardines
In a pan, heat the mineral water and salt until it boils, then leave to cool. Add the vinegar, then submerge the sardine fillets in the liquid and set aside to marinate for about 50 minutes, depending on size. Drain, blot the fillets on paper towels, then place them in a clean bowl and submerge them in the sunflower oil.

To serve
On each plate, lay one sardine fillet, place a rice sheet of roughly the same size on top, then layer on another sardine fillet on top at an angle, then top with a third sardine fillet.

To crown the sardines, sprinkle some chopped pistachios along the length of the final fillet, add a small dollop of tobiko and some flowers, and trickle some of the ajoblanco around it. Sprinkle lightly with lemon salt before serving.

Grandmother's migas, paprika broth, and red jumbo shrimp

Migas de mi abuela, caldo "quemao" y gamba roja

Here, the spectacular scarlet shrimp takes center stage. In eastern Andalusia, it is only fished from the ports of Roquetas and Garrucha. Over in western Andalusia it is known as a *carabinero*. Alejandro's idea was to unite this delicacy with the peasant dish, *migas*, in a fine-dining context. "He always loved migas as a young boy," his mother, Encarna, muses. You can of course substitute the shrimp with crayfish or any other spectacular crustacean.

Paprika broth

1 red bell pepper
2 tablespoons extra virgin olive oil
1 large clove garlic, chopped
3 dry-packed sun-dried tomatoes
Pinch of Guajillo chili powder
3 ½ oz (100 g) ripe Raf tomatoes or plum
  tomatoes (about 3), chopped
½ medium potato, peeled and cut into equal chunks
2 ½ cups (600 ml) good quality fish stock
2 teaspoons mild paprika
½ teaspoon cumin seeds

Migas

1 cup plus 2 tablespoons (270 ml) mineral water
2 teaspoons fine salt
¼ cup (60 ml) extra virgin olive oil
1 tablespoon garlic oil
1 clove garlic, peeled and chopped
Generous ½ cup (3 ¼ oz/90 g) semolina
¾ cup (3 ¼ oz/90 g) yellow cornmeal

Shrimp

1 lb (500 g) jumbo scarlet shrimp
1 teaspoon garlic oil
2 tablespoons shrimp stock (or any shellfish stock)
½ chive, very finely chopped
Sea salt flakes

For the broth

Preheat the oven to 350°F (180°C). Roast the red pepper for 25 minutes until soft. Remove from the oven, cool, and chop, discarding the seeds.

In a deep pan, heat the olive oil over medium heat and sauté the chopped red pepper, garlic, and sun-dried tomatoes, then add the chili powder. Transfer to a blender, leaving any remaining oil in the pan, and process until smooth.

In the same pan sauté the tomatoes; once they are cooked, add the potato pieces and the fish stock. When the potatoes are tender, add the rest of the ingredients and cook for 5 minutes to reduce slightly.

Transfer to the blender, process to a smooth purée, and strain into a jug. Set aside.

For the Migas

In a small pan, bring the mineral water and salt to a boil.

In a large frying pan, heat the oils and add the garlic. Fry until golden, then add the semolina and cornmeal and fry for 5 minutes, stirring occasionally. Pour in the water and simmer over low heat for 10 to 15 minutes until absorbed, stirring continuously to loosen and separate the migas crumbs.

For the shrimp

Preheat the oven to 350°F (180°C), roast the shrimp for just 2 minutes, then peel them, leaving the head and tail intact.

In a saucepan, heat the oil, shrimp stock, and chive until hot.

Put a portion of migas on each plate, lay a shrimp on top and drizzle with a little of the shrimp stock. Sprinkle with flakes of sea salt. Serve with the broth on the side to add at the table.

Serves 6

Lamb confit with couscous
Cordero confitado en su jugo con couscous

Laborious, finicky, time consuming… but it is *so* good! A real labor of love, a tour de force, and a melt-in-your-mouth slab of juicy, compressed meat. If you don't want to make your own gravy, you can use 1 cup (9 oz/250 g) good-quality store-bought lamb gravy. You will need to start about two days ahead.

6 ½ lb (3 kg) lamb necks
Coarse sea salt
1 bushy sprig rosemary
2 large sprigs thyme
1 head garlic, crushed
Sunflower oil

Couscous
1 ¼ cups (300 ml) beef stock
1 ½ cups (9 oz/250 g) couscous
2 carrots, peeled and finely diced
3 ½ oz (100 g) zucchini (1 small),
  peeled and finely diced
Sea salt flakes

Place the lamb necks in a large bowl of water with some coarse salt and set aside for about 8 hours at room temperature to rid them of their blood.

Preheat the oven to 185°F (85°C).

Rinse the lamb necks, pat dry with paper towels, then place them in a roasting pan. Sprinkle with the rosemary, thyme, and garlic, then liberally coat in sunflower oil.

Roast in the oven for 12 to 13 hours until very tender, piercing the meat to make sure they are completely done.

Remove from the oven and allow to cool. Remove the meat from the bones. If you would like to make your own gravy, set the bones aside with any gelatin that seeped into the confit.

To make gravy, put the lamb bones and gelatin in a pan, cover, and simmer over low heat for 2 to 3 hours hours until it thickens.

In an 11 by 7 inch (28 by 18 cm) baking dish, layer the meat to make a terrine about 1 ½ inches (4 cm) thick. When finished, place another dish on top with a weight to compress and "sandwich" the meat. Chill in the refrigerator for 24 hours. Remove from the dish and slice as you wish.

For the couscous
Bring the stock to a boil then tip in the couscous. Remove from the heat and cover with a clean dish towel for 3 minutes. Remove the towel, stir the grains to separate them,

then replace the towel for another 3 minutes. Repeat until the couscous becomes quite dry and loose.

Blanch the carrot and zucchini in boiling water for 1 minute, then transfer to a bowl of iced water. Drain, dry, and stir them into the couscous.

On a grill pan over medium heat, heat the lamb pieces on both sides until they are warmed through. Meanwhile, in separate pans, warm up the couscous and gravy over low heat.

Serve the meat atop the couscous, and finish with the gravy and a few flakes of sea salt.

Spinach soup with white shrimp
Espinacas esparragás con gamba blanca

This is an intriguing dish—half soup, half shrimp cocktail, served tepid or cold, packed with flavors and very nutritious. It's an evolved version of a traditional Roquetas recipe normally made with chard and chickpeas, classic *andalusi* ingredients. Serve it in separate bowls.

¾ cup (3½ oz/100 g) almonds
5 cloves garlic, chopped
¼ teaspoon ground cumin
1 teaspoon chopped parsley
10 cups (10½ oz/300 g) spinach, roughly chopped
Extra virgin olive oil
1 large onion, sliced in crescents
2 medium-large tomatoes, chopped
3 cups (750 ml) vegetable stock
2 cups (500 ml) chicken stock
1 cup (250 ml) ham stock (made by boiling
    bones and cut-offs of ham, then reducing)
1 tablespoon sherry vinegar
Pinch of white pepper
¾ oz (20 g) dry Spanish chorizo
1½ cups (9 oz/250 g) cooked or canned white beans
10½ oz (300 g) white shrimp
Sea salt flakes

In a dry pan, toast the almonds with the garlic until golden, then coarsely grind them in a blender with the cumin and parsley. Set aside.

Blanch the spinach in boiling water then quickly chill in iced water to lock in the goodness. Drain and squeeze dry.

In a large saucepan, heat some olive oil and sweat the onion until tender. Add the tomatoes and simmer for about 10 minutes, then tip in the spinach and cook for 3 more minutes, covered. Stir in the almond mixture and set aside to cool.

In a saucepan, combine the stocks, vinegar, pepper, chorizo, and white beans and bring to a boil. Simmer for about 20 minutes. Remove from the heat and leave to infuse for another 20 minutes, then strain and set the stock aside. (You can use the drained beans and chorizo for another dish).

Peel the shrimp, remove their intestines, and set aside. Briefly sauté the heads in a little oil before squeezing them for their juice.

Share the stock between each bowl, spoon in the spinach mixture, then arrange the shrimp on top, drizzle with the shrimp juice, and sprinkle with salt flakes.

LA ALCADIMA, *Lanjarón, Alpujarras*

Luxuriant green foliage shatters your retina in the gardens of Hotel La Alcadima, a boutique hotel and restaurant on the western side of the Alpujarras. Thanks to abundant springs, the former *cortijo* (farmhouse) once managed the town's water supply until, in the 1950s, it metamorphosed into a pioneering swimming pool. Day-trippers flocked here from Granada, and slowly the hotel took shape.

It is still very much a family affair, with Gonzalo Rodriguez steering the restaurant and his daughter Amanda in charge of the hotel's marketing. "We want to maintain the idea of a small village," says Gonzalo, referring to the many patios that articulate the hotel, resplendent with fruit trees—quince, pomegranate, kumquat, and orange—amid splashes of tropical flowers.

He turns out to be a dedicated, impassioned cook: "I studied traditional recipes and talked to old people who told me about their family dishes. Most of what we serve is Alpujarran as we have such a wealth of ingredients—and we're lucky to have good soil and water. Further south they have to collect rainwater." Witnessing him work in the kitchen is like watching a tornado, his turbulent energy in high contrast to his calm sous chef, Monserrat, who works steadily beside him. "In the end," Gonzalo adds, "it was the mix of Jews, Arabs, and Iberians that produced the richness of our cuisine."

Butternut squash, almond, and bacon soup
Ajillo de calabaza

Gonzalo's multi-layered soup is packed with autumn and mountain flavors, so typical of the Alpujarras, plus a welcome crunch of almonds. The egg may seem superfluous, but its runny yolk adds an incredible unctuousness and binds the soup.

1 lb (500 g) waxy potatoes
1 butternut squash, peeled, halved, and seeded
Salt and freshly ground black pepper
9 oz (250 g) bacon, cut into pieces
2 large cloves garlic, chopped
Generous ¾ cup (200 ml) extra virgin olive oil
1 ¾ cups (9 oz/250 g) blanched almonds, toasted
4 eggs

In a large pot, boil the potatoes until cooked, 15 to 20 minutes. Remove from the pot, retaining the cooking water, peel, and set them aside.

Cut the squash into chunks. In a separate pot, boil the squash in lightly salted water until it is soft to a fork, about 20 minutes. Set aside in the cooking water.

Sauté the bacon in a little oil until crisp. Remove from the pan, reserving the oil. Pour off some of the excess oil, and fry the garlic briefly until it turns golden.

In a large bowl or the bowl of a food processor, combine the potatoes, squash, about 6⅓ cups (1.5 liters) of the cooking waters, and the extra virgin olive oil. Coarsely blend using the food processor or an immersion blender. Add the garlic, almonds, salt, and pepper and continue to mix until you obtain a smooth consistency.

Pour into individual bowls and sprinkle the crisp bacon pieces over the top.

Meanwhile, poach the eggs in boiling water and carefully lay one egg on the top of each bowl. (Alternatively you can fry the eggs.) Serve immediately.

Serves 4 to 6

Fava bean soup
Sopa de habas

This filling soup is packed with the punchy flavors of chorizo and paprika, making it a substantial dinner dish. The creamy texture of the beans perfectly complements the sharp, salty chorizo, and jamón. It is better to use fresh beans, but frozen ones are acceptable alternatives.

2 ½ cups (10 oz/280 g) shelled fava beans,
   from about 1 ¾ lb (750 g) pods
1 cup (250 ml) extra virgin olive oil
1 medium onion, peeled and diced
1 clove garlic, minced
Salt and white pepper
4 ½ oz (125 g) Serrano ham, cut into small pieces
1 orange, halved, one-half cut into pieces
1 large sprig fresh peppermint,
   or 1 ½ teaspoons dried
4 ¼ cups (1 liter) chicken stock
1 ½ teaspoons mild paprika
4 ½ oz (125 g) dried chorizo, sliced thickly

Bring a saucepan of water to a boil and blanch the beans for 1 to 2 minutes. Drain them, then tip them into a bowl of ice-cold water for 1 to 2 minutes to stop the cooking process. Gently squeeze the bright green beans out of their skins, then set aside.

Warm the oil in a large frying pan. Add the onion, garlic, salt, and pepper, stirring until soft but not colored, about 5 minutes. Toss in the ham.

Tip in the fava beans and continue to cook over low heat for 5 minutes, shaking the pan but taking care not to break the fragile beans, then add the orange pieces, so that the skin infuses flavor and fragrance. Cook slowly for 5 minutes more, until the beans change color and texture, then add the mint leaves and remove from the heat.

In a large saucepan, warm the chicken stock. Add the bean mixture and paprika, and squeeze in the remaining orange half, then toss in the chorizo. Bring to a boil, turn the heat down, and simmer for 2 minutes, and the soup is ready.

Serves 4

Alpujarran fried rabbit
Fritailla de conejo

Rabbits are legion in Andalusia and were a favorite source of lean meat in the days of the Moors. Gonzalo's recipe makes a warming winter dish, with ample vegetables and juices to mop up with bread. Serve it with boiled potatoes or rice.

1 cup (250 ml) extra virgin olive oil
2–3 cloves garlic, chopped
Salt
1 rabbit, cut into 4 pieces
2 cups (500 ml) white table wine
2 bay leaves
1 large onion, cut into ½ inch (1 cm) pieces
2 green bell peppers, cut into ½ inch (1 cm) pieces
1 red bell pepper, cut into ½ inch (1 cm) pieces
1 eggplant, peeled and cut into ½ inch (1 cm) pieces
4 plum tomatoes, peeled (see note)
   and coarsely chopped
1–2 teaspoons sugar
Freshly ground black pepper
2–3 sprigs lemon thyme

Note: To peel tomatoes, cut a cross on the top. Plunge them into boiling water for 10 seconds, then immediately plunge into a bowl of iced water. The skin will come off easily.

In a large pan heat 2 tablespoons of the oil, add half of the garlic and a pinch of salt, then brown the rabbit, turning a few times to color evenly. Remove from the heat and pour in the white wine, setting it alight to flambé the meat until the alcohol burns off, then toss in the bay leaves. Set aside.

In a separate pan, heat the remaining olive oil and fry the rest of the garlic and half of the onion until tender. Stir in the peppers, cook for a few minutes until they begin to soften, then add the eggplant and sauté until just tender. Tip in the tomatoes with the rest of the onion and cook for 5 more minutes. Check the flavor, add some sugar to reduce the acidity, and season with salt and pepper.

Combine all of the elements in the largest cooking pan you have and drop in the thyme. Partially cover the pan and bubble gently until the rabbit is cooked, 25 to 30 minutes. Serve hot.

Serves 4

Nazari salad
Ensalada Nazari

Cabbage was popular in Al-Andalus, as was a mix of sweet and savory, so this salad, named after the last dynasty of Granada, lives up to its heritage. The sweet golden raisins and crunchy pine nuts deliciously offset the bitter cabbage. Gonzalo suggests serving it with grilled fish. If necessary, it will keep in the refrigerator for a few days in an airtight container, but do not add the vinegar, olive oil, and oranges until you are ready to serve.

½ Savoy or green cabbage
1 mild flavored apple, such as Golden
   Delicious, peeled and cored
Juice of ½ lemon
Salt and freshly ground black pepper
1 cup (250 ml) extra virgin olive oil
1 clove garlic, peeled and minced
1 ¾ cups (9 oz/250 g) pine nuts
1 ½ cups (9 oz/250 g) seedless golden raisins
3 tablespoons sherry vinegar or any
   good white wine vinegar
2 tablespoons clear honey
1 orange, peeled, outer pith removed, sliced

Clean the cabbage, remove the thick stalks, and finely cut the leaves into strips.

Dice the apple and sprinkle with the lemon juice to prevent discoloring.

In a large salad bowl, mix the cabbage and apple together and lightly season with salt and pepper.

In a frying pan, heat some of the oil then add the garlic and pine nuts, frying until they turn golden. Remove from the heat and let cool for 5 minutes, then spoon this mixture over the cabbage and apple, add the raisins, and mix well.

Stir in the vinegar and the rest of the olive oil, then drizzle the salad with honey. Add the orange slices just before serving.

Serves 4 to 6

Confit of sardines
Moraga de sardinas

This dish looks beautiful, even if it's in a battered, well-used old pan! This traditional technique of preserving fish allowed it to be stored for months in a terracotta dish in a cool, dry pantry. However, unless you are very experienced in home canning with the proper equipment, it is best to serve immediately and store any leftovers in the fridge.

1 lb (500 g) sardines, tripes, scales,
   and heads removed
2 cups (500 ml) extra virgin olive oil
2 cloves garlic, finely chopped
2 tablespoons pine nuts
12 black peppercorns
Salt
1 lemon, sliced
9 oz (250 g) clams, rinsed well
3 bay leaves
½ lemon for juice
Small handful of parsley, chopped

Rinse the sardines well and drain.

In a large wide pan or a terracotta dish, heat the oil over low heat, then add the garlic and the pine nuts and sauté until just beginning to turn golden. Toss in the peppercorns, salt, lemon slices, and clams. Carefully lay the sardines in the oil like the spokes of a wheel, add the bay leaves, then squeeze some lemon juice over the top. Simmer until cooked, about 5 minutes, depending on the size of the sardines (Atlantic ones are bigger than Mediterranean ones), then remove from the heat and scatter with parsley.

Serve at room temperature.

Serves 4

Sweet rice pudding
Cazuela dulce

Cinnamon and rice are ubiquitous in Arab cultures, and this is one Moorish legacy that is still a big hit in Andalucía—and everywhere else in Spain. Refreshing, cool, and sweet, Gonzalo's sloppy, almond rice pudding just slips down—comfort food at its finest. Play around with it, adding a vanilla stick, grating in some nutmeg, drizzling it with honey, or stirring in some thick cream. It can only get richer!

4¼ cups (1 liter) whole milk
1 cinnamon stick
Peel of half a lemon
2 ⅔ cups (9 oz/250 g) ground almonds
1¼ cups (9 oz/250 g) raw sugar
1¼ cups (9 oz/250 g) short-grain white rice

In a saucepan, warm the milk with the cinnamon and the lemon peel over low heat. Once it starts to boil, remove the lemon peel. Using a wooden spoon, stir in the ground almonds and ¾ cup (5½ oz/150 g) of the sugar. Keep stirring to melt the sugar and release the flavors.

When it starts to bubble, remove the cinnamon stick and, little by little, add the rice, mixing it into the other ingredients.

Simmer gently, stirring occasionally so that it does not stick to the pan, until the rice softens and thickens with the milk, 25 to 30 minutes. Test a teaspoonful to make sure the rice is soft but not mushy.

Remove from heat, pour into individual heatsafe bowls, and allow to cool. Sprinkle the remaining ½ cup (3½ oz/100 g) sugar on top and caramelize with a blowtorch, or place under a hot broiler for a few minutes until caramelized.

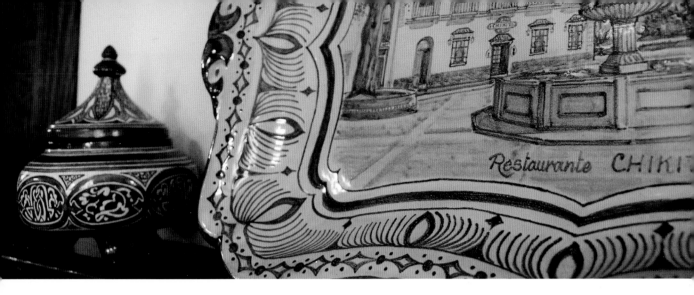

RESTAURANTE CHIKITO, *Granada*

Strategically positioned on a downtown corner, the illustrious Chikito is a magnet for the city's bourgeoisie. Back in 1910, as the Café Alameda, this watering hole became known as El Rinconcillo ("the little corner") and was the meeting place for a dazzling group of artists and intellectuals. Among them were the musician, Manuel De Falla and the ill-fated poet, Federico García Lorca who, in 1936, was dragged out of the café by Franco's fascist troops to be summarily executed. Appropriately, a life-size statue of him now sits in the dining room corner.

A lively tapas bar at the entrance leads to this inner sanctum plastered in celebrity photos (ranging eclectically from the astronaut John Glenn to the actor Benicio del Toro, to writer José Saramago, and footballer Diego Maradona) and some fine Andalusian ceramics.

Chikito is efficiently managed by brothers Diego and Daniel Oruezabal, who alternate as front of house. "Our father opened the restaurant in 1976," Diego tells me. "And all through our early lives we came to help out in the kitchen, so it really is second nature for us." Heading the kitchen is the cheerful chef, Juan Carlos Exposito, who contributes to the sense of a large family working together—from kitchen saucepans to restaurant service. Their *plato estrella* (star dish) is the braised bull's tail—well worth imitating using oxtail (see p. 90).

Serves 4

Alpujarran chestnut soup
Potaje de castañas de la Alpujarra

Don't be put off by the daunting list of ingredients—they make a thick, hearty soup, full of goodness and mountain flavors, with chestnuts taking center stage. A bonus is its palette of autumnal colors. It was developed by Chikito's sous-chef, José Fernandez, who hails from the Alpujarras south of Granada. You can simplify matters by using chicken breast only, skipping the red pepper or scallion, and replacing the chard with any leafy vegetable you have on hand. You will need to soak the chestnuts and chickpeas overnight.

Extra virgin olive oil
1 small carrot, chopped
1 large scallion, chopped
3 tablespoons chopped red bell pepper
1 small plum tomato, chopped
2 tablespoons toasted hazelnuts, chopped
1 clove garlic
1 clove
1 teaspoon saffron
1 dried red pepper or 1 teaspoon sweet paprika
1 teaspoon sweet paprika
1 teaspoon turmeric
1 teaspoon ground anise or ground fennel
Scant ½ cup (100 ml) white wine
1 ½ cups (9 oz/250 g) peeled dried
   chestnuts, soaked in water overnight
¾ cup (5 ½ oz/150 g) dried chickpeas,
   soaked in water overnight, drained
1 bay leaf
¾ oz (25 g) pork, diced
2 large leaves (3 ½ oz/100 g) chard, sliced
1 cup (3 ½ oz/100 g) diced pumpkin
½ cup (2 ¾ oz/75 g) diced potatoes
1 ¾ oz (50 g) chicken breast, sliced
Salt

In a saucepan, heat a little olive oil over medium heat, then sauté the carrot, scallion, red pepper, tomato, hazelnuts, and garlic for about 8 minutes, stirring. Stir in the clove, saffron, dried pepper, paprika, turmeric, anise or fennel, and wine, and cook for a further 2 minutes, or until the vegetables are tender. Remove from the heat and allow to cool briefly. Remove the clove and transfer to a food processor and process to a purée.

Meanwhile, remove any remaining skin from the soaked chestnuts. Drain well and simmer in water until tender, about 45 minutes.

In another pan, combine the chickpeas, bay leaf, pork, and paprika and add enough water to cover them by 2 inches (5 cm). Bring to a boil, lower the heat, and simmer for 1 hour. Stir in the puréed sauce, chard, pumpkin, potato, and chicken. Continue to simmer until everything is tender, about 20 minutes more.

Finally, add the chestnuts with enough of their cooking water to create a thick, textured soup. Add salt and pepper to taste and serve hot.

Serves 4

Chikito's oxtail stew
Rabo de toro de Chikito

Bull's tail is one of Andalusia's great classics—unsurprising given the regional passion for bullfighting. However, the story goes that the stew actually originated as a spin-off of Córdoba's leather industry, when the hides were delivered complete with tails. Waste not, want not—so the tails disappeared into the cooking pot. It is quite glutinous, but washed down with a full-bodied red wine, this stew makes a delicious and sustaining winter dinner. Of course you are unlikely to source bull's tail, but oxtail is widely available and yields the same results. Serve with boiled or roasted potatoes and carrots.

2 cups (500 ml) olive oil
4½ lb (2 kg) oxtail, cut into joints
2 small carrots, chopped
1 tomato, chopped
1 onion, chopped
1 bay leaf
A good pinch of fresh thyme
2 teaspoons chopped rosemary leaves
2 cloves garlic, minced
Salt and ground black pepper
1 dried red pepper or 1 tablespoon mild paprika
2 cups (500 ml) red wine
Handful of chopped parsley

Trim off any excess fat from the oxtail pieces. Heat a little of the olive oil in a frying pan and brown the oxtail on all sides.

In a large saucepan, heat a little more olive oil and add the vegetables, herbs, garlic, salt, pepper, dried pepper or paprika, and the wine. Simmer gently for 15 minutes to obtain a reduction.

Tip in the oxtail pieces and add enough water to submerge them. Bring to a boil over medium heat, then cover and simmer on low heat for about 3 hours (or 45 minutes in a pressure cooker). Stir every 20 minutes or so to ensure they are evenly cooked, and add more water if necessary. When it is ready, the meat will be almost falling from the bone.

Using a slotted spoon, remove the oxtail from the cooking liquid, set the meat aside, then blend the cooking liquid in a food processor to make a smooth sauce. Arrange the oxtail pieces in a large dish, pour over the sauce, sprinkle with parsley, and serve.

Serves 4

Sacromonte omelet
Tortilla Sacromonte

Not exactly Moorish in origin, nor gypsy (Granada's hilltop *barrio* of Sacromonte is famed for its gypsy caves) but this is one of the most succulent omelets I have ever tasted, creamy yet textural from the offal that melts deliciously into the egg. Chef Juan Carlos tells me about its origin. "It came from the abbey of Sacromonte that was built on the spot where San Cecilio was martyred. When the monks did the *matanza* (the winter slaughter of pigs), they used to give away the offal to the poor—then decided to make a dish out of it." Many variations exist, some adding potatoes, chorizo, or green peas, but this one really works. Chikito serves the tortilla with a dramatic dollop of tomato sauce in the center.

7 oz (200 g) lamb's testicles
3 ½ oz (100 g) lamb's brains
1 ½ teaspoons sherry vinegar or red wine vinegar
Extra virgin olive oil
9 oz (250 g) asparagus, finely chopped
½ cup (3 oz/85 g) finely sliced red bell pepper
1 ¾ oz (50 g) Serrano ham, chopped
4 free-range eggs
Salt and white pepper

Tomato sauce (optional)
3 tomatoes
Extra virgin olive oil
1 garlic clove, chopped
1 tablespoon finely chopped onion
Salt and white pepper

First, make the tomato sauce, if using: Bring a pot of water to a boil and plunge the tomatoes in the water until the skins begin to tear. Drain the tomatoes, remove the skins, juice, and seeds, and chop and reserve the flesh.

Heat a little olive oil in a frying pan and sauté the tomatoes, garlic, and onion until the liquid has reduced to a thick sauce, about 10 minutes. Transfer the sauce to a blender and process to a purée.

For the Tortilla
Heat a saucepan of water with the testicles and brains and a little vinegar. Simmer rapidly for about 30 minutes. Drain the water and leave the meat to cool. Remove the skin from the testicles and finely chop the flesh.

In a deep frying pan, heat a little oil and gently fry the testicles and brains over low heat for 5 minutes. Add the asparagus and cook for 10 minutes, then add the red pepper and ham, stirring everything together for about 5 minutes.

Meanwhile whisk the eggs with some salt and pepper.

Adding a little more oil to the pan if necessary, pour the eggs over the meat and vegetables and cook for 5 to 7 minutes until softly set, pushing in the edges with a spatula to build them up, and gently tilting the pan to allow uncooked egg to run underneath as you cook. Place a plate over the pan, flip the tortilla onto it, then carefully slide it back into the pan. Cook the other side until set, about 5 minutes.

Syrup cream cakes
Piononos

In Latin America, the term *pionono* is applied to countless types of wraps, whether sweet or savory. But here, "It's the most typical dessert in Granada!" the waiter exclaims, as he proudly places a plate of them in front of me. He is right—these bite-size cakes appear in patisseries all over the city. Casa Ysla claims "the original" from Santa Fe, just west of the city, where they were allegedly invented in honor of a visiting Pope, none other than Pio Nono, in 1897. Santa Fe's first claim to fame is the place where Boabdil, the last Moorish ruler in Spain, handed over the keys of Granada to the Catholic conquerors—a momentous event marking the end of Al-Andalus. You can add a tablespoon of clear honey to the egg mixture to make the cake more elastic and easier to roll.

Sponge cake
Butter, for greasing
¾ cup (3 ¼ oz/90 g) all-purpose
   flour, plus more for dusting
3 eggs
⅓ cup (2 oz/60 g) sugar
Pinch of salt

Syrup
½ cup (125 ml) water
1 ¼ cups (9 oz/250 g) sugar
1 cinnamon stick
1 tablespoon rum
Ground cinnamon

Custard cream
3 egg yolks
⅔ cup (4 ½ oz/125 g) sugar, plus more to garnish
Scant ½ cup (1 ¾ oz/50 g) cornstarch
2 cups (500 ml) whole milk
1 vanilla bean

First, make the sponge cake: Preheat the oven to 350°F (180°C) and line a 15 by 10 inch (38 by 25 cm) baking sheet with parchment paper that has been greased and dusted with flour.

Separate the yolks from the whites.

In a large mixing bowl, combine half of the sugar and the salt. Add the egg whites and beat to stiff peaks, then set aside in the refrigerator.

In another bowl, mix the yolks with the rest of the sugar and beat energetically or with an electric hand mixer until well combined. Carefully fold in the egg white mixture without losing any of the volume. Sift in the flour little by little, turning with a wooden spoon so that there are no lumps. Always turn from the bottom to the top of the bowl so as not to lose the air in the beaten eggs.

Using a spatula, spread the batter into the lined pan and bake for about 8 minutes, or until a toothpick inserted in the cake comes out clean. Remove and allow to cool in the pan. Once it has cooled to room temperature, turn the pan over onto a large piece of parchment paper, and peel off the lining paper. Divide the cake into two wide halves.

Make the syrup: In a small saucepan, bring the water to a boil. Add the sugar and cinnamon stick and stir. Once it has thickened to a loose, grainy syrup (after about 10 to 15 minutes), remove from the heat and mix in the rum. Pour over the cake halves and sprinkle them with cinnamon.

Make the custard cream: In a bowl, mix the egg yolks with the sugar, then stir in the cornstarch, mixing well.

In a small saucepan, heat the milk and vanilla bean to boiling point and remove from the heat. Whisking continuously, slowly pour the milk into the egg yolk mixture. Return everything to the saucepan and simmer until the mixture thickens to a dense custard, about 15 minutes.

Reserving about 2 tablespoons for the garnish, spread the custard over the top of the cake halves without reaching the edges. Using the paper, carefully roll the cake around the custard like a Swiss roll. Wrap in the paper and refrigerate for 4 hours.

Before serving, remove the paper and slice the cylinders into equal sections. Stand them up and, using a pastry bag or teaspoon, place a small dollop of custard cream on each cake.

If desired, sprinkle some sugar over the top and caramelize with a blowtorch.

PARADOR DE GRANADA, *Alhambra, Granada*

It is hard to beat the location of this hotel restaurant, a revamped 16th century monastery built over a Nazrid palace inside the Alhambra walls. Although the hotel is booked up months in advance, the restaurant is open to any Alhambra visitor, imposing a relentless kitchen rhythm.

Chef Juan Francisco Castro is passionate about the menu, which features several dishes culled from 12th century Nazrid sources. "Their ingredients were good," he tells me. "But for example, fish was never fresh, always salted. And we had to change some cooking times as the initial results were horrible!"

Juan Francisco has spent half his life working in *parador* (state-run hotel) kitchens all over Spain but this one is easily his favorite, since he originates from the nearby Alpujarras and went to catering college in Granada. Even better, he plunders an abundant herb garden inherited from the monks just below the restaurant terrace, facing the Generalife. "We grow about thirty different herbs here. We use coriander a lot in *harira* (a spicy Moroccan soup), also basil, rosemary, oregano, fennel, and thyme." Then he asks if I've ever tasted myrtle, famed from the Court of the Myrtles inside the palace. My negative sends him shooting back to the kitchen only to trot out minutes later holding a dish of ice cream—a scoop of myrtle nestled beside one of lemongrass. Both are divine, their exotic flavors propelling me into time-travel—backwards of course.

Chilled almond soup with apple and fig
Ajoblanco con pan de higo y manzanas

This chilled soup is an absolute Andalusian classic, the precursor of gazpacho and son of *mazamorra* (made without almonds). Cities quarrel over who invented it, with Málaga usually winning, but Granada is a close second. The classic version floats white grapes with a slick of olive oil on top, but Juan Francisco brings an original twist. Use the best almonds you can get hold of (or afford), if possible, the Spanish Marcona variety, which is rounder and more flavorful than the bland, mass-produced (GM) ones. If you cannot make or obtain the fig roll (see p. 132), use a few finely chopped dried figs instead.

1 lb (500 g) blanched almonds
6 cloves garlic, peeled
4¼ cups (1 liter) water
2 cups (500 ml) extra virgin olive oil
Salt
1 tablespoon white wine vinegar, plus more if needed
1 lb (500 g) mild flavored apples like
    Golden Delicious, peeled and cored
9 oz (250 g) fig roll (see recipe p. 132), finely diced
Handful of arugula or dill, to garnish

To make the *ajoblanco*, tip the almonds into a blender, along with the garlic cloves. Add the water and mix slowly on low speed until you have a smooth, homogenous paste. With the machine running, gradually add the olive oil in a steady stream, as if you were making mayonnaise.

Add the salt, vinegar and, if necessary, enough water to obtain a thick but pourable sauce. Strain the mixture into a serving jug, then chill in the refrigerator.

Using a melon baller or round teaspoon, make the apple balls (or dice them).

Divide the apple balls and diced fig roll among serving bowls. Add an arugula leaf or sprig of dill to each bowl. Serve the *ajoblanco* mixture in a jug on the side to be poured at the table.

Chilled tomato and summer vegetable soup
Gazpacho

It is a cliché to have gazpacho in Andalucía, but it is so perfect on a hot summer's day that you're likely to eat it all. If there is any left over, you can keep it in the fridge for a day or so. Traditionally, it was served as a drink rather than a soup, but Juan Francisco serves it in an elegant jug, to be individually poured over ham and sun-dried tomatoes. Serve with chopped tomatoes, cucumber, green pepper, and bread on the side, to be added as wished.

3 ½ oz (100 g) country-style bread or
   sourdough, roughly shredded
1 large clove garlic, chopped
1 green bell pepper, seeded, deribbed,
   and coarsely chopped
7 oz (200 g) cucumber, peeled and coarsely chopped
4 ½ lb (2 kg) plum tomatoes, coarsely chopped
Scant ½ cup (100 ml) extra virgin olive oil
Scant 1 tablespoon white wine vinegar
Salt
7 oz (200 g) Iberian ham, fat removed
3 ½ oz (100 g) dry-packed sun-dried
   tomatoes, cut into fine strips

In a large bowl, layer the bread, then the garlic, pepper, cucumber, and finally the tomatoes on top. Pour over the oil, vinegar, and a large pinch of salt. Pour in just enough water to cover (no more than 1 ½ cups/350 ml). Leave overnight in a cool place outside of the refrigerator.

The next day, transfer to a blender and process to a purée. Strain and adjust the seasoning. Chill in the refrigerator.

Dry out the ham for a few minutes on a dry grill pan over low heat. Finely chop.

Divide the ham and the sun-dried tomatoes equally between the bowls, and allow people to serve themselves from the jug of gazpacho.

Serves 4 to 6

Cod and orange salad with shrimp
Remojón granadino con gamba blanca

This grand old *andalusí* recipe remains a firm favorite in Andalucía as it makes a sustaining yet refreshing salad during the winter orange season. Countless variations exist from Almería to Córdoba (see p 138), but Granada tends to claim ownership, proved by the adjective here, *granadino*. The addition of shrimp and endive is unusual, but raises it from a simple salad to a more sophisticated main course.

4½ lb (2 kg) oranges (6–7), peeled
1 lb (500 g) scallions
About 1 cup (250 ml) mild extra virgin olive oil
4 cloves garlic, peeled and smashed
1 lb (500 g) cod, in large pieces
½ lemon, sliced
9 oz (250 g) shrimp, peeled, leaving tails on
Fine salt
2 heads red Belgian endive, or 3½ loose cups
   (3½ oz/100 g) mixed salad greens
2 hard boiled eggs, quartered
5½ oz (150 g) pitted black olives, thinly sliced

Cut the orange into finger-width rounds, remove the seeds and pith, and cut into segments. Trim the scallions and cut them into fine strips.

In a large saucepan, heat some of the oil, add the garlic, and sauté the cod pieces for a few minutes on each side, until cooked through. Transfer the cod to a bowl and set aside, covered with plastic wrap. Discard the garlic.

Bring a small pot of water to a boil, add the lemon slices, and boil the shrimp until cooked, about 3 minutes. Remove from the heat and plunge into ice water to stop the cooking process.

Roughly flake the cod, add the oranges and scallions, sprinkle with a pinch of salt, and mix carefully with a spoon.

Arrange the endive or salad greens fanning out around a wide, deep salad bowl, then place the cod and orange mixture on top. Place the shrimp in the center. Add the egg quarters, sprinkle with the sliced olives, and finish with a generous slick of extra virgin olive oil.

Serves 8 to 10

Kid goat in garlic sauce
Cabrito al ajillo

Goat is definitely coming up in the world, and is now much easier to source in northern countries, where for years it was scorned as peasant food. Kid goat is a lean, clean meat, low in calories and cholesterol, high in calcium, zinc, potassium, and iron, so altogether very healthy. It never left the kitchens of Andalucía, and you still see goatherds following their bell-tinkling flocks around the sierra. Kid goat meat is tenderer than adult goat, with a subtler flavor. This makes a great, relatively easy dish for a dinner party, hence the larger quantities, but it can be easily halved.

About 1 cup (250 ml) extra virgin olive oil
6lb 10 oz (3 kg) leg of kid goat,
   deboned and cut into chunks
Salt and white pepper
1 teaspoon oregano leaves
1 teaspoon wild thyme leaves
1 long green chili pepper, seeded and finely sliced
2 cups (450 ml) white table wine
2¼ lb (1 kg) potatoes, peeled and cut into chunks
3½ oz (100 g) garlic (about 20 large cloves)
2 dried red peppers, or 1 tablespoon paprika
3½ oz (100 g) country-style bread, broken into pieces
1 lb (500 g) Padron peppers, rinsed and dried
Coarse sea salt

Heat some of the oil in a large frying pan, then sauté the meat and season with salt and pepper. Add the oregano, thyme, and chili pepper and keep turning for 3 minutes or so. Pour in the wine, cover the pan, and simmer gently for 30 to 35 minutes, stirring occasionally.

While the meat is cooking, boil the potatoes in salted water until tender, about 15 minutes.

Meanwhile, heat a generous amount of the oil in a frying pan and fry the garlic, dried chili or paprika, and the bread. Remove from pan then mash into a pulp with a fork. About halfway through cooking the meat, stir this into the pan, making sure it is well distributed.

About 5 minutes before serving, heat a generous amount of oil in a frying pan and toss the Padron peppers in the oil until they blister, turning them frequently to ensure they are cooked all over. Remove from pan and sprinkle with coarse sea salt.

You can mix the potatoes and peppers into the goat, or serve them on the side.

Córdoba and the Caliphate

Now, though, I head for Cordoba's beating heart, the central Judería dominated by the legendary hulk of the Mezquita, once one of the largest mosques in the world. Apart from elaborate gateways, the exterior is austere. Inside, the magic starts—if you ignore the Catholic intrusion, a Renaissance "cathedral" parachuted into its midst after the *reconquista*. A forest of some 850 columns of jasper, onyx, marble, and granite supporting double arches artfully expresses spiritual infinity, culminating at the *mihrab* (altar), where marble, glinting mosaics, and stucco tracery come together in an explosion of symbolic and decorative art. It is spellbinding. Recycled Roman and Visigothic capitals are an art-history bonus, while outside in the forecourt, orange trees, fountains, and water channels offer essential cool when Córdoba's summer temperatures rocket over 100°F (38°C). It is not known as the frying pan of Andalucía for nothing.

After ducking into Bodegas Mezquita, my next source of recipes, I cross the Roman bridge to an Arab tower for a better view of the Alcázar. The high crenellated walls and towers of this Moorish palace enclose a formal garden of aromatic plants and pools that were once irrigated by a waterwheel. Today, theatrically, the wheel stands motionless in the river. This monumental triangle is the hub of Córdoba's golden era of the 8th through 10th centuries, when the mosque, which doubled in size in two centuries, mirrored the unrivalled economic, cultural, and social flowering of Al-Andalus.

Outstanding advances in medicine, philosophy, mathematics, science, astronomy, and agriculture put the caliphate capital on a par with Constantinople and Baghdad. Soaring living standards brought streetlights, hospitals, and universities, while libraries filled up with thousands of handwritten books on that magic new material—paper. While it is thought that Jewish intellectuals were tasked with translating the old Greek classics into Arabic, it was often Muslim women who labored away copying or illustrating them.

Numerous relics of this heyday survive, from the renovated Caliph's baths to the entire labyrinthine Judería, where nooks, crannies, arches, studded doors, patio houses, and fountains encapsulate the urban structure of medieval Al-Andalus. A nocturnal stroll feels like time-travel. Here, too, is a beautiful little synagogue, built in 1315, a few decades before Toledo's Sinagoga del Transito. Just beyond, down a blind alley, I unearth Casa Mazal, a rare restaurant specializing in Sephardic food. Afterwards, intrigued by a recipe for *salmorejo* on glazed wall-tiles in an eponymous alleyway, I find myself in La Fragua, a congenial bar and restaurant throbbing with flamenco. Pepe, the spirited owner, is another fountain of knowledge about traditional Cordoban dishes. Inspired, I order a *tapa* of *mazamorra*, an unctuous, chilled white soup sprinkled with mustard leaves, almonds, and a serpentine trail of olive oil. "It's the father of *ajoblanco* and the grandfather of *salmorejo*," he laughs, and it tastes equally ambrosial.

Modern Córdoba

Córdoba is the Andalusian city where bars, restaurants and craftspeople are most conscious of their rich Moorish heritage. Shops specializing in jewelry, ceramics, and leather line the central streets, while quaint taverns, a handful displaying menus in Arabic, are legion. On every visit I discover new finds down a side street or along the revamped riverside. On the largest square, the arcaded Plaza de la Corredera that was built in the 17th century over a Roman arena, I enter a covered market, a tiny affair that feels local, chatty, and authentic. Suspended rabbits and pigeons await their culinary fate, while pickled deliciousness takes up half the entrance in the form of dozens of incarnations of olives, capers, garlic, and pickles. Jamón from Los Pedroches catches my eye and soon enters my bag, and then it is time for a Vermouth on ice and a tapa at the friendly market bar.

It is time to meet the doyen of Córdoba's revival of *andalusi* gastronomy, Pepe García Marín, who opened his celebrated restaurant, El Caballo Rojo, back in 1962. I am lucky to meet him—since

CENTER
from Córdoba to Málaga
sierra–plains–sea

The truth is that the lines and features of far Arabia still remain in the air of Córdoba and Granada. Federico Garcia Lorca, 1931.

Between Granada and Córdoba an infinite carpet of olive groves undulates north all the way to Jaén, forming Europe's largest area of olive production. Threading my way through it, I follow the so-called route of the Caliphate, a showcase of Andalucian heritage. Row upon row of silvery-green trees contrast with brick-red earth and dizzily change directions with the contours of the sierra like optical art. Then there are stark, jagged limestone peaks, white-washed *fincas* (country houses) draped in necklaces of red peppers, an idyllic valley with a meandering stream, and of course dozens of castles. Zuheros, on the northern flank of the Subbética mountains, has one of the most iconic strongholds, teetering vertiginously on a rocky crag, while Baena's 9th century battlements crown an old quarter simply called Almedina ("the town" in Arabic). To the south, the baroque jewels of Priego de Córdoba surround a sturdy Moorish fortress and a maze-like *moreria* (Moorish quarter) of winding narrow lanes brimming with geraniums. That lightness of spirit is alive and well.

Sierra of olive and wines

Sucked into the vortex of the Subbética mountains, I whip round the bends to reach the charming Finca Las Encinas, source of some authentic rural recipes. Downhill is the silhouette of Iznájar, yet another *pueblo blanco* crowned by a castle. On the way, I pass battered Land Rovers and tractors hauling trailers stacked with purple and black fruit, or see them lined up outside olive mills. It's a race—the

sooner the olives are pressed, the better the ⌐ fact, the entire area is renowned for award-wi extra virgin olive oils made from *hojiblanca, ⌐* or *picuda* olives, ripened by furnace-like sum temperatures and (usually) watered by winter Seasonal workers from Morocco help out duri the intense winter months of harvesting—and ironic hark back. The green nectar is an addic in these parts because, as they say, "Aceite de oliva, todo mal quita!" (Olive oil cures all ills).

Closer to Córdoba, the land morphs into the win country of Montilla-Moriles where, in the folds o ghostly limestone hills, family-owned wine press are announced by large, Ali-Baba style *tinaja* jars regulated wine is one of Andalucía's great oenolo secrets, as the *finos, amontillados, olorosos, palo cortados,* and intense, raisiny *Pedro Ximénez* are close cousins of the sherries of Jerez and every b as good. The dominant Pedro Ximénez grape of ⌐ area ripens at a gallop during the baking hot sum months, ending with the Montilla-Moriles harvest in late August, the first to take place in Spain. Afte pressing, the wine is aged in oak casks, or soleras to become pure nectar. I can't resist stopping at a bar in Montilla itself for a sip of a figgy *oloroso* served with a tapa of silky pork cheeks. Bliss.

After slicing through rolling wheat fields, the highway finally descends to Córdoba, from afar ⌐ dull sprawl beside the banks of the Guadalquivir River. On the horizon I can make out the hills of Los Pedroches where the *dehesa,* that unique ecological balance of meadows and oak-studded woodland, nurtures black Iberian pigs to produce sweet, nutty *jamón iberico de bellota.*

TRAVEL DIARY:

Between Granada and Córdoba an infinite carpet of olive groves undulates north all the way to Jaén, forming Europe's largest area of olive production. Threading my way through it, I follow the so-called route of the Caliphate, a showcase of Andalucian heritage. Row upon row of silvery-green trees contrast with brick-red earth and dizzily change directions with the contours of the sierra like optical art. Then there are stark, jagged limestone peaks, white-washed *fincas* (country houses) draped in necklaces of red peppers, an idyllic valley with a meandering stream, and of course dozens of castles...

my visit, he died aged well into his 90s. Pepe had already left management to his energetic daughter and granddaughter, both named María. It was his discerning palate and personal quest that recovered Moorish dishes like lamb in honey, cod in cinnamon, artichoke hearts, and pine nut marzipan, and subsequently fed a stream of assorted "celebrities" like the dictator, General Franco; also the former King of Spain, Juan Carlos I (a big *salmorejo* fan); and even Jimmy Carter. Every day, Pepe would faithfully lunch at his restaurant and watch the world indulge. "Many of my recipes come from a translated 13th century manuscript," he muses. That gastro-Quran rears its head again.

I am always sad to leave Córdoba. Andalucía's flamboyant postcard traditions of flamenco, horses, and bullfighting may hold strong here (guitar music in a plaza, horse-drawn carriages, or bars plastered in photos of the local hero, the matador Manolete) but they are underscored by a gravitas that seems immune to tourism, perhaps linked to an atavistic sense of having once been the most advanced city in Europe.

Antequera—dolmens, bulls, and all

South of Córdoba, the highway to Málaga branches off past monumental rocky outcrops and farmland of grains, asparagus, and sunflowers to reach Antequera, a town so ancient that it claims prehistoric dolmens, smack in the geographical heart of Andalucía. Behind it rises a rugged escarpment of astonishing karst rock formations, the otherworldly nature reserve of El Torcal, where gigantic boulders look as if they have been tossed down to earth by the gods. From here the views sweep downhill to Málaga and the distant sapphire hues of the Mediterranean.

My first downtown destination is Antequera's ornate bullring, an 1848 structure that was rebuilt a few decades ago to become one of the most striking in Spain—whether you support the "art" (for in Spain it is considered as such) or not. Unusually, it houses a restaurant, the eponymous

Plaza de Toros. Afterwards, I track down a deeply traditional restaurant, Arte de Cozina, in an elegant barrio of 17th and 18th century mansions and churches. Towering high above are the walls of a Moorish fortress built to counter the Catholic advance in the 13th century, when Antequera was a strategic outpost of the Emirate of Granada, before bowing to the inevitable in 1410.

Seaside gastronomy in Málaga

Then it is onwards, south through the hills to balmy Málaga itself, now rimmed by a forest of high-rises. Well before it gained its reputation in the 20th and 21st centuries as the hedonistic capital of the Costa del Sol, with its riotous summer *feria*, its beach bars grilling sardines, and its massed Easter processions, Málaga was a big player in Al-Andalus, number two in the emirate of Granada. The most visible relic is the colossal 14th century fortress of Gibralfaro, peering down from a summit of the Montes de Málaga over today's ambitiously redeveloped port.

Between lofty palm trees in the lower town is a nucleus of eclectic monuments: the spectacular 10th–11th century Alcazaba, a Roman theater and, just beyond, the sharply designed Museo Picasso dedicated to the city's most illustrious son, Pablo. Sipping a chilled *caña*, I spot the signature of his daughter Paloma on a stack of wine barrels at El Pimpi, a popular tapas bar in Málaga's buzziest neighborhood. Nearby, the Mercado Merced, a contemporary food hall, lures me in to visit a stand owned by that oenological stalwart of the city, the Antigua Casa de Guardia—though the ambiance is not quite like the eccentric original. Finally, up a side street, I track down a rare French interloper for some Gallic takes on *andaluz* recipes—proof that even if the adjacent Costa del Sol has become a cultural desert, Málaga retains its creative flair.

Northeast of the city unfolds the bucolic Axarquía region, source of wild honey, almonds, goat cheese, and excellent Muscatel wines, where nearly every village that speckles the hillsides is of Muslim origin. Like Las Alpujarras to the east, La Axarquía fomented the 1569 *Morisco* rebellion, resulting in its inhabitants being exiled or sold into slavery and replaced by Christians brought from the north. Frigiliana, the village where I end this particular road trip, played a key role.

Mercado bliss

In Malaga, I know exactly where to find top Axarquía produce. At the far end of the Alameda, that leafy stretch of exuberant sub-tropical gardens, purple jacarandas, and towering magnolias sandwiched between the traffic lanes, I come to the port's greatest foodie offering: the Mercado de Atarazanas. Once through its horseshoe gateway, I am blown away by the sheer abundance, variety, and quality of the market produce.

Dozens of herbs, dried fruits, nuts, almonds, Málaga raisins, figs (that centuries ago were exported to Baghdad), giant slabs of tuna, lethal-looking swordfish, slippery anchovies, and fat Gordal olives all seduce me. Málaga's constant sunshine and its blessed location between a sea alive with piscine joy and a fertile interior mean mangoes, custard apples, guavas, and avocadoes join more typical apricots, quince, medlars, grapes, and citrus fruits. It is heartening to learn from a stall holder that despite the all-pervasive polytunnels along the coast, many Axarquía villages still use the terracing and irrigation methods of the Moors, and organic farming is spreading.

Then I drive east along the so-called Costa Tropical, swinging up into the hills above Nerja to Frigiliana. The whitewashed village spills dramatically down the hillside in two sections, the newer, 20th century village and the old Moorish labyrinth festooned with orange trees and crimson bougainvillea. Looking across the Mediterranean to North Africa from the terrace of El Jardín, my destination restaurant, it feels like no other place could be more fitting to end a chapter, as here I am truly suspended between sierra and sea.

CENTER
from Córdoba to Málaga
sierra–plains–sea

*The truth is that the lines and features of
far Arabia still remain in the air of Córdoba
and Granada. Federico Garcia Lorca, 1931.*

Between Granada and Córdoba an infinite carpet
of olive groves undulates north all the way to Jaén,
forming Europe's largest area of olive production.
Threading my way through it, I follow the so-called
route of the Caliphate, a showcase of Andalucian
heritage. Row upon row of silvery-green trees contrast
with brick-red earth and dizzily change directions
with the contours of the sierra like optical art. Then
there are stark, jagged limestone peaks, white-washed
fincas (country houses) draped in necklaces of red
peppers, an idyllic valley with a meandering stream,
and of course dozens of castles. Zuheros, on the
northern flank of the Subbética mountains, has one
of the most iconic strongholds, teetering vertiginously
on a rocky crag, while Baena's 9th century battlements
crown an old quarter simply called Almedina
("the town" in Arabic). To the south, the baroque
jewels of Priego de Córdoba surround a sturdy
Moorish fortress and a maze-like *moreria* (Moorish
quarter) of winding narrow lanes brimming with
geraniums. That lightness of spirit is alive and well.

Sierra of olive and wines

Sucked into the vortex of the Subbética mountains,
I whip round the bends to reach the charming Finca
Las Encinas, source of some authentic rural recipes.
Downhill is the silhouette of Iznájar, yet another
pueblo blanco crowned by a castle. On the way,
I pass battered Land Rovers and tractors hauling
trailers stacked with purple and black fruit, or see
them lined up outside olive mills. It's a race—the

sooner the olives are pressed, the better the oil. In
fact, the entire area is renowned for award-winning
extra virgin olive oils made from *hojiblanca, picual*,
or *picuda* olives, ripened by furnace-like summer
temperatures and (usually) watered by winter rains.
Seasonal workers from Morocco help out during
the intense winter months of harvesting—another
ironic hark back. The green nectar is an addiction
in these parts because, as they say, "Aceite de
oliva, todo mal quita!" (Olive oil cures all ills).

Closer to Córdoba, the land morphs into the wine
country of Montilla-Moriles where, in the folds of the
ghostly limestone hills, family-owned wine presses
are announced by large, Ali-Baba style *tinaja* jars. This
regulated wine is one of Andalucia's great oenological
secrets, as the *finos, amontillados, olorosos, palo
cortados*, and intense, raisiny *Pedro Ximénez* are
close cousins of the sherries of Jerez and every bit
as good. The dominant Pedro Ximénez grape of this
area ripens at a gallop during the baking hot summer
months, ending with the Montilla-Moriles harvest
in late August, the first to take place in Spain. After
pressing, the wine is aged in oak casks, or soleras,
to become pure nectar. I can't resist stopping at
a bar in Montilla itself for a sip of a figgy *oloroso*
served with a tapa of silky pork cheeks. Bliss.

After slicing through rolling wheat fields, the
highway finally descends to Córdoba, from afar a
dull sprawl beside the banks of the Guadalquivir
River. On the horizon I can make out the hills
of Los Pedroches where the *dehesa*, that unique
ecological balance of meadows and oak-studded
woodland, nurtures black Iberian pigs to
produce sweet, nutty *jamón iberico de bellota*.

Córdoba and the Caliphate

Now, though, I head for Cordoba's beating heart, the central Judería dominated by the legendary hulk of the Mezquita, once one of the largest mosques in the world. Apart from elaborate gateways, the exterior is austere. Inside, the magic starts—if you ignore the Catholic intrusion, a Renaissance "cathedral" parachuted into its midst after the *reconquista*. A forest of some 850 columns of jasper, onyx, marble, and granite supporting double arches artfully expresses spiritual infinity, culminating at the *mihrab* (altar), where marble, glinting mosaics, and stucco tracery come together in an explosion of symbolic and decorative art. It is spellbinding. Recycled Roman and Visigothic capitals are an art-history bonus, while outside in the forecourt, orange trees, fountains, and water channels offer essential cool when Córdoba's summer temperatures rocket over 100°F (38°C). It is not known as the frying pan of Andalucía for nothing.

After ducking into Bodegas Mezquita, my next source of recipes, I cross the Roman bridge to an Arab tower for a better view of the Alcázar. The high crenellated walls and towers of this Moorish palace enclose a formal garden of aromatic plants and pools that were once irrigated by a waterwheel. Today, theatrically, the wheel stands motionless in the river. This monumental triangle is the hub of Córdoba's golden era of the 8th through 10th centuries, when the mosque, which doubled in size in two centuries, mirrored the unrivalled economic, cultural, and social flowering of Al-Andalus.

Outstanding advances in medicine, philosophy, mathematics, science, astronomy, and agriculture put the caliphate capital on a par with Constantinople and Baghdad. Soaring living standards brought streetlights, hospitals, and universities, while libraries filled up with thousands of handwritten books on that magic new material— paper. While it is thought that Jewish intellectuals were tasked with translating the old Greek classics into Arabic, it was often Muslim women who labored away copying or illustrating them.

Numerous relics of this heyday survive, from the renovated Caliph's baths to the entire labyrinthine Judería, where nooks, crannies, arches, studded doors, patio houses, and fountains encapsulate the urban structure of medieval Al-Andalus. A nocturnal stroll feels like time-travel. Here, too, is a beautiful little synagogue, built in 1315, a few decades before Toledo's Sinagoga del Transito. Just beyond, down a blind alley, I unearth Casa Mazal, a rare restaurant specializing in Sephardic food. Afterwards, intrigued by a recipe for *salmorejo* on glazed wall-tiles in an eponymous alleyway, I find myself in La Fragua, a congenial bar and restaurant throbbing with flamenco. Pepe, the spirited owner, is another fountain of knowledge about traditional Cordoban dishes. Inspired, I order a *tapa* of *mazamorra*, an unctuous, chilled white soup sprinkled with mustard leaves, almonds, and a serpentine trail of olive oil. "It's the father of *ajoblanco* and the grandfather of *salmorejo*," he laughs, and it tastes equally ambrosial.

Modern Córdoba

Córdoba is the Andalusian city where bars, restaurants and craftspeople are most conscious of their rich Moorish heritage. Shops specializing in jewelry, ceramics, and leather line the central streets, while quaint taverns, a handful displaying menus in Arabic, are legion. On every visit I discover new finds down a side street or along the revamped riverside. On the largest square, the arcaded Plaza de la Corredera that was built in the 17th century over a Roman arena, I enter a covered market, a tiny affair that feels local, chatty, and authentic. Suspended rabbits and pigeons await their culinary fate, while pickled deliciousness takes up half the entrance in the form of dozens of incarnations of olives, capers, garlic, and pickles. Jamón from Los Pedroches catches my eye and soon enters my bag, and then it is time for a Vermouth on ice and a tapa at the friendly market bar.

It is time to meet the doyen of Córdoba's revival of *andalusi* gastronomy, Pepe García Marín, who opened his celebrated restaurant, El Caballo Rojo, back in 1962. I am lucky to meet him—since my visit, he died aged well into his 90s. Pepe had already left management to his energetic daughter and granddaughter, both named María. It was his discerning palate and personal quest that recovered Moorish dishes like lamb in honey, cod in cinnamon, artichoke hearts, and pine nut marzipan, and subsequently fed a stream of assorted "celebrities" like the dictator, General Franco; also the former King of Spain, Juan Carlos I (a big *salmorejo* fan); and even Jimmy Carter. Every day, Pepe would faithfully lunch at his restaurant and watch the world indulge. "Many of my recipes come from a translated 13th century manuscript," he muses. That gastro-Quran rears its head again.

I am always sad to leave Córdoba. Andalucía's flamboyant postcard traditions of flamenco, horses, and bullfighting may hold strong here (guitar music in a plaza, horse-drawn carriages, or bars plastered in photos of the local hero, the matador Manolete) but they are underscored by a gravitas that seems immune to tourism, perhaps linked to an atavistic sense of having once been the most advanced city in Europe.

Antequera—dolmens, bulls, and all

South of Córdoba, the highway to Málaga branches off past monumental rocky outcrops and farmland of grains, asparagus, and sunflowers to reach Antequera, a town so ancient that it claims prehistoric dolmens, smack in the geographical heart of Andalucía. Behind it rises a rugged escarpment of astonishing karst rock formations, the otherworldly nature reserve of El Torcal, where gigantic boulders look as if they have been tossed down to earth by the gods. From here the views sweep downhill to Málaga and the distant sapphire hues of the Mediterranean.

My first downtown destination is Antequera's ornate bullring, an 1848 structure that was rebuilt a few decades ago to become one of the most striking in Spain—whether you support the "art" (for in Spain it is considered as such) or not. Unusually, it houses a restaurant, the eponymous

Plaza de Toros. Afterwards, I track down a deeply traditional restaurant, Arte de Cozina, in an elegant barrio of 17th and 18th century mansions and churches. Towering high above are the walls of a Moorish fortress built to counter the Catholic advance in the 13th century, when Antequera was a strategic outpost of the Emirate of Granada, before bowing to the inevitable in 1410.

Seaside gastronomy in Málaga

Then it is onwards, south through the hills to balmy Málaga itself, now rimmed by a forest of high-rises. Well before it gained its reputation in the 20th and 21st centuries as the hedonistic capital of the Costa del Sol, with its riotous summer *feria*, its beach bars grilling sardines, and its massed Easter processions, Málaga was a big player in Al-Andalus, number two in the emirate of Granada. The most visible relic is the colossal 14th century fortress of Gibralfaro, peering down from a summit of the Montes de Málaga over today's ambitiously redeveloped port.

Between lofty palm trees in the lower town is a nucleus of eclectic monuments: the spectacular 10th–11th century Alcazaba, a Roman theater and, just beyond, the sharply designed Museo Picasso dedicated to the city's most illustrious son, Pablo. Sipping a chilled *caña*, I spot the signature of his daughter Paloma on a stack of wine barrels at El Pimpi, a popular tapas bar in Málaga's buzziest neighborhood. Nearby, the Mercado Merced, a contemporary food hall, lures me in to visit a stand owned by that oenological stalwart of the city, the Antigua Casa de Guardia—though the ambiance is not quite like the eccentric original. Finally, up a side street, I track down a rare French interloper for some Gallic takes on *andaluz* recipes—proof that even if the adjacent Costa del Sol has become a cultural desert, Málaga retains its creative flair.

Northeast of the city unfolds the bucolic Axarquia region, source of wild honey, almonds, goat cheese, and excellent Muscatel wines, where nearly every village that speckles the hillsides is

of Muslim origin. Like Las Alpujarras to the east,
La Axarquía fomented the 1569 *Morisco* rebellion,
resulting in its inhabitants being exiled or sold
into slavery and replaced by Christians brought
from the north. Frigiliana, the village where I
end this particular road trip, played a key role.

Mercado bliss

In Malaga, I know exactly where to find top
Axarquía produce. At the far end of the Alameda,
that leafy stretch of exuberant sub-tropical gardens,
purple jacarandas, and towering magnolias
sandwiched between the traffic lanes, I come to
the port's greatest foodie offering: the Mercado de
Atarazanas. Once through its horseshoe gateway,
I am blown away by the sheer abundance,
variety, and quality of the market produce.

Dozens of herbs, dried fruits, nuts, almonds, Málaga
raisins, figs (that centuries ago were exported
to Baghdad), giant slabs of tuna, lethal-looking
swordfish, slippery anchovies, and fat Gordal
olives all seduce me. Málaga's constant sunshine
and its blessed location between a sea alive with
piscine joy and a fertile interior mean mangoes,
custard apples, guavas, and avocadoes join more
typical apricots, quince, medlars, grapes, and
citrus fruits. It is heartening to learn from a stall
holder that despite the all-pervasive polytunnels
along the coast, many Axarquía villages still
use the terracing and irrigation methods of the
Moors, and organic farming is spreading.

Then I drive east along the so-called Costa Tropical,
swinging up into the hills above Nerja to Frigiliana.
The whitewashed village spills dramatically down the
hillside in two sections, the newer, 20th century village
and the old Moorish labyrinth festooned with orange
trees and crimson bougainvillea. Looking across the
Mediterranean to North Africa from the terrace of
El Jardín, my destination restaurant, it feels like no
other place could be more fitting to end a chapter, as
here I am truly suspended between sierra and sea.

TRAVEL DIARY:

Between Granada and Córdoba an infinite carpet of olive groves undulates north all the way to Jaén, forming Europe's largest area of olive production. Threading my way through it, I follow the so-called route of the Caliphate, a showcase of Andalucian heritage. Row upon row of silvery-green trees contrast with brick-red earth and dizzily change directions with the contours of the sierra like optical art. Then there are stark, jagged limestone peaks, white-washed *fincas* (country houses) draped in necklaces of red peppers, an idyllic valley with a meandering stream, and of course dozens of castles…

FINCA DE LAS ENCINAS, *Los Juncares, La Subbética*

Walk through the gates of this converted farmhouse and it feels like entering an oasis. Hidden amid the olive groves of the Sierra Subbética, its spectacular views, beauty, and tranquillity attract a steady flow of international visitors. Many also come to hone their cooking skills with the Welsh chef-owner, Clive Ridout who, together with his Japanese wife, Maki Murakushi, runs this highly personalized gourmet guesthouse.

After catering college and training with a French chef in Cardiff, Clive and Maki moved to London, then Cornwall, before deciding to uproot and escape to rural Andalucía. Over a decade later the rambling *finca* (country house) has matured beatifically. Beneath towering holm oaks (*encinas*), the focal points are the eating areas beside the pool or on a panoramic terrace. Chickens cluck (fresh eggs for breakfast!), dogs and a cat trot between dozens of blossoming plants, while the couple's energetic young son, Cei, zips in and out. Behind the house, Clive's vegetable and herb garden ensures abundant organic produce which, coupled with wild rabbits or quails from neighbors, make perfect ingredients for his focus on traditional Andalusian food. Between Maki's warm intelligence and background in finance, Clive's dry wit and knowledge, and the bucolic setting, Las Encinas achieves that perfect balance between the spirit and the plate.

Serves 4

Arugula and asparagus salad with orange and ginger dressing

Ensalada de rúcula y espárragos con vinagreta de naranja y jengibre

Refreshing, light, and nutritious, this salad is an ideal prelude to Clive's main courses of duck, rabbit, or quail. The complex, aromatic dressing is Maki's creation.

1 lb (450 g) fresh green asparagus
 spears, woody ends snapped off
2 large oranges, peeled, pith
 removed, cut into segments
9 oz (250 g) arugula or mixed salad greens
3 tablespoons extra virgin olive oil
1 tablespoon ginger juice (2–3 tablespoons
 grated ginger pressed through a seive)
1 tablespoon fresh orange juice
½ teaspoon sherry vinegar
½ teaspoon brown sugar
1 teaspoon grated orange zest
Freshly ground rock salt and black pepper
1–2 teaspoons sesame seeds

Cook the asparagus in boiling salted water until just tender, 1 to 2 minutes. Drain and refresh in ice water.

Assemble the asparagus, orange segments, and arugula leaves in a large salad bowl and toss well.

Make the vinaigrette by mixing the extra virgin olive oil, ginger juice, orange juice, vinegar, sugar, and orange zest, and season with salt and pepper.

In a dry frying pan, quickly toast the sesame seeds and sprinkle onto the salad. Mix in the vinaigrette just before serving.

Serves 4 to 6

Asparagus with pine nut and cumin sauce
Espárragos con salsa de piñones y comino

In spring and early summer, Andalucía abounds in fresh asparagus—whether the spindly wild variety foraged by villagers or sold at markets, or the farmed version. Clive's thick sauce makes an unusual alternative to a vinaigrette dip.

1 large ripe plum tomato
1 large bulb of garlic
1 ¾ cups (9 oz/250 g) Spanish pine nuts
1 tablespoon freshly, coarsely ground cumin seeds
1 teaspoon sherry vinegar
1 teaspoon freshly ground sea/rock salt
Scant ½ cup (100 ml) extra virgin olive oil,
   plus more for frying and seasoning
2 ¼ lb (1 kg) fresh green asparagus, ends trimmed
Freshly ground black pepper

Preheat the oven to 350°F (180°C). Roast the tomato and garlic bulb for 15 minutes. Peel the tomato and the garlic cloves. Cut the tomato crosswise and remove the seeds.

Heat a dry heavy bottomed pan over medium heat and toast the pine nuts until golden, shaking the pan frequently. Transfer the pine nuts to a bowl and set aside.

Add a few drops of extra virgin olive oil to the pan and fry the cumin seeds just until fragrant. Remove from the heat and set aside.

In a blender, grind the pine nuts and cumin seeds. Add the tomato, garlic, vinegar, and salt, and process to a smooth consistency. With the machine running, slowly add the olive oil in a trickle to obtain a creamy paste. Set aside.

Season the asparagus with plenty of olive oil and freshly ground salt and pepper. On a hot oiled skillet or grill pan, grill the asparagus for 2 to 3 minutes, turning once.

Serve the asparagus drizzled with top quality extra virgin olive oil and a dollop of the pine nut sauce on top.

Serves 6

Quail in pomegranate sauce
Codornices con salsa de granada

Once common in Al-Andalus, quail has become underrated despite its meat being lean and tasty. Here, it's bathed in pomegranate sauce to make a wonderful centerpiece. You can replace the Iberian *panceta* with unsliced Italian pancetta or bacon. Serve with braised rice (p. 124).

1 tablespoon extra virgin olive oil
3½ oz (100 g) slab of salted Iberico *panceta*,
   roughly chopped (or dry-cured pork belly)
12 quails
Freshly ground sea salt and black pepper
Seeds of 1 pomegranate, to garnish

Sauce
¾ cup (5½ oz/150 g) sugar
½ cup (125 ml) white wine vinegar
⅔ cup (150 ml) dry white wine
1 cup (250 ml) freshly squeezed pomegranate juice
1 stick cinnamon
Peel of 1 lemon

Preheat the oven to 350°F (180°C).

First, make the sauce: In a large pan, combine sugar, vinegar, wine, pomegranate juice, cinnamon, and the lemon peel and bring to a boil. Boil until thick and syrupy, about 30 minutes. Remove the lemon rind and set the sauce aside.

Heat the olive oil in heavy bottomed frying pan and fry the *panceta* until evenly colored. Reserving the oil in the pan, transfer the *panceta* to a large ovensafe dish such as a Spanish terracotta *cazuela*.

In the same pan, brown the quails in batches of four, turning to brown on all sides, then season with salt and pepper. Place them in the *cazuela* with the *panceta*.

Pour the pomegranate syrup over the quails and bake, uncovered, until cooked through, 25 to 30 minutes. Baste regularly.

Remove from the oven; toss the pomegranate seeds over and around the quails, cover with aluminum foil, and return to the oven for 3 to 4 minutes.

Serve immediately.

Duck leg with bay leaf and quince
Pato con laurel y membrillo

This recipe combines two elements that were big favorites in Al-Andalus. The duck used at the time was undoubtedly a mallard, while the very common quince often appeared in *safarjaliyya*, a tangy lamb stew. Clive is a big fan of duck legs, "so much tastier than duck breast or chicken." You will need to marinate the duck overnight.

12 duck legs
Extra virgin olive oil
2 cups (500 ml) chicken stock
2–3 fresh bay leaves

Marinade
1 garlic bulb, peeled and crushed
1 lemon, zest finely chopped, lemon flesh sliced
14–18 black peppercorns, crushed
4–6 cloves, crushed
12 fresh bay leaves, crushed
½ teaspoon freshly ground sea salt
½ teaspoon freshly ground black pepper

Quince
Juice of 2 lemons
3 tablespoon clear honey
2 cups (500 ml) water
1 large pinch of saffron
3 medium quinces, peeled and cored

In a large bowl, combine the marinade ingredients and add the duck legs, turning to cover them well. Refrigerate overnight.

For the quince: In a large saucepan, heat the lemon juice over medium heat. Add the honey, stirring to dissolve, then add the water and bring to a boil. Add the saffron, turn down the heat, and simmer gently for 5 minutes.

Add the whole quinces, turning them in the liquid, and return to a boil. Lower the heat, cover, and slowly simmer for 1 to 1 ½ hours until tender. Pierce with a fork to make sure they are soft without falling apart. Leave to cool in the liquid.

For the duck:
Preheat the oven to 400°F (200°C).

Remove the duck legs from the marinade, scraping off most of the marinade and reserving it.

In a large heavy bottomed frying pan, heat a little extra virgin olive oil over medium heat, then fry the duck legs skin-side down until golden. Arrange the duck skin-side up in a large ovensafe dish such as a Spanish terracotta *cazuela*.

In the same pan, quickly warm all the marinade ingredients and add them to the duck. Pour the chicken stock around the duck, leaving the skin of the duck exposed. Place in the oven and cook until tender, 30 to 40 minutes.

Turn off the oven; remove the duck from the liquid, keeping the duck warm in the oven (but do not cook further).

Strain the cooking liquid through a sieve into a pan. Bring it to a boil, add the bay leaves, and rapidly reduce the liquid until it thickens, about 5 minutes. Remove the bay leaves.

Slice the quince into quarters. Arrange 2 duck legs and 2 pieces of quince on each plate. Top with sauce and serve immediately.

Serves 4

Country style stewed rabbit
Conejo a la campiña

"This is my type of dish," exclaims Clive, and I agree. It is aromatic, with strong citrus notes, a tangy hit from the olives and *fino,* and a huge whiff of the *campo* from the fistfuls of wild thyme. You can imagine the Moors eating this, perhaps without the *fino*. Above all, there is lots of garlic that melts delectably into the sauce. Serve with braised rice (see p. 124) or potatoes.

¼ cup (60 ml) extra virgin olive oil
1 onion, finely chopped
25 cloves garlic, peeled
Scant ½ cup (1 ¾ oz/50 g) all-purpose flour
½ teaspoon freshly ground sea salt
½ teaspoon white pepper
1 rabbit, cut into 4 pieces
1 teaspoon whole black peppercorns
4 bay leaves
2 tablespoons fresh thyme
Generous ¾ cup (200 ml) *fino* wine from
   Montilla-Moriles or dry *fino* sherry
Generous ¾ cup (200 ml) chicken stock
Rind of 1 preserved lemon, sliced thinly
9 oz (250 g) cured green olives
2 tablespoons finely chopped parsley

In an ovensafe pot or a Spanish terracotta *cazuela*, heat some olive oil over medium heat and sauté the onion and garlic until translucent.

Season the flour with salt and pepper and use it to dust the rabbit pieces, before adding them to the onion and garlic in the pot. Add the peppercorns, bay leaves, and thyme, and continue to fry for 5 minutes.

Slowly pour in the *fino* and bring it to a boil, then add the chicken stock and preserved lemon rind. Return to a boil, then lower the heat and simmer for about 40 minutes to reduce, then cover and cook for another 1 hour.

When the rabbit is cooked, toss in the olives and let stand for 5 minutes or so. Sprinkle with parsley before serving.

Serves 4

Braised rice
Arroz perfumado

Scant 1 cup (1 ¾ sticks/7 oz/200 g) salted butter
½ onion, roughly chopped
1 cinnamon stick
1 teaspoon black peppercorns
4 cloves
Large pinch of saffron threads
3–4 bay leaves
2 ¼ cups (14 oz/400 g) long-grain rice
3 ½ cups (800 ml) chicken stock
Salt and white pepper

Preheat the oven to 350°F (180°C).

In an ovensafe dish or pot, heat half of the butter and sauté the onion until translucent. Add the cinnamon stick, peppercorns, cloves, saffron, and bay leaves and gently stir.

Stir in the rice and continue to cook until the rice is translucent, 3 or 4 minutes. Pour in the stock and bring to a boil.

Remove from heat, cover with parchment paper, and bake in the oven until the rice is tender, 15 minutes. Stir in the remaining butter and season with salt and pepper to taste.

Serves 6

Poached quince scented with lavender
Membrillo perfumado de espliego

Lavender is a rarity in Andalusian kitchens today, so I was overjoyed to find Clive using it for this dessert. In the days of Al-Andalus, it was common in syrups, desserts, and even alongside cinnamon in chicken and meat dishes. One Sephardic recipe even adds it to stuffed partridge.

2 cups (500 ml) freshly squeezed pomegranate juice
2 tablespoons freshly squeezed lemon juice
2 tablespoons freshly squeezed orange juice
1 ¾ cups (12 oz/350 g) sugar
6 quince, peeled, keeping stalks intact
1 cinnamon stick
1 teaspoon dried lavender heads

In a large pan, combine the pomegranate, lemon, and orange juices with the sugar and bring to a boil. Lower the heat and simmer to thicken slightly, 8 to 10 minutes.

Add the quince to the liquid, cover the pan, and simmer slowly for 1 ½ to 2 hours, or until tender.

Once cooked, add the cinnamon stick and lavender and leave the quince to steep in this juice for 3 to 4 hours.

Remove the fruit, strain the juice, and serve together at room temperature.

Serves 6 to 8

Almond and olive oil cake
Bizcocho de almendras y aceite de oliva

This deliciously moist cake is light and not overly sweet. It is made with organic Andalusian almonds and olive oil. Eat it alone or with the tangy blueberry coulis—which looks like a culinary stab in the heart—or with mascarpone mixed with light cream and sprinkled with cinnamon.

4 medium eggs
⅔ cup (150 ml) extra virgin olive
   oil, plus more for greasing
1 cup (5¾ oz/165 g) light brown sugar
2 cups (7 oz/200 g) ground almonds
¾ cup (3½ oz/100 g) all-purpose flour, sifted
½ teaspoon baking powder
Handful sliced almonds, toasted

Preheat the oven to 350°F (180°C) and grease a 9-inch (23-cm) round cake pan with olive oil.

In a large bowl, whisk together the eggs, oil, and sugar until light and fluffy. Carefully fold in the ground almonds, flour, and baking powder.

Pour into the prepared pan and sprinkle toasted sliced almonds over the top.

Bake in the oven for 25 minutes or until firm to the touch. Remove from the oven, remove the cake from the pan, and leave on a cake rack to cool.

Blueberry coulis
Coulis de arándanos

1¾ cups (9 oz/250 g) fresh ripe blueberries
½ cup (3½ oz/100 g) vanilla sugar
3½ tablespoons water
Scant ½ cup (100 ml) extra virgin olive oil

In a saucepan, combine the blueberries, vanilla sugar, and water. Bring to a boil, and simmer for 3 to 4 minutes until the sugar dissolves. Remove from heat, and tip into a blender. With the motor running, slowly add the olive oil to obtain a loose purée or coulis. Cool.

ANA PARILLA AREVALO, *home cook in El Higueral, La Subbética*

My neighbor Ana is one of those salt-of-the-earth characters who is rooted in her family, her kitchen, and her beloved geraniums. At most, she will be driven by her eldest son to visit a daughter in a neighboring village; otherwise she never ventures far. All five of her grown children, who once all squeezed inside the same little whitewashed house, live nearby and are devoted.

At eighty, she is as sharp as a pin, knows exactly what is going on in the world (thank you TV), and recites precise recipes to me off the top of her head. Her accent and locution speed are extraordinary, a kind of garbled mountain *andaluz* that even confounds my Spanish friends from the north. It took me a while to realize that both she and her husband, Andrés, are illiterate, having grown up during the Franco era, when rural education was not a priority, yet that hardly cramps their style.

When I'm at my house, she makes little treats, calling out from the gate as she proffers dishes of homemade chorizo, home-cured olives, quince paste, or a tapa of stewed partridge shot by Andrés. Then, when my partner, Richard, and I leave, comes the ritual of the *pan de higo*: she ceremoniously gives one to Richard and one to me with a huge smile. *Hasta la proxima Ana!*

Makes 10 to 12

Ana's fig and almond roll
Pan de higo de Ana

It's a great classic of Mediterranean countries, but I think Ana's is by far the best, though I'm biased. This modest-looking dark brown roll becomes addictive, so beware. A slice or two makes the perfect healthy snack, its sweetness coming only from the figs.

2 tablespoons extra virgin olive
   oil, plus more for oiling
1 ½ cups (7 oz/200 g) blanched almonds,
   plus more to decorate
2 cups (7 oz/200 g) walnut halves
2 ¼ lb (1 kg) dried figs, stalks removed, broken open
2 teaspoons cinnamon
2 teaspoons sesame seeds
1 teaspoon anise
Scant ½ cup (100 ml) brandy or PX sherry

Heat the oil in a pan until hot but not smoking, tip in the almonds and walnuts, and fry until golden, 5 to 7 minutes. Using a slotted spoon, transfer to a plate lined with paper towels and cool slightly.

Reserving some of the almonds to garnish, tip the toasted nuts into a blender, along with the rest of the ingredients, and process to a thick paste.

Oiling your hands, divide the mixture into 10 to 12 equal portions and shape them into rolls or flat round cakes. You can decorate each one with a few extra toasted almonds. Leave in front of an open window to dry for two weeks, then wrap tightly in plastic wrap.

They will keep for months in a cool place.

Serves 6 to 8

Quince paste
Dulce de membrillo

There are few better ways to end a meal than with a hunk of bread, a respectable slab of extra-mature Manchego cheese, and a spoonful of homemade quince paste. It's like Stilton and pear, or Cheddar and chutney—a symbiotic legend. For something more like a dessert, Ana suggests serving freshly made *membrillo* stirred with *requesón* (similar to ricotta) and drizzled with honey.

2 ¾ lb (1.25 kg) quince
Juice of 1 lemon
1 cinnamon stick
Splash of fino sherry (optional)
5 cups (2 ¼ lb/1 kg) sugar

Peel, core, and quarter the quince. As you go, transfer the prepared quince to a large heavy pan and sprinkle with lemon juice to prevent discoloring. When they are ready to go, cover with water and add the cinnamon stick. Bring to a boil and simmer over medium heat for 25 to 30 minutes until the quince is soft when pierced with a fork.

Remove the cinnamon. Use a blender or handheld immersion blender to achieve an even, fine consistency.

Return the mixture to the pan over low heat and add some sherry (if you have it) and the sugar, stirring from time to time with a wooden spoon until it dissolves. After 30 minutes or so it will thicken, change color to a deep pink, and perfume your kitchen. When the spoon stands up in the mixture, it has reached the right consistency.

Remove from the heat, cool slightly, then pour into a large shallow dish or, to store, into plastic containers with lids (the paste can be turned out onto a plate when needed). Chill in the refrigerator for 24 hours, and your quince paste will be ready to eat or to keep for months. It hardens with time.

TABERNA BODEGAS MEZQUITA, *Córdoba*

Just yards from the imposing Mezquita, this tapas restaurant is a landmark on Córdoba's ever-expanding gastro circuit in the twisting lanes of the old town. Owned by the enterprising *cordobés*, Baldomero Gas, the tavern was preceded in 2004 by a sister branch just north of the mosque, both now joined by a gourmet delicatessen of Andalusian products.

The focus of the tavern lies firmly in Córdoba's culinary traditions, resulting in a menu like a hit list of the classics—whether Sephardic or Moorish. "Since we are right next to the mosque, we didn't really have an option—we had to be protagonists!" exclaims Gas, who always seems to have a new culinary project in the works. As a result, it is one of the few places that serves couscous, and people come in droves to devour their honeyed Caliphate eggplants and creamy *salmorejos*. Reflecting such offerings, the décor is typically *andaluz*, though eschewing the clichés, and full of wrought iron, exposed brick, and tiled floors as well as fascinating vintage photos.

Running the kitchen at this Corregidor branch is the sunny Maripaz Parras, a native of Córdoba's Judería who, despite her youth, has worked abroad in Italy and Holland.

Serves 4 to 6

Cod, olive, and orange salad
Remojón

This classic Andalusian appetizer (or lunch main course) is wonderfully refreshing and textural. Every city claims ownership, so there are numerous interpretations (find Granada's on p. 101). Bodegas Mezquita's twist comes from the intense Montilla-Moriles dessert wine (Pedro Ximénez, simply called PX), as well as slow cooking the cod in olive oil to make a *confit*. The advantage of this method is that the fish retains its moisture and is imbued with the flavor of the oil. If you lack the time, just poach the cod in a little water for 5 to 6 minutes.

1 Navel orange, peeled
7½ oz (210 g) cod fillet, about 1 inch (3 cm) thick
1½ cups (350 ml) extra virgin olive
    oil, plus more if needed
2 cloves garlic, finely chopped
Heaped 2 tablespoons toasted
    almonds, roughly chopped
½ hardboiled egg, finely chopped
1 red onion, sliced into half rings
7 pitted black olives, cut into rings
Salt and white pepper
2 teaspoons PX reduction, or simply
    use Pedro Ximénez sherry
Chives (optional)

Divide the orange into segments and remove all seeds, inner skin, and pith.

In a small saucepan, submerge the cod in olive oil. Place over low heat and slowly cook the cod, keeping the temperature as close to 212°F (100°C) as possible (use a kitchen thermometer if you have one). It takes about 50 minutes. Turn the fillets over halfway through.

Once cooked, skim off the white layer that has formed on the surface of the oil (in fact, the fish gelatin), then remove the fillets with a slotted spoon. Allow to cool.

Mix the garlic, almonds, and hardboiled egg.

To serve, arrange the orange pieces on a platter, followed by chunks of the cod, onion, olives, and the almond-egg mixture. Season with salt and pepper.

In a cup, mix the PX sherry with 3 tablespoons olive oil, and drizzle this over the salad, finishing with finely snipped chives.

Serves 6

Mezquita salad of eggplant, tomato, and olives
Ensalada Mezquita de berenjenas, tomate y aceitunas

Versatile eggplant was the most popular vegetable of all in Al-Andalus, and this recipe shows how well it fuses with sugar and honey. It makes a substantial appetizer and is quite sweet, so follow it with a light main course. It looks intriguing—a nest of dark mystery in salad leaves.

5½ lb (2.5 kg) eggplants, very finely diced
6–7 tablespoons extra virgin olive oil
5½ lb (2.5 kg) tomatoes, roughly chopped
1 tablespoon sugar
1 teaspoon ground cumin
Pinch of salt
2½ cups (1¾ oz/50 g) mixed salad greens or arugula
10 pitted black olives, sliced
1 tablespoon clear honey

In a saucepan, heat ¼ cup (60 ml) oil and fry diced eggplant until golden. Transfer to a plate lined with paper towels to absorb the oil, and set aside.

In a saucepan, combine the tomatoes and sugar and simmer over medium heat until the liquid has evaporated and you obtain a thick sauce, 8 to 10 minutes. Stir in the diced eggplant, cumin, and salt. Allow to cool.

Arrange the salad greens on a serving plate, then spoon over the eggplant and tomato mixture, and scatter with the olives.

Mix the honey with the remaining 2 to 3 tablespoons oil, and pour this over the salad before serving.

Serves 6

Mozarabic meatballs in almond and saffron sauce
Albóndigas mozárabes en salsa de almendras y azafrán

Albondigas are yet another legacy of the Arabs that became a stalwart all over Spain. Here they are Mozarabic, referring to the Christians living under Moorish rule. Etymologically, the word *albóndiga* actually derives from the Arabic for hazelnut, *al bundiqa*—that's quite a small meatball! You can replace the chicken thigh meat with chicken breast, though the meatballs may be a little drier. Serve this with rice.

Extra virgin olive oil

Meatballs
1 lb (500 g) ground beef
1 lb (500 g) skinless boneless chicken
   thighs, finely chopped
1 ¾ cups (3 oz/85 g) fresh breadcrumbs
2 whole eggs
1 teaspoon ground cumin
½ teaspoon cinnamon
1 onion, minced
1 tablespoon chopped flat-leaf parsley
Pinch of salt
Pinch of ground black pepper

Sauce
2 tablespoons extra virgin olive oil
3 onions, chopped
6 cloves garlic, peeled and chopped
3 small carrots, diced
⅓ cup (75 ml) water
1 teaspoon curry powder
1 teaspoon saffron threads
Salt and white pepper
½ cup (1 ¾ oz/50 g) chopped almonds
2 ½ oz (70 g) toasted bread, shredded

In a large bowl, combine all the meatball ingredients, mixing well until you have a moist dough. Once it is thoroughly amalgamated, leave to rest for 5 minutes.

Form the meatball mixture into 1 ½-inch (4-cm) balls using the palms of your hands, then let them rest at room temperature for 20 minutes or so.

Heat a little olive oil in a pan, and fry the meatballs for 5 minutes, turning so that they brown evenly. Transfer to a plate lined with paper towels to absorb the excess oil.

Next, make the sauce: In a large sauté pan, heat the olive oil and sauté the onion, garlic, and carrots, until tender, about 5 minutes. Add the water, curry powder, saffron, salt, and pepper. Stir in the almonds and bread and simmer for 10 minutes, or until the mixture thickens, stirring from time to time. Remove from the heat, whisk with a hand mixer or fork, then strain through a sieve into a bowl.

Return the sauce to the pan, add the meatballs, and add enough water to cover the meatballs, stirring carefully to combine. Bring to a slow simmer and cook for about 25 minutes until the sauce has reduced and the meatballs are fully cooked. Serve hot.

Serves 4

Lamb in Pedro Ximénez sauce
Cordero en salsa de PX

Lamb was the favored meat among Al-Andalus' higher echelons, and is still very popular in the region, the best quality being from the Segureña breed. In this recipe, sweet and savory ride high thanks to the intensity of the raisiny PX wine. The dish is relatively easy to make and is great dinner party fodder. Couscous is an excellent accompaniment.

1 tablespoon extra virgin olive oil
8 cloves garlic, minced
3 onions, finely chopped
2 ¼ lb (1 kg) boneless leg of lamb, fat trimmed, cut into chunks
3 teaspoons salt
Freshly ground black pepper
1 teaspoon ground thyme
1 ¼ cups (300 ml) Pedro Ximénez dessert wine
¼ cup (1 oz/30 g) pitted prunes
1 ½ tablespoons honey
2 ½ tablespoons toasted pine nuts

In a pan, heat the extra virgin olive oil and sauté the garlic and onion.

Season the lamb with with the salt, pepper, and thyme and add it to the pan. Fry over high heat, moving the meat around until it is entirely browned.

Add the wine, cover, lower the heat, and leave to simmer for about 1 hour until the meat is tender, keeping an eye on the liquid level (add more water if necessary), and stirring occasionally.

During the last few minutes of cooking, stir in the prunes and honey. Simmer for a few minutes more, then sprinkle with pine nuts before serving.

Serves 4

Marinated turkey
Pavo en escabeche

This light and tangy dish is perfect on a sunny terrace with a glass of chilled white wine. Although turkey is hardly an Old World beast (it was brought to Spain from the Americas by Jesuits in the 16th century and in fact the Yucatan has a recipe very similar to this one), the technique of cooking or marinating in vinegar is very *andalusí* and packs a delicious punch. The turkey will keep in its *escabeche* (marinade) for up to a week in the refrigerator.

14 oz (400 g) turkey breast, rinsed, fat removed
¼ cup (60 ml) extra virgin olive oil
2 tablespoons vinegar
1 large carrot, halved lengthwise
½ onion, thinly sliced
7 cloves garlic
1 bay leaf
10 black peppercorns
Salt
1 tablespoon sliced cornichons
1 tablespoon pitted black olives

Put all the ingredients, except the pickle and olives, into a saucepan, and add just enough water to submerge. Bring to a boil, lower the heat, and simmer, covered, for 30 minutes or so until the turkey is cooked through (the timing will depend on its thickness).

Using a slotted spoon, remove the ingredients from the pot, reserving the marinade to store leftovers, and leave to cool. Thinly slice the meat, dice the vegetables, and arrange these on a plate with the pickles and olives.

Serves 6

Eggplant fritters in Pedro Ximénez syrup
Berenjenas a la miel de Pedro Ximénez

Eggplant was the queen vegetable of Al-Andalus, originally from Persia. Again, etymology proves this fact—as the word transited from the Persian *bahhimjan* to the Arabic *badinjan* to the Spanish *berenjena*. Eggplant fritters, an absolute classic of Córdoba that has conquered Andalucía, are usually drizzled in honey or molasses—you can substitute either for the Pedro Ximénez reduction used here.

2 eggplants (about 2 ¼ lb/1 kg total)
About 1 cup (250 ml) milk
Extra virgin olive oil, for frying

Pedro Ximénez reduction
Generous ¾ cup (200 ml) Pedro
   Ximénez dessert wine
⅓ cup (2 oz/60 g) sugar

Batter
1 ½ cups (6 ½ oz/180 g) flour
1 egg
1 teaspoon yeast
Generous ¾ cup (200 ml) beer
½ teaspoon salt
10 sprigs flat-leaf parsley, finely chopped

First, make the PX reduction: In a saucepan, combine the wine and sugar and simmer over medium heat for about 30 minutes, until syrupy, stirring regularly to dissolve the sugar. Remove from the heat—it will thicken further as it cools.

Next, make the batter: Using a hand mixer, beat all the ingredients together until smooth then set aside for 30 minutes to settle.

Cut off the stalks and slice the eggplants in half lengthwise. Cut into ½-inch (1-cm) thick half moons. Soak the slices in milk until shortly before you want to fry them (this is to prevent oxidization).

In a large frying pan, heat 1 ½ inches (4 cm) olive oil over high heat. In batches, shake the milk off the eggplant slices, dip them in the batter, and fry until golden brown, 3 to 5 minutes per batch. Remove with a slotted spoon and drain on a plate lined with paper towels.

Serve the hot fritters drizzled in the syrup.

CASA MAZAL, *Córdoba*

"House of Fortune" is the Hebrew name of this rare Sephardic (Judaeo-Spanish) restaurant down a side alley of the medieval Judería. Whether all was sweetness and light among Jews, Christians, and Muslims during the golden age of Al-Andalus is a moot point, but Casa Mazal does an impressive job of keeping Sepharad culinary traditions alive.

Ironically named Jesús, the manager is a ball of frenetic energy, in high contrast to the calm young chef, Nicolas Montés, who prepares intricate Kosher dishes behind the scenes. "We don't serve pork, shellfish, or milk products," Jesús Guerrero López points out. "And we use lots of herbs like cilantro and rosemary, keeping a balance of sweet and spicy." Dishes like chicken with honey, dates, and raisins; couscous with chicken and lemon; and *pishkado* or "fish in plum sauce" are all redolent of North Africa and the Middle East.

Although the Jewish owner leaves management to Jesús, her influence is visible in decorative features like the embedded Ottoman wall-tiles, a ceramic Star of David, the vivid paint colors, and the low, inlaid tables. Music is the other major strand at Casa Mazal, bringing evening performances to the central patio overlooked by a gallery. On a balmy night, lulled by a haunting Sephardi song, those authentic dishes gain even deeper significance.

Serves 4

Chicken salad with pomegranate, almonds, and orange

Ensalada de pollo con granadas y almendras y naranja

Chicken and strawberry? Such eclectic sweet and salty ingredients make up this elaborate salad, with most of the work in the preparation. You can leave out some ingredients, but try to maintain the contrast of flavors and textures. Fry the chicken pieces at the last minute, since they should be hot.

6 loosely packed cups (5¾ oz/165 g)
   mixed salad greens
1 orange, peeled, pith and seeds
   removed, cut into small pieces
Seeds of 1 pomegranate
2 medium carrots, finely diced or grated
1 red onion, peeled and finely diced
1 tomato, cored and diced
9 oz (250 g) boneless skinless
   chicken breasts or thighs
2 tablespoons sesame seeds
2 tablespoons extra virgin olive oil
¾ cup (3 oz/85 g) chopped almonds or walnuts
10–15 g mustard shoots (optional)
½ cup (3 oz/85 g) sliced strawberries

Vinaigrette
1 level tablespoon Dijon mustard
3 tablespoons clear honey
2–3 tablespoons extra virgin olive oil

In a large bowl, mix the salad greens, orange, pomegranate seeds, and diced vegetables.

Cut the chicken into small chunks, coat in the sesame seeds, and fry in extra virgin olive oil over medium heat until cooked through, 5 to 7 minutes. Mix into the salad.

Just before serving, sprinkle the chopped nuts, mustard shoots, and strawberries over the top. Add the vinaigrette, tossing to distribute evenly.

Serves 6

Slow-roasted lamb jam
Confitura de cordero

This is a stunning dish, possibly a precursor to Mexican *mole* sauce, with its chocolate and dried fruits. It is said to have been invented by nuns. You can skip making the confit potatoes and simply boil them, though you will miss out on an incredible velvety texture and unique taste. Equally, you can replace the honey rum with a Spanish brandy.

Lamb
4½–5 lb (2-2.25 kg) boneless leg of lamb,
    trimmed of fat, and butterflied (from an
    8 lb/3.6 kg lamb leg on the bone)
Salt and white pepper
1 branch of rosemary, leaves finely chopped
8 pitted prunes, chopped

Sauce
⅔ cup (150 ml) honey rum
2 tablespoons molasses
1 tablespoon chocolate syrup
3 tablespoons dried fruit, such as
    raisins or golden raisins

Confit of potatoes
10½ oz (300 g) heirloom potatoes, washed
A few sprigs of fresh rosemary and thyme
Sea salt
Extra virgin olive oil

Vegetables
1 large onion, sliced into thin wedges
4 carrots, sliced
2 cups (9 oz/250 g) diced zucchini
1 red bell pepper, seeded, deribbed, and chopped

Asparagus
Extra virgin olive oil
8 asparagus spears
Salt

Preheat the oven to 220°F (100°C).

Season the lamb with salt, pepper, and rosemary then stuff with the prunes.

Carefully and tightly roll up the meat to form a large sausage, then place in an oiled baking pan or dish.

Roast very slowly for 2½ hours, then turn the oven up to 350°F (180°C) for another 30 minutes. Remove from oven, allow to cool, then cut into slices.

Meanwhile, make the confit of potatoes. Fit the potatoes snugly in a baking dish with a few springs of rosemary and thyme, sprinkle with salt flakes, and completely submerge in olive oil. Place them in the oven with the lamb, and cook for about 2 hours. Test with a fork to ensure they are cooked through.

Heat a little oil in a frying pan and sauté the vegetables, stirring from time to time; they will take about 10 minutes to become tender.

While they are cooking, return to the lamb. Heat 2 tablespoons of olive oil in a frying pan over medium heat, then slip in the lamb slices to reheat. Add the honey rum and alight to flambé. Stir in the molasses and chocolate, mixing well, then for the last minute of cooking, add the dried fruit. It will reduce to a thick, sticky sauce—a real jam.

In a separate frying pan, heat a splash of olive oil over medium heat and sauté the asparagus with a sprinkle of salt for 10 minutes or so, until bright green and tender.

To serve, place the lamb in the center of each plate, spooning the sweet sauce over it, and crown with 2 asparagus spears each. Arrange the potatoes and vegetables on the side and serve immediately.

Serves 4

Duck couscous
Couscous con pato

This is a star dish at Casa Mazal and, yet again, assembles an incredible variety of flavors. It shouldn't be difficult to source the prepared duck confit. Nicolas suggests adjusting the quantities of molasses and soy sauce according to taste. The *mil flores* tea used to subtly flavor the couscous is a typical *andaluz* product, an intense mixture of black tea leaves with sunflower, rose, cornflower, and safflower. The nearest aromatic alternative would be Earl Grey.

2 confit duck thighs
1 onion, peeled and thinly sliced
2 tablespoons extra virgin olive
   oil, plus more for frying
2 teaspoons soy sauce, or more to taste
1 teaspoon salt
1 tablespoon molasses
3½ tablespoons vegetable stock
1½ cups (6½ oz/180 g) chopped vegetables
   (carrots, zucchini, celery)
1 cup (250 ml) boiling water
1 teabag Mil Flores tea
1 cup (6 oz/175 g) couscous
½ teaspoon salt
2 tablespoons toasted pumpkin or sunflower seeds

Preheat the oven to 175°F (80°C).

Shred the duck meat, removing the bones. In a baking dish, stir together the onion, oil, soy sauce, salt, molasses, and vegetable stock. Add the shredded duck, mixing well, and bake for 10 minutes.

Meanwhile, heat some olive oil in a frying pan and sauté the vegetables until tender, about 10 minutes.

Steep the teabag in the boiling water. Place the couscous in a heatsafe bowl, sprinkle with salt, and pour the tea over it. Mix well with a fork, cover, and set aside for 5 to 7 minutes, until the tea has been absorbed. Fluff with a fork to separate the grains before serving.

To serve, arrange the couscous, duck mixture, and vegetables on a plate and sprinkle with pumpkin or sunflower seeds.

Serves 4

Chili chicken
Pollo harissa con lombarda

The flavor of this chicken dish with its mild chili hit improves even further if you marinate the chicken in the sauce for a few hours in the refrigerator before cooking. Harissa is actually a fiery North African sauce of roasted red peppers, chilies, and spices—so since chilies came from the Americas, it could not have existed in Al-Andalus. It was after the expulsion of the Jews from Spain, who in many cases went to North Africa, that they discovered this potent seasoning.

2 large mild green chili peppers,
   such as guindilla, seeded
1 tablespoon ground cumin
2 cloves garlic, chopped
1 roasted red pepper, roughly chopped
1 tablespoon tomato paste
1 tablespoon white wine vinegar
1 tablespoon paprika
2 tablespoons extra virgin olive oil,
   plus more for cooking
2 medium onions, chopped
⅔ cup (150 ml) white wine
1½ lb (700 g) boneless skinless chicken
   breast, cut into chunks
Salt
⅔ cup (150 ml) soy creamer
Snipped chives, to garnish

First, make the harissa sauce: In a food processor, combine the chili, cumin, and half of the garlic, and process to a paste. Add the red pepper, tomato paste, vinegar, and paprika, and process until smooth. With the machine running, slowly pour in the olive oil.

Heat a little olive oil in a large pan, and sauté the onion and remaining 1 clove garlic until translucent, then add the white wine. Simmer for about 3 minutes until reduced slightly, then stir in the chicken pieces, season with salt, and cook for about 5 minutes, before tipping in the harissa sauce. Simmer until the chicken is cooked, about 10 minutes. When done, stir in the soy creamer to thicken the sauce.

Scatter some snipped chives over the top before serving.

Red cabbage

1 red cabbage
Extra virgin olive oil
1 large leek, julienned
2 teaspoons apple cider vinegar
Salt and white pepper

Prepare the red cabbage by stripping the outer leaves, cut it into quarters, then remove the tough central core. Finely slice the leaves.

In a saucepan, heat some extra virgin olive oil, sauté the leek until translucent, then stir in the red cabbage with the vinegar. Cover and cook over low heat for about 30 minutes or until tender. Season with salt and pepper, and allow to cool; for this dish it is served cold.

Makes 12 to 14 cookies

Almond cookies
Almendrados

Casa Mazal orders their almond cookies from a specialist Kosher baker, but this recipe should do the trick. Serve with dollops of jam and fresh mint tea.

¾ cup (1 ½ sticks/6 oz/170 g) butter,
   at room temperature
½ cup (3 ½ oz/100 g) sugar
1 egg
Heaped 1 cup (4 oz/110 g) ground almonds
Zest of 1 lemon
1 teaspoon cinnamon
Heaped 1 tablespoon poppyseeds
1 ⅔ cups (7 oz/200 g) all-purpose
   flour, plus more for flouring

Preheat oven to 350°F (180°C).

In a large bowl cream the butter and sugar together until fluffy, then add the egg, beating well. Stir in the almonds, lemon zest, cinnamon, and poppyseeds. Mix thoroughly then add the flour, beating energetically to make a smooth dough. Refrigerate for at least 1 hour so it is less sticky.

Cut out two pieces of parchment paper about the size of your baking sheet and flour them. Roll the dough out between the pieces of floured parchment paper to an even thickness of ½ inch (1 cm). Remove the top sheet of paper and use a cookie cutter dipped in flour to cut out shapes, leaving about 1 inch (2.5 cm) between them. Remove the trimmings and transfer the paper to a baking sheet. Keep the trimmings to roll out again between two new sheets of floured parchment paper and repeat the process.

Place in the oven and bake for about 20 minutes, or until just golden around the edges. Leave to cool slightly then remove form the pan using a knife, and place on a rack until completely cool. Store them in an airtight container, though they won't last long.

RESTAURANTE PLAZA DE TOROS, *Antequera*

I had never before been offered a table in the middle of a bullring—until I came to this celebrated restaurant in Antequera. Flinging open the wooden gates, Inma Jiménez, the sparky young manager, offered me the entire sandy terrain. In good weather, diners flock there to eat beneath the stars as, uniquely, the restaurant is slotted under the seats of the stands. Inside, the sloping beamed ceilings and stone walls plastered with bullfighting memorabilia are seconded by a museum of the taurine "art" like Ronda's. Although opened in 1985, the restaurant languished for some years until Inma took over in 2014 and gave it a new lease on life. Now chef Diego Solis toils away on recipes showcasing Antequera's seasonal produce, some that are old stalwarts like·the local *porra* (*salmorejo*) while others are less common, like carpaccio of young bull. Naturally, the *croquetas* are made of bull's tail and *toro* sneaks into countless other dishes, but vegetarian options exist too.

Antequera's Moorish credentials are impressive, as it was one of the last defenses of the emirate of Granada. After integration into Catholic Spain, it became a hotbed of Renaissance thought, a strategic commercial crossroads, and home to over thirty churches. The bells really toll loudly here when not drowned out by a *pasodoble* introducing the matadors into the ring.

Serves 4 to 6

Antequera's chilled tomato soup
Porra Antequerana

This thick, creamy, chilled soup is very different from its cousin, gazpacho. Under the banner *salmorejo*, it hails from Córdoba (usually with an extra edge of vinegar and garnished with chopped boiled egg and jamón), but Antequera, only 60 miles (100 km) to the south, hotly disputes this. Diego explains that some cooks peel the tomatoes, but he merely cores them.

2 ¼ lb (1 kg) juicy plum tomatoes
1 clove garlic
1 red bell pepper, seeded, deribbed, and quartered
1 lb (500 g) dry rustic bread, roughly torn
1 tablespoon sherry or wine vinegar
Salt and white pepper
3 ½ tablespoons extra virgin olive oil

Garnish
2 hardboiled eggs, quartered
3 ½ oz (100 g) jamón, diced
1 large tomato, quartered
5 oz (140 g) can good quality tuna
    in olive oil (optional)
Extra virgin olive oil

Using a sharp knife, core and coarsely chop the tomatoes. Add them to a food processor with the garlic and red pepper and process to combine. Add the bread and process further until you obtain quite a thick purée. Add the vinegar and season to taste. With the machine running, gradually pour in the oil.

Strain the soup into a large bowl and allow it to cool (or place in the refrigerator until chilled). Divide between soup bowls and garnish each one with egg, diced jamón, tomato, a dollop of tuna, and a generous trickle of olive oil.

Serves 4

Chickpea and spinach soup
Potaje de garbanzos y espinacas

Chickpeas were, famously, one of the staple legumes introduced by the Moors and remain favorites for soups and stews to this day. This traditional soupy dish is a star of Semana Santa (Easter week), when austerity rules and meat becomes rare. It is real comfort food, easy to make, and perfect for a healthy, light supper. You can use canned chickpeas (about 1 ½ x 14 oz/400 g cans), but aim for organic and make sure you rinse them well.

1 ½ cups (10 ½ oz/300 g) dried chickpeas,
  soaked in water overnight
Salt
1 bay leaf
3 small-medium potatoes, peeled and chopped
Extra virgin olive oil
2 large onions, peeled and minced
3 cloves garlic, peeled and minced
2 ripe tomatoes, peeled (see p. 77) and chopped
2 carrots, peeled and finely chopped
1 teaspoon saffron
9 cups (9 ½ oz/270 g) spinach
Sweet paprika

Drain and rinse the chickpeas under cold running water. Drain and tip into a large saucepan. Add 1 liter (4 ¼ cups) water, a pinch of salt, and the bay leaf. Bring to a boil, lower the heat, and simmer until tender, 1 to 1 ½ hours, depending on the age of the chickpeas. Add more water if the level gets low. About 15 minutes before they are done, add the potatoes and cook until tender.

Meanwhile prepare the *sofrito*, or base sauce: In a large, deep saucepan, heat plenty of olive oil over low heat and gently sweat the onion and garlic for 3 or 4 minutes. Stir in the tomatoes and carrots and continue to cook for 5 minutes or so until it becomes a homogenous sauce. Add the saffron and turn off the heat.

In a separate large pan, bring 2 ½ cups (600 ml) water to a boil. Add the spinach, lower the heat, and simmer, covered, for about 3 minutes or until the spinach wilts. Drain the spinach and add it to the tomato sauce. Stir over medium heat for about 5 minutes. Add the paprika and remove from the heat.

Once the chickpeas are cooked, add them to the sauce with enough of the cooking water to make a hearty soup. Season to taste with salt and pepper, stir well, and bring to a simmer. Serve hot.

Serves 2 to 4

Stewed partridge perfumed with rosemary
Perdiz estofada al aroma de romero

Diego developed this recipe to make full use of red-legged partridges, which are high on the list of Andalusian hunters every autumn. In fact, Andalucía boasts the most diverse and extensive hunting in the developed world—luckily it's tightly regulated. Villagers often place caged partridges in the *campo* to attract wild ones—then crack go the shotguns. You can source imported partridges seasonally from gourmet food stores such as D'Artagnan, or you can substitute guinea hens. Serve this dish with fried potatoes, sliced bell peppers, and/or cooked whole tomatoes.

2 large partridges, skin on
Salt and white pepper
All-purpose flour, for dusting
Extra virgin olive oil
12 dried Malaga figs
1 ¼ cups (300 ml) red wine
1 ½ teaspoons sugar
1 teaspoon ground cinnamon
2 large scallions, finely sliced
4 cloves garlic, chopped
3 ripe tomatoes, peeled (see p. 77), seeds
   removed, and finely chopped
2 carrots, peeled and sliced into thick rounds
1 cup (250 ml) white wine
2 sprigs fresh thyme
2 sprigs fresh rosemary
2 sprigs fresh oregano
1 bay leaf
4 ¼ cups (1 liter) chicken stock

First wash the partridges under running water and pat dry using paper towels. Sprinkle with salt and pepper and tie them so they keep their shape. Lightly dust with flour.

In a large deep saucepan, heat a generous amount of olive oil over medium heat. Sear the partridges, turning them until they are golden all over. Remove the partridge and set aside, reserving the oil in tha pan.

In a separate small pan, combine the figs, red wine, sugar, and cinnamon, and simmer until the figs are plump, about 10 minutes. Drain them, discarding the cooking liquid, and set aside.

Drain the partridge oil from the pan, leaving just enough to sauté the scallions and garlic over low heat. After about 10 minutes, add the tomatoes without their juice. Cook until any remaining liquid from the tomatoes has evaporated, and stir in the carrots. Pour in the white wine and bubble for 5 minutes to reduce the mixture.

Add partridges and herbs to the pan and pour in the stock. Bring to a boil, lower the heat, cover the pot, and simmer for about 20 minutes. Add the figs, and continue to simmer until the meat is tender (check it again after 5 minutes; if it is not cooked, continue to simmer—it can be a tough bird and sizes vary).

You can serve the dish from the pot or, more elegantly, remove the partridges and figs, discard the herb sprigs, and use an immersion blender to purée the sauce until smooth and glossy. Place the birds on a serving dish, untie them, and pour the gravy over them—it should have a lacquer-like sheen.

Serves 4

Fresh artichokes sautéed with Iberian ham
Alcachofas naturales salteadas con jamón ibérico

Globe artichokes were much loved in Moorish times. They originally grew wild throughout the Mediterranean basin but it is thought that superior cultivated versions came to Al-Andalus from North Africa. The Spanish name, *alcachofa*, actually derives from the Arabic, *al khurshuuf*. Artichokes are very nutritious: low in calories, high in antioxidants, fiber, and minerals and help combat cholesterol. In fact, the Greeks and Romans were the first to extol their health-giving properties. Here, their subtle flavor is lifted by velvety *jamón Ibérico* (hardly Muslim), which you can replace with the cheaper *jamón serrano*. An alternative recipe from the Córdoba area is *Alcachofas a la Montillana*, where sweated onion, saffron, and a glass or two of punchy Montilla white wine enter the last stage of cooking. Not bad at all.

1 lb (500 g) young artichokes
1 lemon, halved
1 tablespoon plus 1 teaspoon flour
Salt
3 tablespoons extra virgin olive oil
7 oz (200 g) thinly sliced Iberian ham
⅓ cup (75 ml) white wine
Chives (optional)

Clean the artichokes, removing the tough outer petals, and slice off the base of the stems; you will need only the tender inner leaves and upper stem. (If the artichokes are large, quarter them and remove the chokes.) As you work, rub the stems with the lemon to prevent discoloring.

Boil a large saucepan of water, add 1 teaspoon of the flour and a pinch of salt, then drop in the artichokes, and simmer for about 15 minutes, or until the stems are tender.

If eating immediately, drain the artichokes well, making sure no water remains (if preparing them in advance, leave them in the cooking water, cool, and refrigerate until you are ready to finish the dish).

Heat some olive oil in a large frying pan and sauté the artichokes with the ham, turning with a wooden spoon, until the artichokes are lightly colored, about 3 minutes. Transfer to a plate, leaving the oil in the pan, and set aside.

Return the pan to low heat, stir in the remaining 1 tablespoon flour and allow it to thicken for a minute or so. Squeeze in the remaining lemon half and add the white wine, mixing well to form a light sauce. Serve the artichokes and ham slices drizzled with extra virgin olive oil and the lemon-wine sauce and garnished with chives.

Serves 4 to 6

Antequeran sponge and almond cake
Bienmesabe Antequerano

I love the word *bienmesabe*, which literally means, "tastes good to me." With a name like that, it could be applied to dozens of desserts throughout the Hispanic world. Diego's version derives from the cloistered nuns of Antequera's Convent of Belén, ten of whom survive and churn out industrial quantities of cookies and cakes. It is thought that these impassioned cooks inherited the recipe from the Moors, kings of the sweet tooth. Antequera's other *bienmesabe* variations all include almonds, syrup, and cinnamon.

1 ¾ cups (9 oz/250 g) toasted almonds
4 ½ oz (125 g) package Italian ladyfingers
   (*savoiardi*) or sponge cake fingers
1 cup (250 ml) water
Generous 2 cups (15 oz/425 g) sugar
15 oz (425 g) can pumpkin purée
6 eggs, beaten

To Decorate
Ground cinnamon
Confectioner's sugar
Sprigs of fresh mint (optional)

Coarsely grind the almonds in a food processor.

Line the base of a 10 inch (25 cm) square baking dish with the ladyfingers.

In a small saucepan, heat the water and sugar over low heat, stirring well until the sugar dissolves and you obtain a syrup. Spoon a little under half of this over the ladyfingers, keeping the rest in the saucepan.

Spread the pumpkin purée thinly over the syrupy ladyfingers.

Stir the almonds and beaten egg into the remaining syrup, mixing well, then return to low heat to simmer gently for 3 minutes to thicken. When it is ready, pour this mixture over the ladyfingers, blanketing them entirely. Leave to cool and refrigerate until you are ready to serve.

Just before serving, sprinkle with cinnamon and confectioner's sugar. Cut into squares and serve garnished with mint.

ARTE DE COZINA, *Antequera*

Charo Carmona is a powerhouse on the culinary map of Málaga province. Now in her early sixties, she has spent over twenty years resurrecting traditional recipes of this region to serve in her tapas bar and restaurant. The grand 17th century building with a flagstone patio and upper galleries is in the heart of old Antequera, just yards from the central food market. "Food markets are like museums of the landscape, the colors and smells changing with the seasons," muses this culinary purist.

Aided by her son, Francisco, who also runs the family vineyard, Charo steers the kitchen with a rigor and zeal that have brought several accolades. "My mother-in-law introduced me to food when I became engaged at fifteen. She was a genius in the kitchen, very imaginative and picked up ideas in Catalunya on frequent trips. I have strong "taste memories" from that time. The emotions of food are so important. One day an old man in the restaurant ordered *Maimones* (a simple garlic soup). After a spoonful, tears started rolling down his cheeks. He said he hadn't tasted it in sixty years, and ended up having two bowls!"

For Charo, contemporary Andalusian cuisine is *una riqueza* of Phoenician, Roman, Jewish, and Moorish input, as well as bountiful produce. "But now I need to pass these recipes on," she adds. Taste memories for the future, no doubt.

Chilled soups
Porras

Porra (meaning "pestle," from a mortar and pestle) is the Antequeran version of Córdoba's *salmorejo*, a thick, creamy tomato emulsion or chilled soup. Its age-old *andalusí* ingredients of breadcrumbs, olive oil, vinegar, garlic, salt, and water become the *salmorejo* we know today when united with the New World tomato. This very unusual orange *porra* is a dazzling plate of sunshine.

Serves 4

Chilled orange soup
Porra de naranja

1 lb (500 g) day-old sourdough bread, loosely torn
2 cups (500 ml) freshly squeezed
   orange juice, strained
1 clove garlic
⅔ cup (150 ml) extra virgin olive
   oil, plus more to garnish
Salt
Chopped almonds and Spanish jamón, to garnish

Soak the bread in the orange juice
for about 30 minutes.

Blend in a food processor with the garlic, olive oil, and a pinch of salt until you have a fine, even consistency. Refrigerate just until chilled, but not for too long, or the orange will lose its freshness.

Garnish with generous trickles of extra virgin olive oil and a scattering of chopped almonds and jamón.

Serves 4

Chilled white soup
Porra blanca (Mazamorra)

1 lb (500 g) day-old sourdough
   bread, loosely shredded
4–5 garlic cloves, peeled and chopped
Salt
1 cup (250 ml) extra virgin olive
   oil, plus more to garnish
Sherry vinegar
2 hard-boiled eggs, chopped
Sprig of mint

Soak the bread in just enough water to cover for 5 minutes until it swells up nicely. Remove the bread and squeeze dry. If you like you can remove the crust, but it's not essential.

Tip the bread into a food processor with the garlic and a pinch of salt and blend to a smooth paste. With the machine running, add the oil in a trickle, then the vinegar. Continue to blend until you have a fine, fluid texture, glistening with olive oil. Some people add a little water to make it lighter.

Garnish with boiled egg, mint leaves, and a trickle of olive oil.

Serves 4 to 6

Country-style suckling kid
Chivo a la pastoril

This traditional Antequera recipe is best made with suckling kid goat, about one month old, however, since this is not always available, the next best thing is a 12-month-old meat breed goat (that is, not raised for dairy purposes). Despite being classified as red meat, goat is leaner and contains less cholesterol, fat, and protein than either lamb or beef. It needs relatively slow cooking to preserve its tenderness and moisture. For the sauce, Charo uses twenty-five-year-old sherry vinegar, since this has a subtle taste with depth and does not overpower the other flavors. She stresses that the bread is essential to thicken the sauce, but that the almonds can be left out. Serve this dish with fried potatoes.

Extra virgin olive oil
Handful of blanched almonds (optional)
Slice of sourdough bread, broken into pieces
½ head garlic, peeled and finely sliced
½ kid goat or calf liver (7–9 oz/200–
    250 g), coarsely chopped
1 teaspoon dried oregano
4½ lb (2 kg) suckling kid goat, cut into chunks
Salt and ground black pepper
1 sprig of thyme
Scant 1 tablespoon sweet paprika
About 1 cup (250 ml) sherry vinegar

In a large sauté pan, heat a generous glug of olive oil and sauté separately, one after the other, the almonds, bread, garlic, and the liver, until tender. Remove each ingredient with a slotted spoon, leaving the remaining oil in the pan, and set aside on a plate. In a large mortar and pestle, crush them together thoroughly to make a paste, and mash in the oregano. Set aside.

Season the chunks of goat with salt and pepper, then sauté in the same frying pan until browned on all sides. If necessary, spoon out any excess oil. Stir in the thyme, paprika, and vinegar, then cover with water. Bring to a boil, lower the heat, and simmer for 25 minutes.

Stir in the liver, bread, and almond mixture and simmer vigorously for 5 more minutes, until you have a thick sauce. Taste and add more salt and pepper, if needed.

Makes 12

Sweet cheese buns
Almojábanas

The name of these soft cheesecakes derives from the Arabic *al-muyabannat* meaning, quite simply, "made with cheese." They may look quite solid, but are actually light as a feather, with an added crunch. Charo suggests serving them in pairs, sandwiching the pieces with a slice of goat cheese or quince paste.

½ cup (125 ml) extra virgin olive
   oil, plus more for greasing
2 cups (9 oz/250 g) flour
Salt
1 cup (250 ml) water
3½ oz (100 g) very firm goat cheese, shredded
1½ teaspoons baking powder
3 eggs, beaten until frothy
Ground cinnamon
½ cup (125 ml) honey or molasses

Preheat the oven to 350°F (180°C) and lightly grease a baking sheet with olive oil (or use a nonstick baking sheet).

In a bowl, mix the flour and a pinch of salt.

In a pan, bring the water and oil to a boil. Remove from the heat. Stirring continuously with a wooden spoon, gradually add the flour mixture, a little at a time, mixing until you have a smooth, unctuous dough. Add the cheese and baking powder, and continue to mix until the cheese has been absorbed. Set aside to cool for 5 minutes.

Once the dough has cooled, incorporate the beaten eggs and knead gently to an even consistency.

Form the dough into 2 inch (5 cm) balls with well-greased hands. Flatten them slightly with the palm of your hand, and arrange on the prepared pan, leaving about 2 inches (5 cm) between them. Bake for 20 to 25 minutes until golden.

Remove from the oven, sprinkle each ball with cinnamon, and drizzle with honey.

LA LUZ DE CANDELA, *Málaga*

Phoenicians, Carthaginians, Romans, and Moors were all successively lured by the idyllic site of Málaga, cradled by mountains and embracing the sea. Over the last few decades, despite being the cosmopolitan gateway to the sybaritic beaches of the Costa del Sol, it has forged a dynamic cultural life. La Luz de Candela, tucked away up a steep street a few blocks north of the Picasso Museum, is run by two French brothers, Mathieu (the manager) and Charlie Dusser (the chef). A thousand years ago, this same hillside was grazing ground for the city's cattle; today it is home to dozens of fashionable watering holes.

The menu features intriguing twists on local specialties. "I don't focus exclusively on fish like so many restaurants here," Charlie tells me. "I wanted to do something different but still use local ingredients. I'll add something like hummus and use techniques like *escabeche*." That doesn't stop the Frenchman from sneaking in *ratatouille* (*pisto* in Spanish), Dauphinoise potatoes, or Roquefort cheese.

A native of Bourges, in the Loire region, Charlie learned to cook from his mother, whose father was a chef, then worked in top London restaurants for several years, before finally landing in Málaga to be near his Franco-Spanish daughter, Candela. So the restaurant name is a typical Gallic *double entendre*, referring both to her and to candlelight.

Pickled mussels and clams
Escabeche de mejillones y almejas

Escabeche was a typical Moorish technique for conserving seafood and meat (no fridges in those days) using vinegar and spices. There must be a Spanish ancestral taste for it, since numerous types of canned seafood *en escabeche* now fill supermarket shelves and top brands are neatly displayed in the windows of old-fashioned grocery stores. Charlie's version has real bite, tempered by a portion of spicy hummus (recipe on next page). You need to make it at least 24 hours before eating.

About 2 cups (500 ml) white wine
6 cloves garlic, peeled and finely chopped
1 onion, chopped
1 lb 10 oz (750 g) mussels
1 lb 10 oz (750 g) clams
1 cup (250 ml) vinegar
Sprig of parsley
2–3 carrots, sliced
1 bay leaf
2 shallots, finely chopped

In a large saucepan, warm half of the wine with half of the garlic and the chopped onion over medium heat. Add the shellfish and steam for up to 5 minutes or until the shells open. Remove the shellfish, discarding any unopened ones, and set aside. Discard the liquid.

In a small saucepan, combine the remaining wine and garlic, and the vinegar, parsley, carrot, bay leaf, and shallots. Bring to a boil and bubble for 20 minutes. Leave to cool.

Meanwhile remove the mussels and clams from their shells.

Combine the vinegar sauce with the shellfish, transfer to a container, add a trickle of olive oil, and cover. It is ready to eat after 24 hours and will keep refrigerated for one to two weeks.

Charlie's hummus
Humus de Charlie

This hummus has some unusual flavors, although much depends on quantities. The apricots (a very *andalusí* fruit) leave a sweet aftertaste. Charlie merely says, "Find your own balance!" It's best to start with half a teaspoon of each spice and keep adding, tasting as you go. Although chickpeas have been common in Andalucía ever since they came from the Middle East, hummus itself is only slowly appearing in younger, more hip restaurants.

3 ½ oz (100 g) dried apricots
2 cups (10 ½ oz/300 g) cooked or canned chickpeas
⅔ cup (150 ml) light cream
1 large green chili pepper, roughly chopped
½ clove garlic
Juice of ½ lemon
Ground cumin
Ground ginger
Turmeric
White pepper
Sweet or hot paprika
Salt

Soak the dried apricots in warm water for 30 minutes and drain.

Tip all the ingredients into a blender and process to a smooth paste. Adjust the spices to your liking.

Salmon tartare
Tartare de salmón

This light tartare can be an appetizer or a main course—it is easy to adjust the quantities, or even vary some ingredients; for example, you can substitute tuna for salmon. Try Charlie's version though, since the ginger and the asparagus give an unusual (Moorish) twist to what is quite a French classic. He often serves it with his hummus (p. 183). The following recipe makes a generous appetizer.

2 green asparagus spears
14 oz (400 g) fresh salmon fillets, skin removed
Scant ½ cup (2 oz/60 g) capers, finely chopped
¼ yellow bell pepper, seeded and finely chopped
1 clove garlic, minced
2 teaspoons minced fresh ginger
2 shallots, minced
Chopped dill and/or chives
Sea salt and white pepper

Vinaigrette
1 tablespoon lemon juice
3 tablespoons extra virgin olive oil

Bring a small pan of water to a boil and blanch the asparagus for 3 minutes, then transfer to a bowl of ice water to cool.

Mix the vinaigrette ingredients together, season with salt and pepper, and set aside.

Chop the salmon fillets into small cubes then tip them into a large bowl. Cut the asparagus to roughly the same size. Gently mix the capers, pepper, garlic, ginger, shallots, and the dill or chives into the salmon, being careful not to break up the fish. Stir in the vinaigrette and add salt and pepper to taste. Chill in the refrigerator for 15 minute or so in order for it to come together.

Fish, potato, and mayonnaise soup
Gazpachuelo

This hot soup came from the Málaga fishermen who warmed their chilled bones with it in the winter. Charlie's version is far superior to the norm—the fish fillets are generous in size and the toast with aioli is an extra treat, altogether making a delicious and filling dinner dish. If you cannot face making the fish stock, use a top quality, ready-made one. The same goes for the mayonnaise.

2–3 leeks, sliced diagonally into 1 inch (3 cm) lengths
3 cups (750 ml) homemade or good
  quality fish stock (see p. 188)
10½ oz (300 g) waxy potatoes, peeled
  and cut into thick ovals
Extra virgin olive oil
4 fillets of sea bass, sea bream or monkfish
  (each about 3½ oz/100 g), skin on
⅔ cup (5½ oz/150 g) good quality
  mayonnaise (see p. 188)
4 small slices of bread, preferably
  baguette or sourdough
4 teaspoons aioli (see p. 188)
Handful of chives, finely chopped
Sea salt flakes

Bring a small pan of salted water to a boil, add the leeks, and simmer for about 5 minutes until tender. Allow to cool.

In a saucepan, bring 1 cup (250 ml) of the fish stock to a boil, add the potatoes, and simmer until tender, about 20 minutes. Remove and set aside, reserving the stock in the pan.

In a large pan, heat a little extra virgin olive oil over medium heat, then place the fish fillets in the pan skin-side down and fry until cooked, 5 to 7 minutes, depending on thickness.

Meanwhile, add the remaining fish stock to the stock used for cooking the potatoes. In a large bowl, dilute two tablespoons of the mayonnaise with about ¾ cup (175 ml) of this stock, then return it to the pan, stir, and bring it to a simmer before removing from the heat. You should have a thick, creamy broth.

Toast the bread and spread each slice with aioli.

Divide the potato and leek slices among the soup bowls. Pour the broth over the top, then arrange the sea bass fillets and the toast on top.

Finish with the chopped chives, a few salt flakes, and a trickle of extra virgin olive oil.

Makes 1 cup (9 oz/250 g)

Mayonnaise

3 egg yolks
1 teaspoon mustard
Salt and white pepper
½ teaspoon lemon juice or vinegar
⅔ cup (150 ml) sunflower oil
Scant ½ cup (100 ml) extra virgin olive oil

Make sure all of the ingredients are at room temperature. In a bowl, beat together the yolks, mustard, salt, pepper, and vinegar with a fork until combined. Whisking continuously with a wire whisk, slowly add the oil (drop by drop at first). Once it starts to thicken, you can add the remaining oil in a thin stream, still whisking, ending with the olive oil. Store in a sealed jar in the refrigerator for up to a week.

Fish stock

In a large stockpot, combine 1½ to 2 lb (700 to 900 g) fish bones and heads, ½ chopped fennel bulb, 1 chopped carrot, 1 sliced onion, 1 chopped celery stick, a few springs of parsley, chopped green ends of 2 leeks, 1 bay leaf, and 2 peeled cloves of garlic. Add enough water to cover the ingredients, bring to a boil, then skim off the foam that collects on the top. Add ½ cup (125 ml) white wine and simmer gently, covered, for about 20 minutes.

Remove from the heat and let it sit for 10 minutes before straining through a fine sieve. If you are not using the stock immediately, cool a little longer, then cover and place in the refrigerator (it will keep for up to a week) or freeze.

Aioli

In a mortar and pestle, crush 1 garlic clove with a pinch of salt and transfer to a bowl. Whisking continuously, gradually mix in a scant ½ cup (100 ml) extra virgin olive oil until you have a thick cream. Store leftovers in a sealed jar in the refrigerator for up to a week.

Serves 4

Andalusian ratatouille
Pisto andaluz o ratatouille

This looks like a convoluted way of making ratatouille, or *pisto*, but by following Charlie's technique of cooking each vegetable separately, you avoid what can sometimes become a shapeless, sloppy mush. The result is a perfect textural balance, with each vegetable retaining its form and crunch. For a light, healthy dinner, serve it with a fried fillet of sea bass or mackerel.

2 eggplants, cut into cubes
Sea salt
Extra virgin olive oil
2 cloves garlic, crushed
6 large, ripe tomatoes, peeled (see
    p. 77), seeds removed
Bouquet garni: a few sprigs each of thyme,
    rosemary, parsley, and bay leaf tied together
Freshly ground black pepper
1 green bell pepper, seeded, deribbed, and quartered
1 red bell pepper, seeded, deribbed, and quartered
1 onion, sliced
2 medium zucchinis, cut into chunks
Fresh basil (optional)

Place the eggplant cubes in a colander and sprinkle with salt. Set aside for 30 minutes to 1 hour to rid them of their moisture. Rinse and pat dry.

In a large saucepan, heat a little olive oil then toss in the garlic. Once it turns golden, add the roughly chopped tomatoes. Add the bouquet garni, a pinch of sea salt, and a few grinds of pepper, then simmer on very low heat without a lid for about 1 hour. Do not let it come to a boil.

Heat a little olive oil in a frying pan. Place the red and green peppers skin-side down in the hot oil until they soften, then remove from the pan and peel off the skins. Dice the peppers, return them to the frying pan, and cook over medium heat for about 5 minutes until they soften. Transfer to a colander and set aside.

Adding some more oil, if necessary, sauté the onions until translucent, then remove from the pan and set aside.

Tip the eggplant cubes into the pan with a splash more oil and cook for about 5 minutes over low heat until they soften, but without letting them brown. Remove from the pan and set aside.

Finally, add the zucchinis to the pan with a glug of oil and sauté until they gain some color, about 5 minutes, then drain and set aside.

To serve cold, arrange the ingredients in a salad bowl, alternating each layer of vegetable with some tomato sauce. You can add a few basil leaves to perfume the mixture. Once everything has cooled to room temperature, place in the refrigerator.

To serve hot, combine the vegetables with the tomato sauce in a large saucepan, cover, and simmer for 20 minutes.

EL JARDÍN, *Frigiliana, Málaga*

Less than an hour east of Málaga, the quintessential Andalusian village of Frigiliana seems to have tumbled down a hillside of La Axarquía, its Moorish jigsaw of whitewashed houses commanding peerless views across the Mediterranean to North Africa. Near the top of the steep, winding streets is El Jardín, also known as The Garden, due to its English owner. Here, curtains of bougainvillea and floppy banana palms frame a large terrace with a jaw-dropping panorama that seduces a steady flow of clients. Seated in the balmy sunshine, they indulge in chef Robert Grimmond's visually stunning and eclectic, Middle Eastern-inspired food.

It sounds like a culinary nod to Al-Andalus but, ironically, Grimmond devised his dishes while living in London, avidly pillaging a local Lebanese grocery store. After training at the prestigious Leith's cooking school, he returned to his childhood getaway of Andalucía (his parents had a house in nearby Nerja) and in 2005 opened this restaurant.

In fact, Frigiliana played a crucial role in Al-Andalus gastronomy due to a landmark sugar mill that processed sugarcane grown along the coast. Though the mill survives, times have changed and today the mellow pace, balmy climate, and scenic beauty are balm to the souls of a community of foreign artists and sybarites. Nonetheless, every August the village remembers its history with a festival of the Three Cultures: Muslim, Jewish, and Christian.

Citrus Salad
Ensalada citrica

This plate of sizzling color is perfect in the sunshine and, with its sweet-salty dressing,
mixed with mint and complex chermoula (itself composed of a long list of spices),
plus the fresh bite of pomegranate seeds, it brings potent hints of the Middle East.
As for the flowers, Robert suggests tuberous begonias for their citrus flavor.

4 oranges
2 grapefruit
1 tablespoon honey
½ teaspoon salt
1 tablespoon lime juice
1 tablespoon extra virgin olive oil
Seeds of ½ pomegranate
Small bunch of mint, chopped
1 teaspoon Moroccan chermoula spice mix
About 6 cups (5 ¾ oz/165 g) mixed salad greens
2 avocados, diced
Fresh edible flowers (optional)

Slice the ends off the oranges and grapefruit,
pare off the skin, segment the grapefruit,
and slice the orange into rounds.

In a small bowl, mix together the honey,
salt, lime juice, olive oil, pomegranate seeds,
chopped mint, and chermoula spice.

Arrange the fruit segments around the edge of a
serving bowl and fill the center with the salad greens
and avocado, then decorate with edible flowers.

Serves 4

Falafel with beet tahini, hummus, and pickled chili
Falafel con tahini de remolacha, hummus y chilli

Falafel is one of those Middle Eastern street foods claimed by everyone from the Palestinians to the Lebanese and Israelis. The same goes for hummus. Robert's studied presentation is rather different and the deep crimson of his tahini adds an almost Miro-esque quality. The four elements together create delectable textural contrasts. *Hawayej* is a Yemeni spice mixture, mainly comprised of turmeric and cumin, with coriander, cardamom, and black pepper.

1 large onion, roughly chopped
2 tablespoons flat-leaf parsley, chopped
2 tablespoons cilantro, chopped
1 ½ teaspoons baking soda
1 teaspoon salt
1 teaspoon ground cumin
1 teaspoon *hawayej* spice mix
⅔ cup (4 ½ oz/125 g) dried chickpeas, soaked overnight, drained
1 tablespoon chickpea flour, if needed
1 tablespoon sesame seeds and/or flaxseeds
Sunflower oil, for deep-frying

Garnishes
Beet Tahini (see p. 196)
Robert's Hummus (see p. 196)
4 pickled chili peppers (optional)
Handful pomegranate seeds (optional)

In the bowl of a food processor or blender, combine the onion, parsley, cilantro, baking soda, salt, cumin, and spice mix. Process to obtain a spicy onion salsa.

Add the chickpeas and blend briefly until you have a coarsely ground mixture. If it looks a little wet, add the chickpea flour to bind it.

Spread the seeds out on a shallow plate. Using your hands, form the mixture into 1 ½ inch (4 cm) balls, flatten them slightly, then press them into the seeds.

In a large deep saucepan, heat sunflower oil to a depth of 3 inches (8 cm) until very hot and spitting. Fry a few of the felafel at a time until crisp and golden brown, about 3 minutes on each side. Using a slotted spoon, transfer to a plate lined with paper towels to drain.

Serve with beet tahini and hummus and decorate with a large pickled chili. Sprinkle with pomegranate seeds if you have them.

Makes about 2 cups (1 lb/500 g)

Beet Tahini
Tahini de remolacha

Make your plate sing with a generous smear of this vivid crimson dip. Robert suggests making it in advance, since it keeps for a couple of days in the refrigerator. If it thickens too much, loosen it with a little water.

1 cup (250 ml) tahini
Generous ¾ cup (200 ml) water
3½ tablespoons freshly squeezed lemon juice
1 ready-cooked and peeled beet
Salt

Combine all of the ingredients in a blender and blend at a high speed until you have a smooth, creamy mixture.

Makes about 3¼ cups 1 lb 12 oz (800 g)

Robert's Hummus

Hummus is just one of those things—everyone claims ownership and everyone has a different recipe. Wars have been fought over it—well not quite, but a documentary ("Make Hummus not War") compared dozens of versions by possessive Middle Eastern cooks. With olives and cumin and no garlic, Robert's recipe is unusual, but above all he uses ice, and says, "I prefer my hummus very smooth so I tend to add all the ice at once and blend for a long time."

3 cups (1 lb/500 g) cooked or canned chickpeas
⅓ cup (80 ml) tahini
3½ oz (100 g) pitted Kalamata olives
¼ cup (60 ml) freshly squeezed lemon juice
2 teaspoons ground cumin
Scant ½ cup (100 ml) extra virgin olive oil
1½ teaspoon salt
5½ oz (150 g) ice cubes (5–6 cubes), crushed if large

In a blender, process all the ingredients except the ice on high speed, then add the ice cubes, little by little, until you reach your desired consistency.

Serves 4

Citrus and herb-roasted cod with chorizo sauce
Bacalao al horno con hierbas y salsa de chorizo

Served with Pea, mint, and cilantro puree and Black garlic potatoes (p. 200), this is another one of Robert's pictures on a plate, where diverse elements merge brilliantly.

1 lb 9 oz oz (720 g) fresh cod fillet with skin
Salt and white pepper
Extra virgin olive oil

Chorizo sauce / Salsa de chorizo
2 shallots
1 tomato, diced
2 fresh Spanish chorizos, skinned and diced
½ cup (125 ml) red wine
½ cup (125 ml) chicken stock
½ cup (½ oz/15 g) mixed salad greens, to garnish

First, make the sauce: In a deep frying pan, heat a little olive oil and sweat the shallots for 5 minutes, then add the tomato. Cook for about 3 minutes before adding the chorizo, then fry for another 5 minutes to gain color and release the sausage oils. Pour in the wine, bring to a simmer, and let it bubble for 5 to 7 minutes until it has reduced by half, then add the stock and bring back to a gentle boil.

Continue to cook for about 5 more minutes until it begins to thicken, remove from the heat, then coarsely blend with an immersion blender. The sauce will have a fair amount of texture due to the chorizo. Set aside.

Preheat the oven to 350°F (180°C).

In a frying pan, heat 2 tablespoons of the olive oil over medium heat. Season the cod fillet and place it skin-side down in the hot oil, and cook for 2 to 3 minutes until skin is crisp and golden. Flip over and transfer to an ovensafe dish. Bake for about 5 minutes until just tender.

Arrange the cod on a plate surrounded by the chorizo sauce, pea purée, and potatoes. Garnish with salad leaves to finish.

Serves 4

Pea, mint, and cilantro purée
Puré de guisantes con mienta y cilantro

The sweetness of this puree makes a perfect accompaniment to the Citrus and Herb-Roasted Cod on p. 198.

2 tablespoons butter
2 shallots or 1 small onion, finely chopped
4 ½ cups (1 lb 5 oz/600 g) frozen peas
½ cup (125 ml) vegetable stock
Small handful of fresh mint
Small handful of cilantro
Salt

In a large saucepan, heat the butter and sauté the shallots or onion until translucent, then add the peas and stock. Bring to a simmer and cook until the peas and onions are tender. Using a ladle or slotted spoon, transfer to food processor, keeping half of the stock in the pan. Add the herbs and blend to a smooth purée. If you prefer it thinner and smoother, add more stock until you reach your desired consistency. Season with salt to taste. If you wish to reheat the purée, add a little water and stir over low heat.

Serves 4

Black garlic mashed potatoes
Puré de patatas al ajo negro

Although black garlic (fermented garlic) originated in Asia, these tasty beauties are now produced in La Mancha and are widely available in Spain and elsewhere. Serve this rich side dish alongside meat and fish dishes such as Citrus and Herb-Roasted Cod (p. 198).

1 lb 12 oz (600 g) peeled potatoes
½ cup (1 stick/4 oz/115 g) butter
⅔ cup (150 ml) light cream
6 cloves peeled fermented black garlic
Salt and white pepper

Boil the potatoes until tender, drain, and set aside to steam-dry for a few minutes.

In a small pan, heat the butter and cream until the butter has melted.

In a large bowl, mash the potatoes with the butter, cream, and garlic. You can use an electric mixer, but do not over-mix, or you'll end up with what Robert calls, "a sticky mess."

Season with salt and pepper to taste. To reheat, just add a sprinkle of water and warm over low heat.

Serves 4

Coffee roasted Medjool dates with labneh
Dátiles Medjool asados con labneh (requesón)

At last, this exquisite, unusual dessert makes use of dates (and Medjool, the best quality available), once a classic product of the desert-like conditions of eastern Andalusia. Today the fruit is, sadly, rarely picked so try and source Palestinian dates from Jericho, which are excellent. Here, combined with the labneh, the Middle East sings loud and clear. You will need to start the recipe the night before.

Generous ¾ cup (200 ml) orange juice
¼ cup (1 ¾ oz/50 g) sugar
Generous ¾ cup (200 ml) strong coffee
16 Medjool dates, pitted
4 cardamom pods
1 cinnamon stick

Labneh
1 lb (500 g) good Greek yogurt, strained
  through a cheesecloth overnight
Grated zest of 1 orange
1 tablespoon honey
1 teaspoon orange blossom water

Pour the yogurt into the center of a large piece of cheesecloth or a very fine mesh strainer. Suspend over a bowl and leave to drain overnight.

The next day, combine the strained yogurt with the rest of the labneh ingredients and set aside.

Preheat the oven to 400°F (200°C).

In a saucepan, combine the orange juice, sugar, and coffee. Simmer, stirring occasionally, until you obtain a thin syrup, 10 to 15 minutes.

Arrange the dates in a baking dish, coat with the orange-coffee mixture, and add the spices. Bake for 20 minutes, shaking the dish from time to time to prevent the date skin from burning. Once cooked, remove from the oven and set aside to cool in the cooking liquid.

Once it has cooled, pour the liquid into a saucepan, place over medium heat, and simmer for 5 to 7 minutes, until reduced by half.

Peel the skin off the dates, drizzle with the glaze, and arrange them on a serving dish, alternating with spoonfuls of labneh.

TRAVEL DIARY:

Peering skywards at the Giralda, I try to mentally time travel
to its construction in the 12th century, but unlike in Córdoba,
Granada, or Almería, that leap of time and faith isn't easy. For
a start, the minaret is now crowned by a spinning statue of, yes,
Faith, planted by the conquering Catholics beside their cavernous
cathedral built over the mosque. Not only that, despite this iconic
tower (in which the *muezzin* would canter heroically up a ramp on
horseback to deliver the call to prayer), Seville's Moorish past is
overlaid by a heavy cloak of baroque frills and flamenco flounces…

WEST
from Seville to Cádiz
forest–hills–beaches

Peering skywards at the Giralda, I try to mentally time travel to its construction in the 12th century, but unlike in Córdoba, Granada, or Almería, that leap of time and faith isn't easy. For a start, the minaret is now crowned by a spinning statue of, yes, Faith, planted by the conquering Catholics beside their cavernous cathedral built over the mosque. Not only that, despite this iconic tower (in which the *muezzin* would canter heroically up a ramp on horseback to deliver the call to prayer), Seville's Moorish past is overlaid by a heavy cloak of baroque frills and flamenco flounces. Even the dazzling Mudéjar interior of the neighboring Alcázar somehow lacks soul, not surprising given that King Pedro of Castilla gave it an extensive makeover. Then there is the Torre del Oro, an Almohad military watchtower once attached by a chain to a twin fort across the river to create a kind of garrote for enemy ships. Yet even this ingenious Moorish monument later gained a baroque penthouse—*olé*!

Ultimately Seville is a hedonistic city of flamenco, tapas (the birthplace no less), art, orange trees, tourism, commerce, social contrasts, and of devotion to the Virgin Mary. Spilling over the Guadalquivir River to Triana, once a gypsy enclave and before that a *Morisco* ghetto, its numerous highlights include elaborate mansions, baroque churches, and a lavish bullring. However, one place, more than any other, sets my pulse racing—the Casa de Pilatos. This 16th century family mansion is a must-see tour de force by Mudéjar craftsmen, where astoundingly crafted *zelij*, carved plaster and inlaid wooden ceilings, compete with Roman statues. The

lush, shaded garden is perfect for whiling away a scorching afternoon, book in hand.

The Abbadids, Catholicism, and the New World

As I soak up the atmosphere of the sprawling city crackling with energy and legions of tourists, I think of its zenith under the Abbadid dynasty from the 1020s until the agonizing siege of 1248 that ended Muslim rule. With rich, fertile land to the southwest bordering the natural trading outlet of the Guadalquivir River, it thrived on olive oil, sugar cane, and, more curiously, a valuable crimson dye found in beetles that fed on native holm oaks. Ranches, stud farms, and minerals all compounded the wealth that had existed even 1800 years earlier when it was allegedly Tartessos, that semi-mythical land much lauded by the Greeks. Gobbling up territory from Ronda to the Algarve, the Abbadid rulers poured profits into the arts, bringing spinoffs such as a famed ceramic tile industry and the manufacture of musical instruments.

This cultural high point crashed with the *reconquista* when Seville's role darkened into the capital of the tyrannical Inquisition, the seat of which is now buried beneath Triana market. All changed again when the city became the stepping stone for the New World and the happy recipient of galleon-loads of gold and silver booty, as well as the next culinary revolution shaped by the tomato, pepper, squash, chocolate, and potato. The gorgeous purple jacaranda trees that stud Seville's streets came too. The curtain finally dropped in the early 1600s when the Guadalquivir river

silted up and maritime trade shifted to Cádiz.

Today's city is essentially the fruit of that prosperous time. Now Spain's fourth largest city, it is dynamic, creative, and youthful, yet also deeply Catholic. Christ seemingly lugs his cross through every street and square, while La Dolorosa weeps in bars and markets. I'm talking about ceramic wall plaques, photos, and paintings, offshoots of the fervent processions of Semana Santa. With typical Sevillian panache however, this holy week is countered by the riotous Feria de Abril, or Spring Fair, bringing immaculately attired horse-riders, a tsunami of flamenco frills and fluttering fans, and much concentrated sherry-drinking.

Bull's meat, berries, and tapas

I marvel at the bountiful and diversified markets, whether in touristy Triana, at the prodigious Mercado de Feria, or at the slickly rebuilt Encarnación beneath the gigantic, undulating *setas* (mushrooms), Seville's controversial 21st century landmark. The city is still the heartbeat of wheat fields, olive groves, and vineyards stretching south to Jerez, while the bucolic Sierra del Norte is plundered for its game, honey, and vegetables. There is bull's meat straight from the *corridas*, wild asparagus, white truffles, and mountains of fragrant stone fruit and berries from neighboring Huelva province, together with velvety Iberian hams and charcuterie from pigs fattened on acorns. Fishmongers, too, do a roaring trade backed up by small *freidurias* feeding a local craving for fried fish.

And those tapas? I can't resist a pilgrimage to El Rinconcillo, a legendary bar (opened in 1670) manned by the same barmen for decades. They may get a little greyer but still scrawl your tally on the counter with chalk that slips neatly into their breast pockets. Then, at a corner bar displaying a *caracoles* sign, I stop for a *caña* and a plate of tiny, slightly bitter snails to celebrate these gastropods, a seasonal passion shared by (or inherited from?) the Moroccans.

Many Seville bars have traded their soul for fusion and tourists, but I happily return to Eslava for the purposes of this book; it still seriously rocks. Later in the evening, a Sevillian friend steers me to Casa Vizcaíno, packed with locals of all ages and types. Without flourishes or modernity and with rock-bottom prices, this ninety-year-old temple to cold beer and house vermouth limits its tapas to olives, *habas* (big beans), and mussels. It breathes old Seville and egalitarian conviviality and I love it.

The next morning before I leave, I weave through narrow streets, past orange trees, and horse-drawn carriages in the touristy Judería to find Bodega Santa Cruz, another long-term survivor that, at this hour, is packed with cheery workers digging into traditional breakfasts of *pan tostado* and *manteca*. Seville is not lost.

To the pigs!

The time has come to travel northwest into the Sierra de Aracena, renowned as the home of snuffling Iberian pigs. Even though the Muslims and Jews banned pork, it is impossible to write about Andalusian food without mentioning it

and indeed enjoying it (see p. 286). Pork is the favored meat among country people and its many incarnations orchestrate Spanish food culture.

Yet there is a surprise in store. Swinging around the bends of the verdant hills, past cascades of yellow broom, trickling streams, and cork oaks partly shorn of their bark, I make for a tiny village called Almonaster la Real. Here, crowning the hilltop, a 9th century mosque surveys pristine forests and *dehesa* as far as Portugal. Built over a Visigothic church and later returned to that function before ending as a monument, the serene colonnaded interior still incorporates a *mihrab* though the exterior minaret was truncated long ago. Outside, timeless sounds envelop me: a lazy fly, wheeling, screeching swifts, a chirruping cricket, the crowing of distant roosters, wind rustling the trees and wildflowers, and the tinkle of the fountain inside the mosque. Time travel works here.

In nearby Alájar where I spend the night, the narrow lanes and excruciatingly tight corners are built for mules not cars, so I'm amazed to discover that this village of 700 people claims thirteen bars and restaurants, all in full swing. It must be the pure air. In an even smaller village nearby, Linares, I return to an unexpectedly sophisticated restaurant, Arrieros, for some serious pork insight. The other highlight of this sierra is mushrooms, dozens of types from *boletus* to *gurumelos*, devoured with gusto in the restaurants of Aracena itself. Here too is a celebrated 142-year-old institution, the dauntingly calorific Confitería Rufino, a wonderland of delicate sweets and cakes, many of Moorish or Jewish origin and handmade at their workshop.

The sherry triangle

On the road again, next stop Jerez, I hurtle through dull agricultural plains south of Seville to enter the golden sherry triangle completed by Sanlúcar de Barrameda and El Puerto de Santa María. Parallel to the road stretches a vast patchwork of rice fields bordering the Guadalquivir river that segue into one of Europe's most bird-rich wetlands, Coto Doñana. This is the destination for Andalucía's and Spain's greatest *romería*, El Rocio, a bawdy pilgrimage of one million faithful on horseback, on foot or in horse-drawn wagons who somehow mix a religious cult with hard partying every Pentecost.

My priority though is the source of sherry. Our word "sherry" is an Anglo abomination of Jerez, that in turn derived from the Arabic, *Xeres*. The English wine merchants were to blame, or praise, for the prospering of this fortified wine that today is undergoing a bit of a renaissance worldwide. The city itself is a proud one, its recent regeneration revitalizing the bodegas and *tabancos* (the local word for tapas bar), while it remains the definitive horse capital of Andalusia. Like Seville, few Moorish relics survive other than a mosque and baths inside the Alcázar. Javier, a local entrepreneur, explains, "After Jerez was re-conquered in the 13th century and the Muslims left, a stream of gypsies and Jews replaced them." One result is a vibrant flamenco culture, a fusion of Arab, Jewish, and Oriental sounds possibly deriving its name from the Arabic *felag mengu* ("fugitive peasant") referring to the influx of North Indian tribal people via Egypt. The other legacy is a characteristic Jewish quarter, though its walls and synagogues have long disappeared.

I revel in the tangle of central streets, the plazas dotted with palm trees, the animated covered market, and the odd glass of *oloroso*. After enjoying a glass with creamy *croquetas* at La Moderna, a hardly modern 1930s bar that integrates a section of the old city walls and attracts an eccentric, mature clientele, I navigate the maze to find a more youthful Alboronía, my destination restaurant.

Cádiz, seafood, and the Atlantic

Laurie Lee movingly described Cádiz as "a scribble of white on a sheet of blue glass, lying curved on the bay like a scimitar and sparkling with North African light." It is an absolute delight, one of my favorite cities in Andalucía with history bouncing back 3000 years to the Phoenicians from Tyre (in today's Lebanon) and its focus resolutely on the ocean, whether for ultra-fresh seafood or, centuries ago, trade from the New World.

Washed by limpid Atlantic light, this ancient city of Gadir, home to the Spanish constitution of 1812, easily seduces thanks to its ice-cream-colored façades, merchants' watchtowers, palm-studded plazas, and sense of looking outwards, across the ocean. In contrast, its link to the mainland is a slender arm of land dominated by unappealing 1960s and 70s high-rises. One side of the arm is home to the cargo, ferry, and cruise ship port, while the other is a far more alluring stretch of sandy beach lined with *chiringitos* and brasseries. Here, I drop into La Marea, a classic seafood restaurant, to sample a tapa of *fideos con almejas* (noodles with clams) with a glass of crisp manzanilla: just right.

But it is inside the old walls that the *gaditano* pulse truly beats. At another old favorite, Taberna La Manzanilla, gregarious Pepe regales me (again) with stories of this 1940s bar where eighteen sherries are served straight from the casks. More colorful still is the *barrio* of La Viña, whose volatile streets started life with fishermen, flamenco artists, and lowlife, but now blossom during the riotous February carnival (Spain's largest) and offer an appealing

trail of tapas bars. I return to a pivot of matador memorabilia, Casa Manteca, where they serve cured pork on squares of wax paper. I wash it down with a *copa* of red Barbazul, a vibrant, aromatic Cádiz wine that is making waves in the wine trade.

Next, it is time to hit the top end at El Faro, a sophisticated restaurant and tapas bar famed for flawless seafood, to dig up some house recipes amid the joking of a well-run kitchen. Just a block away lurks a treasure-trove of sheer sensory indulgence: the food market. In this phenomenal temple to the ocean, dozens of fish species vie with crustaceans and mollusks on a spectacular scale, so fresh that the very air is pure, salty, and Atlantic. I am swept away by the abundance, shapes, sizes, and even expressions of these piscine creatures, the interaction of clients and vendors, and the passion shared by all. Exiting the stone walls, I discover rickety tables set up by locals to sell their minimal catch. It's impossible to resist an oyster, or six, freshly shucked, in this case by a weathered *gaditano* who recounts collecting them that morning in the *marismas* of San Fernando; the minerally taste lingers in my mouth for hours.

Across the bay

Cádiz embraces a huge bay that is faced on the mainland by another major port, El Puerto de Santa María. This once fashionable town of sherry bodegas has developed quite a foodie reputation, much thanks to the brilliance of Ángel León, "chef of the sea," and his triple Michelin-starred restaurant, Aponiente, as well as timeless seafood bars beside the Guadalete river like the 1950s gem, Romerijo. However, when I hop off the ferry from Cádiz after a blustery half-hour crossing, I head straight for a restaurant called El Arriate in search of innovation and eclecticism. Later, traces of Al-Andalus unexpectedly turn up inside El Puerto's imposing castle, where the remains of a 10th century mosque bring a flicker of the past to a place that moved on long ago.

Medina Sidonia, fighting bulls, *retinto*, and village *ventas*

South of Cádiz straggles the Costa de la Luz, a gorgeous, breezy coastline of white-sand beaches dotted with small resorts and tempting fish restaurants, and a mecca for kite-surfers. Here too is Cape Trafalgar, renowned for its role in a momentous naval battle between Spain and Britain back in 1805. Contrarily, I choose to head inland in search of authentic rural food around Medina Sidonia. This striking, once aristocratic hill town is allegedly the oldest town in Europe—like Cádiz, it dates from the Phoenicians. More relevant to my quest is the fact that in 712, barely a year after the Muslim armies invaded Hispania, it became capital of the Sidonia province (*medina* is Arabic for "town"). Many of the local cakes date from those days, notably the *alfajores* (from the Arabic *al-hasù*, meaning "filled"), delectable little cylinders of honey, almonds, hazlenuts, and spices, made by two more of Andalucía's venerable *confiterias*, Nuestra Señora de la Paz and Sobrina de las Trejas.

Winding, cobbled streets take me panting up to the castle ruins, catching my breath on the way at an impeccable Moorish horseshoe arch. At the top, 360-degree views stretch from the Sierra de Grazalema to the north all the way southwest to the Atlantic and even, in the far distance, to the faint outline of the Rif Mountains of Morocco. In between are rolling pastures dotted with fighting bulls and cattle, the cork oak forests of Los Alcornocales Natural Park, and a distant *pueblo blanco*, Vejer de la Frontera.

One feature of this area of La Janda is the concentration of *ventas*. Uniquely Andalusian, *ventas* were originally modest roadside inns feeding itinerant workers with sustaining, tasty meals. Even if some have gone upmarket, at others you still find family dishes cooked with love and served with pride in simple, authentic settings. So I make for Venta El Soldao, a local legend thanks to its elderly matriarchal owner and delicious, affordable food. The family welcomes me, introduces me to their peacock, goats, chickens, and wild ducks before one son, Paco, whisks me off to see the family farm of *toros bravos*—fighting bulls. As I snap a picture of an impressive specimen from the open car window, it lurches towards me, those ferocious horns just inches away. With a shudder I sense that I am tapping into deeply rural, highly traditional Andalucía.

The home strait

From the *venta* hamlet it is a short drive through pine forests to the coast, past sparkling, picture-postcard Vejer whose sugar-cube houses, Moorish structures, and sub-tropical vegetation are hugely popular with foreign residents. Then, finally, I am on the coast in *almadraba* territory, like the kitesurfers blown by the infamous *levante* wind through Barbate, Zahara, and Bolonia with its striking Roman ruins. As it is the season, I stop for a lunch of luscious Bluefin tuna tartare, making me feel both epicurean and primitive, as this food is so ancient. Back on the road, I feel dwarfed by gigantic hilltop wind farms, a 21st century version of Don Quixote's "hulking giants." Later I learn that hidden inside coastal caves and beneath ledges is an astonishing gallery of Paleolithic rock art, the most extensive in Andalucía, just a few thousand years older than the *almadraba*.

Finally I reach Tarifa, the southernmost point of Western Europe, and head for the old quarter where an imposing castle overlooks the Tangier ferry terminal and the glittering Mediterranean. I have come full circle, ending my gastronomical odyssey where the Moors began theirs, with Morocco barely 9 miles (15 km) across the strait and my starting point, the Cabo de Gata, 250 miles (400 km) to the east. Dodging the bohemian surfers thronging the bars, I climb to the ramparts of the castle originally built in 960 by Abd-er Rahman III, that enlightened caliph of Córdoba. In front, across the cerulean channel, stretches the hazy silhouette of Morocco. I reach out—I can almost touch it.

- TORREDEROS ROSADO

- ZUCCHINI CHARLOTTE
- LITTLE SLOW-COOKED LEEKS WITH TARTARA
- ARTICHOKE WITH COLD FISH—3'50   SAUCE
- BEEF TATAKI (SLOW-COOKED)—4'50   —2'90
- ROASTED MACKEREL WITH DICED TOMATO, ONION
- DEEP-FRIED BABY SARDINES—2'90   AND PEPER STRIPS
- BABY RED-MALE FRIED ——— 2'90   2'90
- DEEP-FRIED ANCHOVIES FROM MALAGA 2'90
- SLOW-COOKED EGG SERVED ON BOLETUS CAKE
          WITH CARAMELIZED WINE REDUCTION
       (1st PRIZE SEVILLA EN BOCA DE TODOS 2010)
- "A CIGAR FOR BECQUER" ——— 2'90
  BRIK PASTRY CIGAR

CALABACIN
VERDURAS
TARTARA   2'10
BROCCOLI BOLETUS
"TAM BECQUER"
DE PAN AVELLANA   3'50
FRUTAS BACALAO   8'50
            2'90
HUEVO y JAMON —— 2'90
MAYONESA DE SOJA — 4'50
ROCA ESCRITA A VINO TINTO — 2'90
MALLO   2'90
BOLETUS   2'90
CHORIZO   2'90
CORVINA   2'90

TINTOS
- LA PLANTA (RIBERA DEL D
- TORREDEROS ROBLE (RIBERA
- PROTOS ROBLE (RIBERA DE
- MARTINEZ LACUESTA (RIO
- 6 AL REVÉS (RIBERA DEL
- PICARO DE MATSU (TO
- HABLA DEL SILENCIO (E
- BARBAZUL (ARCOS DE LA F
- ENATE (SOMONTA

ESLAVA, *Seville*

Eslava, a thirty-year-old landmark on Seville's gastro map, goes from strength to strength in the increasingly hip *barrio* of San Lorenzo. The original tapas bar was opened in 1988 by Sixto Tomar and his wife Rosa, together with Isabel Capote, so initiating a symbiotic trio. "I was very young when I started here—I had just finished a five-year course in hotel and catering," she tells me between juggling pans and produce. Once they opened a restaurant next door, the rest, as they say, is history.

Isabel is calm and highly organized, steering a large kitchen team working in two shifts from morning until well after midnight. The restaurant opens its doors for classic Spanish eating hours but, unusually, the bar is open all day. If you drop in during the afternoon you are surrounded by foreign foodies busy Instagramming; go much later and the decibels have risen to authentic Spanish levels and the place is heaving.

As we talk, a huge pan of pork ribs bubbles away in honey nectar. "That's one of the dishes our clients just won't let us give up! Our salmorejo, too," she sighs. Rosa joins us, another Sevillian beauty with an equally measured temperament. Between them, with input from Sixto, they conceive new dishes for the stylish modern restaurant and small plates for the tapas aficionados. Such constant quality and creativity has been rightly recognized by several national awards.

Amuse-bouche of anchovy with almond cream and clementine and lime spheres
Combinado de boquerón con ajoblanco, esferas de mandarina y lima

Although Isabel uses the evocative word *mazamorra* to denote this spoon of wonder, it is theoretically *ajoblanco*, since it contains almonds. Anchovies, *mazamorra*, and *ajoblanco* are all classics of Muslim Spain, but be warned, this tricky recipe requires on and off preparation over a period of more than twenty-four hours. Yet the textures and flavors are so skillfully mastered that the amuse-bouche won Isabel a major culinary award, so it is worth persevering. Isabel suggests that if the clementine spheres seem too complicated, replace them with spoonfuls of clementine jam. And if there is any almond cream left over, don't worry, it will see another day as a chilled appetizer.

Ajoblanco (almond cream)
¾ cup (3 ½ oz/100 g) blanched almonds
1 oz (30 g) slice of dry rustic bread
½ cup (125 ml) sunflower oil
1 clove garlic
Salt

Clementine and lime spheres
Sunflower oil
2 ½ tablespoons clementine juice
2 ½ tablespoons lime juice
1 ½ tablespoons sugar
2 teaspoons agar agar

Amuse-bouche
12 fresh anchovies, cleaned and filleted
2 clementines
1 lime
3 tablespoons apple vinegar
1 ½ tablespoons soy sauce
½ teaspoon smoked salt
Extra virgin olive oil
½ cup (2 oz/60 g) pitted black olives,
    very finely chopped

Place the anchovies in the freezer for 24 hours.

To make the *ajoblanco*, combine the almonds, bread, oil, and garlic in a blender and process to a smooth cream, adding a little water if necessary (it should be quite thick). Season with salt to taste.

To make the clementine and lime spheres, Pour some sunflower oil into a bowl and refrigerate until it is very cold, about two hours.

In a saucepan, heat the clementine juice and limejuice with the sugar and agar agar. Once it is tepid and the agar agar has dissolved, pour the liquid into a dropper, and drop small amounts into the chilled sunflower oil. These will coagulate to form small, jelly-like spheres that should be drained, arranged on a plate without touching, and placed in the refrigerator.

Defrost the anchovies. Grate the zest of 1 clementine and squeeze the clementine and lime juice. In a bowl, combine the juice, zest, vinegar, soy sauce, and smoked salt. Use this liquid to marinate the anchovies for 4 hours.

Remove the anchovies from the marinade, pat dry with paper towels, then shape each one around a generous dollop of *ajoblanco* in a small serving bowl or large spoon. Top the crown of each one with some clementine and lime spheres, drizzle with olive oil, and scatter the entirety with finely chopped black olives. Serve immediately (if you plan to keep them in the refrigerator for a short while, drizzle the olive oil just before serving).

Serves 4

Foie gras with date and walnut crumble and quince paste

Micuit de foie con migas de dátiles y nueces con compota de membrillo

Get out the violins. In this luscious symphony of flavors, Isabel creates her usual balance of sweet and salty, in this case with the added richness of the creamy foie gras. You can buy foie gras already deveined, which makes life easier.

14 oz (400 g) ethical mi-cuit foie gras (goose)
Scant 1 tablespoon sugar
3 tablespoons sweet raisiny wine
  such as Pedro Ximénez
3 tablespoons brandy
Salt and white pepper
½ cup (1 ¾ oz/50 g) walnut halves
½ cup (2 ½ oz/70 g) pitted dates
1 cup (10 ½ oz/300 g) quince jam
Extra virgin olive oil
Sage leaves

Soak the foie gras in water for half an hour, drain, dry with paper towels, then pull out the fine veins. In a bowl, combine the sugar, wine, brandy, salt, and pepper and macerate the liver for two hours.

Using plastic wrap to help, shape it into a roll about 1 inch (3 cm) in diameter.

Add water to the bottom of a steamer and bring to a vigorous simmer (150°F/65°C). Unwrap the roll and steam for about 15 minutes, checking that the foie gras does not break up. Carefully remove the roll, let it cool, then refrigerate for 12 hours.

Very finely chop the walnuts and dates, and mix them together to form a crumble.

On each plate, arrange three dollops of quince jam next to a bed of date and walnut crumble. Arrange three spoonfuls or slices of foie gras on the crumble and sprinkle with olive oil. Garnish with sage.

Serves 4

Duck breast with fermented honey and kumquat
Magret de pato con meloja de miel y naranjas kumquat

The tangy bitterness of the kumquats makes an unusual balance for the sweet honey of the sauce, raising a quality *magret* to heavenly heights. This is a quick dish to prepare with minimal ingredients— and of course the sweet and salty mix is truly Moorish. Mead is a sweet alcoholic drink made from fermenting honey with water. If you can't find any, substitute dark clear honey with a strong flavor.

2 duck breasts with skin, about 14 oz (400 g) each
Salt and white pepper
12 kumquats, chopped, plus more to garnish
5 tablespoons (3½ oz/100 g)
   fermented honey or mead
Small handful of pea shoots, to garnish

Preheat the oven to 340°F (170°C).

Season the duck breasts and quickly sauté them in a dry frying pan for about 2 minutes on the skin side and 1 minute on the flesh side. Remove, leaving the fat in the pan, slice the breasts, and set them aside on an ovensafe dish in a warm place.

Return the pan to medium heat, add the kumquats and honey, and cook, stirring to reduce, for about 15 minutes until a purée is formed.

Trickle the purée over the duck slices, then heat the entire dish in the oven for 1 minute. Remove, garnish with the pea shoots and remaining kumquats, and serve immediately.

Serves 6

Spring leg of lamb with honey, currants, and pine nuts
Pierna de cordero a la miel con pasas de corinto y piñones

Bathed in a dark, silky sauce speckled with pine nuts, this tender young lamb makes an extremely striking dinner dish. In Al-Andalus, the Arab and Berber penchant for mixing sweet and savory meant all kinds of fruits are added to meat—such as prunes, quince, or apples, along with the eclectic flavors of fennel, citrus, cumin, saffron, cinnamon, and coriander. Lamb really was a moving feast.

4½ lb (2 kg) bone-in leg of young lamb
Salt and white pepper
About ¾ cup (175 ml) extra virgin olive
   oil, plus more for sautéing
2 onions, finely chopped
3 green bell peppers, finely chopped
1 bay leaf
1 cup (250 ml) white wine
½ cup (125 ml) brandy
2 teaspoons saffron threads
1 tablespoon mild paprika
½ cup (2¾ oz/75 g) pine nuts
½ cup (2¾ oz/75 g) currants or seedless raisins
2½ tablespoons honey, heated
   slightly to become liquid
1 tablespoon all-purpose flour, dissolved in
   ½ cup (125 ml) warm water (optional)
Rosemary sprigs, to garnish

Preheat the over to 350°F (180°C).

Season the lamb leg with salt, lay it in a large oven dish or roasting pan, and generously coat with the olive oil. Roast in the oven for 30 minutes to seal the meat.

Meanwhile, make the sauce: In a saucepan, heat 2 or 3 tablespoons of oil and sauté the onion, green peppers, and bay leaf for 3 to 5 minutes, until the onion turns golden. Add the wine, brandy, saffron, paprika, and 2 tablespoons water. Simmer for about 15 minutes to reduce the sauce.

Once the lamb has roasted for 30 minutes, pour the sauce over it and reduce the oven temperature to 325°F (160°C). Roast until the lamb is cooked to your liking, about 1 hour for medium-rare. Remove from the oven, transfer to a serving plate, cover with foil, and set aside while you finish the sauce.

Toss the pine nuts, raisins, and honey into the juices left behind in the pan. If you would like to thicken the sauce, stir in the flour water.

Serve the lamb, topped with the sauce and garnished with rosemary.

Spareribs baked in honey
Costillas a la miel

This easy dish is served as a tapa in the bar adjoining Eslava's restaurant. It is one of those perennial favorites that go back years, and were it scratched from the blackboard a revolution would surely kick off. You can use the same recipe for cooking chicken thighs.

4½ lb (2 kg) spareribs, halved
Salt and white pepper
Extra virgin olive oil
¾ cup (9 oz/250 g) honey
Scant ½ cup (3½ oz/100 g) butter
1 tablespoon curry powder
2 tablespoons Dijon mustard
Fresh thyme

Preheat the oven to 400°F (200°C).

Spread the ribs over a lightly oiled baking pan in a single layer. Season with salt and pepper and drizzle with olive oil, then bake for 45 minutes, turning occasionally so that they brown evenly. Add some water if they start to stick.

Meanwhile, in a saucepan set over low heat, gently heat the honey, butter, curry powder, and mustard for 5 minutes or so, stirring to combine.

Remove the ribs from the oven, drizzle with the honey sauce, and sprinkle generously with thyme. Lower the oven temperature to 325°F (160°C) and return the ribs to the oven for a further 15 minutes. They should be well done, golden, and sticky; if not, bake a little longer. You can also reheat them on the stovetop.

LA SALMORETECA, *Mercado Lonja del Barranco, Seville*

Chef Juanjo Ruiz has turned into somewhat of a star thanks to just one dish—*salmorejo*. Cleverly reinterpreting this traditional Cordoban emulsion, he replaces, or adds to, the base ingredient (tomato) then piles on a dizzying variety of toppings. The result is a menu of exotic chilled soups served at food halls in Seville, Córdoba (the Mercado Victoria), and Fuengirola. Corn, truffle, and mushroom; squid ink, asparagus, celery, squash, fennel, and cumin; orange and cod; lemon and apple; and molasses and mustard are just some of the flavor combinations. Sweet *salmorejos* sneak in too, such as white chocolate, dark chocolate, or grape with pink pepper.

Juanjo, a cheerful, motivated extravert in his mid-thirties from Córdoba, started cooking school in Seville then attended the French Culinary Institute of New York before going to university in Madrid. These travels clearly fuelled his imagination. More recently he has attacked another classic, the *tortilla*, or Spanish omelet, conjuring combinations such as chorizo and potatoes, mushrooms with blue cheese, or potatoes, saffron, and mustard, altogether creating a palette of wild colors.

In summer, Seville's air-conditioned food hall brings welcome relief from the baking hot streets and, even better, if you sit outside on the terrace above the banks of the Guadalquivir River, a gentle breeze will waft over your tray of zingy *salmorejo* tasters.

Serves 4

Mushroom salmorejo
Salmorejo de boletus y setas

Flexible ingredients and toppings mean you can adjust to your liking, adding black truffle if you like, or you can replace the almond garnish with fried chopped garlic and diced jamón for extra flavor.

3 ½ oz (100 g) mixed mushrooms, chopped
Salt
1 lb 5 oz (600 g) juicy plum tomatoes,
  roughly chopped
3 cloves garlic
2 ½ oz (70 g) rustic bread, roughly shredded
Scant ½ cup (100 ml) extra virgin olive
  oil, plus more for sautéing
1 teaspoon grated black truffle (optional)

Garnish
1 hardboiled egg, chopped
2 tablespoons almonds, toasted and chopped

In a frying pan, heat a little olive oil and sauté the mushrooms with some salt until tender, about 5 minutes. Set aside.

Tip the tomatoes and garlic into a blender and process until combined, then mix in the bread and the olive oil. Season with salt, and process on a low speed until you have a thick purée.

Lastly, add the mushrooms and truffles and blend just until you obtain a creamy emulsion.

Pour into glasses and garnish with the chopped egg and almonds.

Serves 4

Beet salmorejo
Salmorejo de remolacha

1 lb 10 oz (750 g) ripe plum tomatoes,
  roughly quartered
1 clove garlic
3 ½ oz (100 g) bread, shredded
½ teaspoon salt
½ cup (125 ml) extra virgin olive oil
9 oz (250 g) cooked beets, roughly
  chopped with some of their juice

Garnish
3–4 tablespoons toasted sunflower seeds or pine nuts
4 anchovies in olive oil, halved and rolled up
1 tablespoon capers

In a blender, process the tomatoes on a low speed until coarsely chopped, then add the garlic, bread, and salt. With the machine running, add the olive oil and process until you have a smooth emulsion.

Add the beets and process for 2 more minutes until the entire mixture is thick and creamy.

Pour into glasses or bowls and scatter with sunflower seeds, anchovies, and capers.

Serves 4

Avocado salmorejo
Salmorejo de aguacate

This is very subtly flavored, and slips down in seconds. Juanjo tops it with diced ceviche (fish marinated in lime juice), but smoked salmon is just as good.

Flesh of 4 ripe avocadoes
3½ oz (100 g) dry rustic bread, crumbled
1 clove garlic, peeled and roughly chopped
1 large juicy tomato, cored and chopped
1 teaspoon salt
Scant ½ cup (100 ml) extra virgin olive oil

Garnish
2 hardboiled eggs, chopped
Diced ceviche or chopped smoked salmon
Grated lime zest (if using ceviche)

Toss all of the salmorejo ingredients into a blender and process on a low speed until you have a thick, creamy emulsion.

Spoon into glasses, garnish with the hardboiled eggs, and top with chopped ceviche and lime zest, or smoked salmon.

Serves 4 to 6

Mushroom and blue cheese omelet
Tortilla de setas y queso azul

A *tortilla de patata*—you see it everywhere as a stalwart of the tapas bars, of Spanish kitchens, and of pilgrimages like Andalusia's boisterous El Rocio with its one million followers. Juanjo's evolved version oozes flavor and should look like a golden pillow— before you slice into its velvety heart. Follow his example by playing with the ingredients, but make sure you have mastered the basic flipping technique.

Extra virgin olive oil
1 lb 12 oz (800 g) potatoes, peeled and diced
8 eggs
1 teaspoon salt

Mushroom purée
4 cloves garlic, finely sliced
Scant ½ cup (100 ml) extra virgin olive oil
14 oz (400 g) mixed mushrooms, coarsely chopped
1 ¾ oz (50 g) blue cheese, crumbled or diced

First, make the mushroom purée: In a frying pan, sauté the garlic in olive oil until golden, add the mushrooms, and continue to fry until tender, 6 to 8 minutes. Mix in the cheese, lower the heat, and cook over low heat for 5 minutes. Tip into a blender and process to a purée, then set aside.

In a large frying pan, heat some oil over low heat and gently fry the potatoes until they are soft but not colored, 6 to 8 minutes. Remove then set aside to cool.

In a large bowl, beat the eggs with the salt, add the potatoes, then stir in the mushroom purée, combining all of the ingredients well.

Heat a clean non-stick frying pan over medium heat. Once hot, swirl in some olive oil to cover the base. Tip in the egg mixture, tilting the pan to distribute it. Cover with a lid and cook for 3 to 5 minutes, until loosely set. Remove the lid and using a spatula, push the edges towards the center to firm them up. Place a plate on top of the pan and flip the omelet onto it. If necessary, add a little more oil to the pan, then carefully slide the omelet back into the pan to cook the other side. Cook, uncovered, until set to your liking, 3 to 5 minutes.

Slide the omelet onto a plate and serve either hot or cold.

ARRIEROS, *Sierra de Aracena*

Chef Luismi López and his wife, Adela Ortiz, are seated at their local café carved out of a former bullring. Above it towers the village church, and downhill stretches a web of cobbled streets and whitewashed houses. "Linares only has about 300 inhabitants," Luismi points out. "So our clients come from nearby towns like Aracena and Alájar. They dress up to come for dinner—for them it's an occasion."

Arrieros is a cool, rustic-chic restaurant that flows outside onto a sunny, flowery terrace. Here, neighbors' chitchat and church bells vie with a cacophony of hundreds of birds nurtured by the surrounding nature reserve that stretches to the Portuguese border. The verdant woodlands are also famously home to Iberian pigs, which end up as superlative *solomillo* or *jamón ibérico,* so it is no surprise that Luismi loves cooking with pork.

"Things have changed in the village since I grew up here," he muses. "As a child we ate lamb, kid goat, brains, and liver—now I want to revive goat and offal, it's something we have lost." Adela, elegant and energetic, tells me how, twenty years ago, they tossed a coin to see who would be chef and who would be front of house. Luismi got the cooking job, leading to two years of catering school and work at a Michelin-star restaurant. That experience shows in his incredible attention to detail and passion for local food. It also means that some people consider Arrieros to be the best restaurant in the entire province of Huelva.

Serves 4

Marinated Iberian pork with raisin couscous
Presa Ibérica en escabeche con cuscus de pasas

Escabeche (pickle or brine) is one of the great cooking techniques bequeathed by the Arabs, originally designed to preserve meat before the days of refrigeration. The sweet-sour taste and tender Iberian pork is balanced by grainy couscous. "We used to serve it with potatoes, but they weren't as good" Luismi tells me. "Everyone cooks couscous differently," he adds, but Luismi's technique works well. If you can't find Iberian pork, then source the best quality, organic pork available.

Extra virgin olive oil
1 lb 5 oz (600 g) Iberian pork loin
1 head garlic, broken into cloves
2 carrots, peeled and sliced
1 leek, roughly chopped
Scant ½ cup (100 ml) *fino* sherry or white wine
Scant ½ cup (90 ml) aged sherry vinegar
3–4 cloves
1 teaspoon cumin seeds
1 tablespoon fresh oregano
1 bay leaf
Salt and black pepper
Sprigs of cilantro, to garnish

Couscous
Extra virgin olive oil
2 cloves garlic, finely sliced
1 small onion, finely chopped
1 red bell pepper, seeded, deribbed,
    and finely chopped
1 teaspoon ground cumin
4 thin asparagus spears, woody ends removed, halved
⅓ cup (1 ¾ oz/50 g) seedless raisins
Salt
1 cup (250 ml) vegetable stock
1 ½ cups (9 oz/250 g) couscous

Bring the pork to room temperature an hour or so before cooking.

Heat some olive oil in a frying pan over high heat and quickly brown the pork on both sides. Lower the heat to medium and cook for 1 minute more on each side. Transfer the pork to a plate, leaving the oil in the pan.

Toss in the garlic, carrots, and leek. Sauté until tender, then add the wine, vinegar, and spices, season with salt and pepper, and simmer for 15 to 20 minutes. Remove from the heat and submerge the pork loin in this *escabeche* (marinade) for 4 hours.

Meanwhile, make the couscous: In a large saucepan, heat some olive oil over low heat and sauté the garlic, onion, and pepper for 5 minutes or so. Add the cumin and asparagus, and continue to cook until the vegetables are tender. Stir in the raisins, season with salt, and set aside.

In a separate saucepan, heat the vegetable stock. Once it starts to boil, tip in the couscous and remove from the heat. Allow the grains to absorb the stock for 3 minutes. Return the pan to low heat, stir in 1 tablespoon extra virgin olive oil, and fluff up the grains with a fork to separate them. Tip the couscous into the saucepan of vegetables and stir to combine.

Finally arrange the couscous on a serving dish, lay the pork loin on top, and garnish with a sprig or two of cilantro.

Iberian pork tenderloin stuffed with dates in quince and chocolate sauce

Solomillo ibérico relleno de dátiles en salsa de membrillo y chocolate

So modest in appearance, yet so complex in flavor, this is one of Luismi's mini-masterpieces. The tender Iberian pork works deliciously with the sweetness of the dates. If you can't find Iberian pork, then source the best quality organic pork available.

2 Iberian pork tenderloins, about 10 oz (280 g) each
Salt and freshly ground black pepper
Extra virgin olive oil
½ cup (3¼ oz/90 g) finely chopped shallots
3 pitted dates, finely chopped
Handful of basil leaves, finely sliced
3½ tablespoons sweet dessert wine

Quince and chocolate sauce
Extra virgin olive oil
1 onion, chopped
Generous ¾ cup (200 ml) meat stock
1¾ oz (50 g) quince paste
3½ tablespoons brandy
¾ oz (25 g) dark chocolate, broken into pieces

First, make the sauce. In a saucepan heat a little oil and sweat the onion until translucent but not brown. Add the onion, stock, quince, and brandy, bring to a simmer, and cook for 20 minutes. Add the chocolate pieces, stirring until they have melted. Remove from the heat, transfer to a food processor, and blend to a thick sauce.

Preheat the oven to 195°F (90°C).

Using a sharp knife, make a lengthwise cut down the center of each tenderloin, making sure you don't cut all the way through, and open it up like a book so it lies flat. Season with salt and pepper and set aside.

In a frying pan, heat a little olive oil over low heat, and sauté the shallots, dates, and basil until the shallots have softened. Add the wine and simmer until the mixture has reduced to a thick paste, 5 to 7 minutes.

Spread this paste evenly over the top of the tenderloins, roll them up like a jelly roll, and tie them with kitchen twine.

Heat a little oil in a frying pan over high heat and sear the meat briefly on all sides. Transfer to a roasting pan and bake in the oven until just tender, 10 minutes.

Finally slice the meat into medallions, coat with the quince sauce, and serve.

Sautéed vegetables in vanilla oil
Salteado de verduras y vainilla

This is a delicate presentation of an assortment of vegetables given an unusual fruity edge by the vanilla oil. If you can't buy it, make it at least a week in advance. You'll have some left over to try out drizzled over crustaceans like lobster or shrimp.

9 oz (250 g) pumpkin, peeled
2 red bell peppers, seeded and deribbed
2 small zucchinis
2 onions
Extra virgin olive oil
Sea salt flakes and black pepper

Vanilla oil (or use store bought)
1 cup (250 ml) good quality olive oil
1 vanilla bean

To make your own vanilla oil, split a vanilla bean, scrape out the seeds, and place the seeds and pod in a small jar or bottle of quality olive oil. Store in a cool pantry and shake it daily for a week or so before use.

Finely dice the vegetables into equal-size pieces. Sauté each one separately in olive oil until tender, then mix together, season with salt flakes and pepper, and drizzle with vanilla oil.

Serves 4

Lemon and ginger mousse
Mousse de limón y genjibre

Rich and creamy with sharp pings of lemon zest and ginger, this easy
mousse makes a perfect indulgent end to a rich pork meal.

2–3 unwaxed lemons
1 cup (7 oz/200 g) sugar
Scant ½ cup (100 ml) freshly squeezed lemon juice
1 ½ cups (375 g) lemon whole-milk yogurt
2 cups (500 ml) heavy whipping cream

Garnish
Sesame seeds
Ground ginger
Ground cinnamon
Mint leaves

Zest the lemons and finely slice the pulp.

In a large bowl, use a whisk to mix the sugar,
lemon juice, zest, and yogurt. In a separate bowl,
whip the cream to firm peaks. Carefully fold the
whipped cream into the yogurt mixture, transfer
to serving dishes, and chill in the refrigerator.

Before serving, lightly sprinkle with sesame
seeds, ginger, cinnamon, and chopped
lemon pulp, and garnish with mint.

ALBORONÍA, *Jerez de la Frontera*

Adelina Pandelet and Victor Marin opened Alboronía in 2013 in the shaded patio of an artisan center, just off the beaten track of central Jerez. Unusually, Adelina's background combines catering school with a degree in art history, specializing in Islamic art, while Victor inherited expertise on flamenco from his father, a flamenco writer. "For years I worked in Seville, also in Holland," Victor recounts. "But at one point became unemployed. Living with Adelina I thought, I have a cook with me, so let's open a tapas bar!" This they did successfully in a small town outside Seville before moving back to Victor's hometown of Jerez to shift to a more ambitious scale.

"We have mountains of books at home, some on cooking and a lot on the mix of cultures in Andalucía—it's so rich. Deciding on the name Alboronía fused history, food, and the Arab culture, and meant that people who come here know what to expect." Adelina, more reserved than the jovial, outgoing Victor, adds, "I love the combination of salty and sweet in Moroccan food but you have to be careful in the balance. Everything I make is quite elaborate and seasonal." In the sherry-obsessed city of Jerez, Alboronía makes an exotic option with deep *andalus* roots. And, naturally, Victor will serve you a glass of *fino* too.

Summer vegetables with goat cheese
Alboronía con queso de cabra

It makes absolute sense for this Andalusian classic to be served by its eponymous tapas bar. Allegedly, the dish was cooked to great applause for the Caliph Abder Rahman II in 9th-century Córdoba, obviously without New World tomatoes and peppers. One legend maintains that Ziryab, that medieval multi-tasker (see p. 8 and p. 20), originally prepared it in his native Baghdad for the princess Alburan, thus it was dubbed Alburaniyya; another version makes Buraniyya the chef-creator. Whatever its origins, it later became known as *pisto andaluz*, a cousin of southern France's *ratatouille*. It's a moveable feast in which potatoes and/or chickpeas sometimes find their way into the pot, and quince is optional. The goat cheese drizzled with honey is a delicious addition from Alboronía (the bar).

3 eggplants, peeled and cut into chunks
5 tablespoons extra virgin olive oil
1 onion, finely chopped
3 cloves garlic, peeled and minced
1 green bell pepper, seeded, deribbed,
   and finely chopped
1 quince, cored and cut into chunks (optional)
7 oz (200 g) pumpkin, peeled and cut into chunks
2 medium zucchinis, chopped
¼ cup (¾ oz/50 g) chopped tomatoes, with their juice
Salt and freshly ground black pepper
3½ oz (100 g) cylindrical goat cheese, sliced
¼ cup (60 ml) clear honey

Place the eggplant pieces in a colander and sprinkle with salt; set aside for 30 minutes, then rinse and pat dry.

In a large saucepan, heat the olive oil and gently fry the onion, garlic, and green pepper for 5 minutes or so. Stir in the quince, pumpkin, zucchinis, and tomatoes, carefully turning to mix.

Cover the pot and simmer over low heat for 25 to 30 minutes until the vegetables are tender but not falling apart. Season to taste with salt and ground black pepper.

Transfer the mixture to an ovensafe dish, top with the goat cheese then place under the broiler for a few minutes until the cheese turns golden. Remove from the oven, drizzle lightly with honey, and serve.

Serves 4

Layered mackerel and lentil hummus with cucumber cream
Milhojas de lomo de caballa con humus de lentejas y crema de pepiño

This is like a club sandwich of lentil hummus and mackerel, drizzled in a gently perfumed cucumber cream, perfect on a hot summer's day. Serve as an appetizer or tapa with a glass of *fino* sherry.

Extra virgin olive oil
4 mackerel fillets, halved lengthwise
Mint leaves, to garnish

Lentil hummus
¾ cup (5½ oz/150 g) cooked green lentils
3 tablespoons plain yogurt
1 clove garlic, chopped
Juice of ½ lemon
2 tablespoons sunflower oil
2 tablespoons ground cumin
1 tablespoon toasted sesame seeds
1 teaspoon salt

Cucumber cream
3 tablespoons plain yogurt
1 cucumber, peeled and diced
½ clove garlic, chopped
3 mint leaves, plus more to garnish
2 tablespoons mild extra virgin olive oil

To make the hummus, combine all the ingredients and purée using a food processor or immersion blender. Set aside in the refrigerator.

Next, make the cucumber cream. Combine the yogurt, cucumber, garlic, and mint and purée using a food processor or immersion blender. With the machine running, slowly add the oil in a trickle to make an emulsion. Place in the refrigerator.

In a frying pan, heat a little oil and flash-fry the mackerel fillets for 30 seconds on each side.

Place a piece of mackerel on each serving plate. Top with a heaped teaspoon of hummus, followed by another piece of mackerel to make a sandwich. Finish with a spoonful of cucumber cream and garnish with mint leaves.

Spicy chicken tagine with ginger and apricots
Tajin picante de pollo, genjibre y albaricoques

This Jerez tagine has a complex mixture of flavors—the slight burn of the cayenne pepper is tempered by the sweet apricots and honey as well as the dry couscous, while the ginger really sings. Adelina was inspired by the tagines she sampled in the Moroccan town of Chefchaouen, though she has added her own twist. The couscous is finished in the oven, but if you are in a hurry, you can skip this step.

3 tablespoons extra virgin olive oil
1 onion, peeled and finely chopped
3 sprigs of fresh rosemary, leaves finely chopped
2 thumb-size pieces (1 ½ oz/40 g) fresh
    ginger, peeled and minced
1 teaspoon cinnamon
1 teaspoon cayenne pepper
4 large bone-in chicken thighs
¾ cup (3 ½ oz/100 g) dried apricots,
    preferably organic, halved
14 oz (400 g) can of whole tomatoes
2 tablespoons honey
Salt and white pepper
Rosemary sprigs, to garnish

Couscous
1 ¾ cups (10 ½ oz/300 g) couscous
Pinch of salt
1 ⅔ cups (400 ml) hot water
2 tablespoons olive oil

Preheat the oven to 350°F (180°C) (if you plan to oven-steam the couscous).

In a heavy bottomed pot or a tagine dish, heat the oil, then sauté the onion, rosemary, ginger, cinnamon, and cayenne over medium heat until tender. Add the chicken thighs and turn them until they are golden all over. Stir in the apricots, tomatoes, and honey.

Bring to a boil, then lower heat to a simmer, cover, and bubble gently for 25 to 30 minutes until the chicken is cooked. Season to taste with salt and pepper.

Next, make the couscous: Place the couscous grains in an ovensafe dish, sprinkle with salt, and cover with the hot water. Set aside for 5 minutes to allow the water to absorb. Trickle the olive oil over the grains and stir with a fork. Cover with aluminum foil and place in the oven to dry, about 15 minutes. (If you are in a rush, you can prepare the couscous by pouring boiling water over the grains. Cover with a lid and set aside for 5 minutes or so, before fluffing with a fork to separate the grains.)

Spread the couscous over the base of a tagine or serving dish, lay the chicken thighs on top, spoon over the apricot mixture, and garnish with a sprig or two of rosemary.

Serves 4

Duck fillets with almond and pistachio sauce, turmeric couscous, and rose petals

Solomillo de pato con majado de almendras, pistachos, pétalos de rosa y cuscús de raíz de curcuma

4 boneless, skinless duck breasts, sliced into 12 pieces
Exra virgin olive oil

Sauce
1 large pat of butter
2 cloves garlic, peeled and finely sliced
¼ cup (1 oz/30 g) toasted almonds
¼ cup (1 oz/30 g) shelled salted pistachios
1 tablespoon rosewater
2 tablespoons clear honey
Scant ½ cup (100 ml) duck stock, or any meat stock
Salt and white pepper

Couscous
1 ¾ cups (10 ½ oz/300 g) couscous
Pinch of salt
1 ⅔ cups (400 ml) hot water
2 tablespoons olive oil

Garnish
Fresh turmeric root
Edible rose petals (optional)
Mint leaves

Preheat the oven to 350°F (180°C) (if you plan to oven-steam the couscous).

Make the sauce: In a large saucepan, heat the butter and gently fry the garlic.

In a mortar and pestle or food processor, combine the almonds, pistachios, and sautéed garlic (leaving the butter in the pan) and crush to a coarse nutty texture.

Return the mixture to the pan and stir in the rosewater, honey, and stock. Cook over low heat for about 3 minutes, until the mixture reduces and thickens. Season with salt and pepper to taste.

Next, make the couscous: Place the couscous in an ovensafe dish, sprinkle with salt, and cover with the hot water. Set aside for 10 minutes to allow the water to absorb. Trickle the olive oil over the grains and stir with a fork. Cover with aluminum foil and place in the oven until tender, about 15 minutes. (If you are in a rush, you can prepare the couscous by pouring the boiling water over the grains. Cover with a lid and set aside for 5 minutes or so, before fluffing with a fork to separate the grains.)

Heat some oil in a frying pan over high heat and sauté the duck until just cooked, about 30 seconds on each side. Season with salt and pepper.

Arrange the couscous on a serving plate, place the duck on top, drizzle with the sauce, then grate some turmeric over it. Garnish with a few rose petals and mint leaves.

EL FARO DE CADIZ, *Cadiz*

As the grandson of the founder of the legendary Faro restaurant, youthful Mario Jimenez Córdoba belongs to the greatest food dynasty of Cádiz. It's a lot to live up to, and although initially Mario embarked on a commercial career in Madrid, restaurant life lured him back. "I first worked in top restaurants in northern Spain before becoming kitchen manager here—and I really love cooking!" he remarks cheerfully. He is extremely lucky to work beside Manolo Ojeda, a great hulk of a man who has headed the Faro kitchen for thirteen years—an impressive stretch. "That's nothing," chuckles Manolo. "There's a waiter who has just retired after fifty years, and a couple of kitchen hands who have both worked here for twenty years."

Mario is on a mission for change though. "This place opened back in 1964," his eyes widen, "so there's a lot to renovate." But nothing alters the steady rhythm of the piscatorial seasons or El Faro's reputation as *THE* place for fish, rice, and seafood in Cádiz whether at the packed tapas bar or in the calmer restaurant. Right now red mullet is ending, and the famous *almadraba* season is beginning. "We just had 60 pounds (27 kg) of fresh Bluefin tuna delivered from Barbate!" He summons the kitchen "fisherman" who emerges clutching a giant *corvina*, then shows me mountains of shrimp from Sanlúcar. In this treasure trove of the ocean, every dish reflects tradition, freshness, and long experience.

Serves 4

El Faro's fish soup with orange
Caldillo de perro

Typical of El Puerto de Santa Maria, the port across the bay from Cadiz, this tangy fish soup is said to date back to the Reconquista when its odd Spanish name was coined. Allegedly, Christians who were brought from the north to live in Cádiz called all pork-averse Muslims "dogs" (*perros*). For some reason, the fish soup gained the same nickname. What's in a name though? The soup is delicate with a faint orange flavor, and since Mario insists that, "odd numbers are very important in a garnish," make it three fennel fronds, not two.

2 tablespoons olive oil
6 cloves garlic, skinned and sliced
2 onions, chopped
4¼ quarts (4 liters) hot water
2 potatoes, sliced into half-moons
Salt
1 lb 5 oz (600g) fresh white fish steaks,
   such as hake, with bones and skin
Generous ¾ cup (200 ml) freshly
   squeezed orange juice
Zest of 1 orange
Fennel fronds, to garnish

In a deep saucepan, heat the oil and fry the garlic until golden. Remove with a slotted spoon, leaving the oil in the pan, and set aside for the garnish.

Add the onion to the pan and sauté until translucent. Pour in 8½ cups (2 liters) of the water, add the potato slices, and season with a pinch of salt. Simmer vigorously until the potatoes are nearly done, though still firm at the core, about 10 minutes. Lower the fish steaks into the liquid and pour in the rest of the water with the orange juice. Continue to simmer vigorously until the fish is cooked, about 7 minutes.

Remove the fish and set it aside. Using a slotted spoon, remove the potatoes and divide them among serving bowls. Arrange the fish pieces on top, cutting them if necessary, sprinkle with orange zest, and garnish with fried garlic and some fennel fronds. Pour the broth into a jug to serve at the table.

Serves 4

Mozarabic monkfish with a sauce of sweet wine, raisins, and pine nuts
Rape mozarabe con vino dulce, salsa de pasas y piñones

This sweet, raisiny fish dish is really unusual and yet again recalls the days of Al-Andalus, when these flavors were combined so often and so successfully. The finished dish, with its thick sauce, has a lovely glaze. Serve it in a bowl with some coarse bread for mopping up the sauce.

3 tablespoons extra virgin olive oil
2 onions, finely chopped
2 medium carrots, finely chopped
¼ cup (1½ oz/40 g) raisins
2½ tablespoons pine nuts
1 lb 12 oz (800 g) steaks of monkfish, anglerfish, or porgy
⅓ cup (80 ml) Pedro Ximénez wine
4¼ cups (1 liter) homemade or quality fish stock
Salt
1–2 teaspoons cornstarch, dissolved in 2–3 tablespoons water

In a frying pan, heat the olive oil and sauté the onion and carrot for a minute or two before adding the raisins and pine nuts. Continue to cook until the pine nuts are toasted.

Lay the fish in the pan then tip in the wine and bring to a simmer. Turn off the heat and light the wine with a long match to flambé the fish.

When the flame has extinguished, return the pan to the heat, pour in the fish stock, add a pinch of salt, and simmer vigorously until the fish is cooked, about 7 minutes. In the last minute of cooking, stir in the cornstarch, half at a time, until the sauce has thickened. Don't overdo it—less is more.

Clams with spinach and brandy
Almejas con espinacas al brandy de Jerez

This may not be the prettiest of El Faro's dishes, but it is one of the tastiest, with its creamy, garlicky, eggy, brandied sauce. It works well as a main course; but, of course, with fewer clams it can be an appetizer. It was developed some thirty years ago by Fernando Córdoba, Mario's uncle, who heads El Faro del Puerto, the sister restaurant across the bay. His original recipe poaches, rather than scrambles the eggs—more spectacular and worth trying—carefully lower the raw egg into the spinach and cream mixture and cook for just a couple of minutes (the yolk should be soft enough to run when the dish is served).

Extra virgin olive oil
6 cloves garlic, peeled and finely sliced
8 cups (9 oz/250 g) spinach, chopped
2 cups (500 ml) shellfish stock
20 large clams, about 1 lb 12 oz (800 g)
½ cup (125 ml) brandy
2 eggs

Heat the oil in a large frying pan then sauté the garlic for 1 minute, before adding the spinach and stock. Stir to combine, then add the clams. Tip in the brandy; once it bubbles, turn off the heat and carefully light it on fire to flambé. Flames will shoot up so step back and enjoy the spectacle for a minute before they die down.

Return to the heat, and once the clams begin to open, stir in the eggs, which will loosely scramble in the sauce. Continue to cook for a few minutes more until the clams have opened but be careful not to overcook the egg—it is a fine balance. Discard any clams that do not open and serve in bowls.

Serves 4 to 6

Shrimp fritters
Tortillitas de camarones

If there is one *tapa* that El Faro is famed for throughout Andalucía and indeed Spain, it is shrimp fritters. Nowhere are they surpassed in delicate laciness and fine, crisp texture, although restaurants in Sanlúcar de Barrameda put up a strong fight. The recipe originated in San Fernando, a working town on the mainland at the start of the Cádiz isthmus, where salt flats and marshes are much loved by tiny shrimp (*camarones*). The crustacean even gave their name to the town's much loved hero, the flamenco singer Camarón de la Isla. According to Mario, "The most difficult part of the recipe is the temperature of the oil." You need a large paella or frying pan for this. If you can't find chickpea flour, use more all-purpose flour.

Pinch of salt
2 cups (500 ml) cold water
1½ cups (5½ oz/150 g) chickpea flour
1¼ cups (5½ oz/150 g) all-purpose flour
3–4 scallions, finely chopped
1 tablespoon flat-leaf parsley, leaves finely chopped
9 oz (250 g) head-on Spanish *camarones* (very tiny shrimp), left whole, or peeled regular-size shrimp, sliced thinly
Extra virgin olive oil, for frying

In a large bowl, combine the salt and water then, little by little, add the two types of flour, stirring with a wooden spoon to obtain a smooth batter. It should be quite loose, slightly thicker than milk. Stir in the scallions, parsley, and shrimp, cover with a lid, and place in the refrigerator.

In a large paella pan or frying pan, add the oil to a depth of about ¾ inch (2 cm). Heat the oil over medium-high heat until almost smoking, about 300°F (150°C). Test a teaspoonful of dough, dropping it into the oil; it should expand to create an irregular circular fritter without breaking up.

Once the oil is at the correct temperature, drop tablespoonfuls of the cold batter into the oil to fry, turning over any fritters that are too thin and cooking too fast. It will take about 5 minutes for them to become golden and crisp. Do this in several batches. Adding too many can alter the temperature of the oil and affect the texture of the fritters. Using tongs, remove the fritters from the pan, shake off excess oil, and arrange on a plate. You can keep them warm in the oven at a very low temeperature while you work, and keep the batter in the refrigerator to maintain its cool temperature. Serve immediately.

Tapioca pudding with lemon and bitter orange
Tapioca, limón y naranja amarga

This is El Faro's version of Spain's ubiquitous *arroz con leche*, or rice pudding, in this case using tapioca, a jelly-like substance full of glistening pearls that's made from the cassava root. Welcome back—I haven't eaten this since my school days, and it is an epiphany. The El Faro version is dreamily gelatinous and not too sweet, with hits of citrus—absolutely delicious. You'll need to start a night in advance, but you can keep it in the refrigerator for up to 5 days, then briefly microwave before serving.

4 ¼ cups (1 liter) rice milk
4 ¼ cups (1 liter) water
Zest of 1 lemon
¼ cinnamon stick
1 cup (7 oz/200 g) sugar
1 ¼ cups (7 oz/200 g) tapioca pearls

Bitter orange jam
1 lb (500 g) oranges
1 ¼ cups (9 oz/250 g) sugar

Garnish
1 lemon, peeled, seeds and pith
  removed, cut into tiny slices
Fennel fronds (optional)
Edible flowers (optional)

In a large bowl, mix the rice milk, water, lemon zest, and cinnamon together and place in the refrigerator overnight.

Next, make the bitter orange jam: Wash and quarter the oranges, removing as many seeds as possible. Place in a blender and process on high speed until coarsely chopped. Transfer to a bowl and mix in the sugar. Refrigerate overnight or for at least 12 hours.

Remove the oranges from the refrigerator and transfer to a saucepan, adding about a tablespoon of water if it has solidified. Simmer for about 5 minutes to heat through. Return the mixture to the blender and blend to a loose purée. Set aside.

Next, make the pudding: In a saucepan, combine the chilled rice milk mixture and the sugar and bring to a boil over medium heat. Add the tapioca pearls and cook, whisking constantly with a wire whisk, until the mixture starts to thicken and the pearls become translucent, up to 20 minutes. Reduce the heat for the last minute, still stirring. Remove from the heat entirely, but continue to stir until it has cooled slightly.

Spoon the pudding into individual bowls, decorate with the lemon slices and 3 teaspoons of orange jam in each. Add a fennel frond and scatter with edible flowers, if available. Serve warm.

El ARRIATE, *El Puerto de Santa María*

Funky El Arriate is in calle Los Moros, street of the Moors, right by the dock for the catamaran from Cádiz and surrounded by the sherry bodegas that made El Puerto prosper. Right opposite the restaurant is the renowned Osborne, that bodega of the iconic bull silhouette that pops up on hilltops beside the freeway. Yet El Arriate whisks you into a very different world. Beyond a serene garden of orange trees you enter a cavernous, boho-chic space packed with eccentricities, color, and with a cool jazz soundtrack. In the tiny kitchen, David Méndez, the chef-owner, and two sous-chefs produce complex morsels that bring together different worlds from Japan to Mexico to Al-Andalus—his soul food.

David actually hails from a small town in the *campiña* of Córdoba, where the tediously long, hot afternoons of his adolescence inspired him to cook. Fast-forward a few decades and here he is, swinging the pans in an acclaimed restaurant with his bubbly wife Eva at the front of house. Amid the creative disorder, David knows what he is doing. "Don't burn the paprika and don't put a lid on it," he insists as he produces an *arroz negro* full of texture.

After fifteen years, he knows the Cádiz area well and is generous in his appraisals. "Gutiérrez Colosía is the best sherry bodega here, and for authentic *gaditano* food you can't go wrong in Sanlúcar de la Barrameda—nowhere is bad there!" But for *andaluz* innovation, El Arriate rides very high.

Serves 4

Avocado balls in sweet-and-sour sauce
Croquemoles

There is really no translation for David's most sought-after dish, a play on words combining Spanish *croqueta* with Mexican guacamole. These crisp avocado balls are wonderfully exotic, full of imaginative flavors, yet not difficult to make. And don't be put off by the long list of ingredients— you will probably find most of them in your pantry. Persevere—it is very much worthwhile.

Avocado balls
1 lb (500 g) bag tortilla chips
5 ripe avocadoes
2 teaspoons curry powder
2 teaspoons ground cumin
1 tablespoon chopped coriander leaves
1 teaspoon salt

Sweet-and-sour sauce
Extra virgin olive oil
2 small carrots, finely chopped
½ leek, finely chopped
½ red bell pepper, seeds removed, finely chopped
½ stick of celery, finely chopped
½ head of garlic, peeled and finely chopped
½ onion, finely chopped
1 fennel bulb, finely chopped
3 tablespoons ketchup
3 tablespoons soy sauce
1 ½ cups (350 ml) pineapple juice
2 teaspoons sugar
1 tablespoon Jerez sherry vinegar
1 teaspoon cornstarch

First make the sauce: Heat some oil in a large frying pan and add the carrots, leek, pepper, celery, garlic, onion, and fennel. Sauté for 5 minutes. Stir in the ketchup, soy sauce, pineapple juice, sugar, vinegar, and cornstarch and maintain at a vigorous simmer for about 6 minutes, until the liquid has reduced. The vegetables should maintain their shape while the sauce becomes quite concentrated. Spoon the sauce onto a serving plate.

Next, make the avocado balls: On a board, smash the tortilla chips into small pieces. Spoon the avocado pulp into a bowl, add the spices, and mash together to combine. Shape the mixture into 1 ½ inch (4 cm) balls and roll them in the broken chips to coat them entirely. Lay the avocado balls on top of the sauce and serve.

Serves 4 as a sharing plate

Razor clams in pickled lemon sauce with potato purée
Navajas en escabeche de limón y pure de patatas

Intriguingly architectural in appearance, this appetizer is perfect for sharing—though may entail a fight over the last clam. There is an incredible mixture of flavors in the sauce, and you can even toss in a few capers for extra bite.

1 thumb-size piece fresh ginger, peeled and grated
½ stick lemongrass, grated
1 teaspoon cayenne pepper
Juice of 2–3 lemons
2 potatoes, peeled and boiled
Scant 1 cup (1¾ sticks/7 oz/200 g) butter
1 egg yolk
3 tablespoons gomasio (Japanese
   sesame and salt seasoning)
⅓ cup (1¾ oz/50 g) blanched almonds,
   toasted and chopped
⅓ cup (1¾ oz/50 g) sesame seeds, toasted
1 tablespoon salted lard
16 razor clams

For the escabeche (pickled sauce), mix the ginger, lemongrass, cayenne, and lemon juice and set aside.

Mash the potatoes with the butter and egg-yolk.

In a small bowl, mix the gomasio, almonds, sesame seeds, and lard, then stir this into the potato purée. Place in a pastry bag.

Heat a grill pan over high heat. Place the razor clams briefly on the pan, just until they start to open. Remove them immediately, ease the shells apart, keeping them hinged, and then fill each empty side with the potato mixture.

Spoon some of the escabeche sauce over the clams, then carefully stack them on a serving plate, alternating the direction of the shells. Serve with the remaining escabeche on the side, to be spooned over.

Black rice with cuttlefish
Arroz Negro con choco

Despite the ferocious color, squid ink is used for its delicate, briny flavor, and is widely present in Spain's rice-obsessed Levant region of Valencia, and also Catalunya. Andalucía, too, loves it, and David's dish with cuttlefish or squid uses local rice from the Doñana marshes just to the north. "It is very absorbant rice," he advises. "So it needs three times its quantity in water. The Valencians developed it here in the 19th century when they discovered how perfect the conditions were." You can replace it with round-grain Bomba or Arborio rice. Whatever the type, it looks dramatic in black! For extra kick and as a homage to El Puerto's bodegas, tip in a small glass of *oloroso* sherry.

12 oz (350 g) cleaned cuttlefish or squid
Extra virgin olive oil
1 red bell pepper, seeded, deribbed, and chopped
2 cloves garlic, peeled and sliced
3 tomatoes, chopped
3 ½ oz (100 g) seaweed such as Wakame,
  salicornia, or samphire
1 tablespoon sweet paprika
¾ cup (175 ml) *fino* sherry or white wine
2 ½ cups (1 lb/500 g) Bomba or Arborio rice
Salt
6 ⅓ cups (1.5 liters) good quality fish stock, warm
5 teaspoons (16 g) squid ink
1 clove garlic
1 tomato
Handful chopped parsley

Rinse the cuttlefish or squid well, pat dry, and slice or dice the body and tentacles. Set aside.

In a large saucepan, heat a generous glug of olive oil over medium heat and sauté the bell pepper, garlic, tomatoes, and seaweed for 3 minutes, stirring. Add the paprika and wine, then tip in the rice, cuttlefish or squid, and a pinch of salt. Add the stock, mix well, then stir in the squid ink. Bring to a gentle boil and cook until the water is absorbed and the rice is tender, about 18 minutes.

In a mortar and pestle, crush the garlic, tomato, and chopped parsley together. Just before serving, stir this mixture into the rice.

Skirt steak macerated in orange with spelt and pickles
Entraña de retinta macerada con naranja, espelta y encurtidos

This is another of David's complex creations made using the local breed of *retinta* beef. The marinade tenderizes what can be quite a tough cut of meat, and David's ingredients combine strong echoes of the East with hints of Andalusian citrus. For the spelt, David suggests that once cooked it is fried in whatever chopped vegetables you wish—shitake mushrooms, fennel, carrot, etc.

1 lb 12 oz (800 g) skirt steak
1 onion, finely chopped
Pickled cauliflower and radish, to serve (optional)

Marinade
Peel of 2 oranges
Peel of 2 lemons
Juice of 2 oranges
1 tablespoon extra virgin olive oil
1 tablespoon algae nori (Japanese dried seaweed)
1 teaspoon ground ginger
1 tablespoon black sesame seeds
1 tablespoon white sesame seeds
1 hot chili pepper
1 tablespoon Szechuan pepper

Spelt
2½ cups (625 ml) chicken stock, plus ½ cup (125 ml) more if needed
3 tablespoons soy sauce
2 tablespoons Jerez brandy or amontillado
1¼ cups (7 oz/200 g) spelt berries, rinsed

Dry the orange and lemon peel in the sun for two days, or heat in the oven for 3 hours at 300°F (150°C), then finely chop.

In a large bowl, combine the marinade ingredients and add the skirt steak, turning to ensure the meat is well covered. Refrigerate 12 hours.

After the meat has marinated, make the spelt: In a saucepan, mix the stock, soy sauce, and brandy or amontillado, then tip in the spelt. Simmer vigorously, uncovered, for about 40 minutes, or until tender (keep checking since cooking time can vary). If it becomes dry add ½ cup (125 ml) more stock. Drain any excess liquid and set aside.

Remove the meat from the marinade, slice it, and sprinkle it with the onion pieces. Heat a grill pan over high heat until very hot. Sear the meat on all sides, turning a couple of times until almost charred. Allow to rest a few minutes and scrape off the onion.

Serve with pickled cauliflower and radish and a neat mound of spelt.

VENTA EL SOLDAO, *Los Badalejos, Medina Sidonia*

Teresa Montero, pushing ninety, is a legend in the Janda region of Cádiz. The charming, warm-hearted matriarch still runs a country restaurant or *venta* (a typically Andalusian roadside inn) that opened in 1953. Here she is supported by a fluctuating cast of her eleven offspring who help in the kitchen, serve in the bar and restaurant, or look after the clucking ducks, chickens, and turkeys outside. One son, José, supplies freshly baked bread, while another, Enrique, manages the lovely family *cortijo* as a hotel and restaurant. Burly Carlos runs the cattle farms of fighting bulls and the local breed of *retinto*; both meats feature on the restaurant menu, leaving imposing trophies (heads) on the walls.

In the kitchen on a busy weekend, daughters Tere and Sofia prepare huge vats of bubbling stews using only their own or local produce. Another son, Paco, adjusts a rice dish, the house specialty, cooking it with chicken, venison, rabbit, partridge, or pheasant. Meanwhile, a Moroccan kitchen helper prepares mountains of toast for late breakfasts.

Teresa herself, bright-eyed and smiling, gives me a few tips. "With meat I like using nutmeg, also black pepper, but never cumin—you can't digest it. And the quality of your olive oil is *really* important!" She kisses her fingers expressively. "You know with a business like this, you must do things little by little." After sixty years, with customers from Spain's former Prime Minister, Felipe Gonzalez, to the late Colombian writer, Gabriel García Marquez, she has certainly succeeded.

Serves 4

Red pepper, onion, and tuna salad
Ensalada de pimientos rojos asados, cebolla y atún

This Andalusian classic is easy to prepare and makes a colorful, flavorsome appetizer, since the charring of the peppers brings an unusual smoky edge. Teresa's advice is not to roast the peppers in the oven or they will become too soft. "Peppers need to be crunchy."

1 lb 10 oz (750 g) red bell peppers
3 onions, thinly sliced
2 hard-boiled eggs, quartered
5 oz (120 g) can good quality tuna
2–3 tablespoons extra virgin olive oil
1 tablespoon sherry vinegar

Heat a griddle over medium heat and roast the peppers for 10 to 15 minutes, turning often so that they blacken and char. Transfer the peppers to a plastic bag, place this in a bowl, and cover with a lid. Set aside to cool.

Once the peppers have cooled, peel off the blackened parts with your fingers and briefly rinse them under running water. Slice the peppers and and arrange them on a plate with the onion, egg, and spoonfuls of tuna.

Dress generously with oil and vinegar and serve.

Serves 4

Carrot salad
Zanahorias aliñadas

There is a hint of Morocco in this easy, healthy appetizer that is a classic in the tapas bars of Cádiz. Play with the dressing by adding some paprika and/or parsley, but the oregano is fundamental. At Venta El Soldao the carrots also come with chunks of fried beef liver—a delicious combination.

1 lb (500 g) organic carrots, scrubbed
Salt
2 cloves garlic, peeled and diced
1 tablespoon fresh oregano
1 teaspoon ground cumin
1 ½ teaspoons sherry vinegar
2 tablespoons extra virgin olive oil, plus more to serve

Boil the carrots in salted water for 15 to 20 minutes, until tender but not soft. Drain and cool at room temperature, then slice into rounds.

In a bowl, mix together the garlic, oregano, cumin, vinegar, olive oil, and 1 teaspoon salt. Mix well, crushing the garlic with the back of your spoon. Pour this mixture over the carrots, cover, and set aside somewhere cool for around 2 hours to macerate. To serve, trickle generously with olive oil.

Serves 4

Enrique's tomato salad
Ensalada de tomate de Enrique

It is very hard to come anywhere close to the quality of Andalusian tomatoes in summer. Only use the best in-season tomatoes to make this simple light appetizer that will counter-balance a heavier main course.

3 beefsteak or large heirloom tomatoes
2 cloves garlic, peeled and finely diced
1 tablespoon fresh oregano
Salt and black pepper
Extra virgin olive oil

Core and thinly slice the tomatoes. Arrange the slices on a plate, scatter with garlic and oregano, season with salt and pepper, then trickle generously with olive oil. Serve immediately.

Serves 6

Chicken and rice
Pollo con arroz

Teresa's most popular dish is applauded throughout the region. It surely must have contributed to the gold medal she was awarded for working excellence, a national distinction. This dish is creamy comfort food at its best and requires top quality free-range or organic chicken for utmost flavor. The rice will be quite sloppy immediately after cooking but soon thickens. Teresa suggests using the same technique for rabbit, partridge, pheasant, pork, or venison.

Scant ½ cup (100 ml) extra virgin olive oil
4 cloves garlic, finely sliced
2 large onions, finely sliced
4 lb (2 kg) whole free-range chicken,
    cut into pieces, skin removed
1 cup (250 ml) white wine
1 bay leaf
Salt
1 large ripe tomato, peeled (see p. 77) and diced
1 ¾ cups (12 oz/350 g) short-grain rice,
    such as Bomba or Arborio
2–3 tablespoons cooked peas

In a large saucepan heat the oil over medium heat and fry the garlic and onion. Add the chicken pieces, turning them in the sizzling oil until golden. Then add the wine, bay leaf, and 2 teaspoons salt, cover the pan, turn down the heat, and simmer gently until the meat is cooked, about 30 minutes.

Meanwhile, make the rice: In a saucepan, heat 2 tablespoons of the chicken sauce over medium heat. Stir in 6 cups (1.4 liters) water and the diced tomato and bring to a boil. Tip in the rice and a pinch of salt, stir with a wooden spoon, and simmer vigorously until the rice is just tender, 10 to 15 minutes (taste a few grains to check). Add the chicken pieces and continue to simmer for 5 minutes.

Place the rice and chicken in a serving dish, scatter with the cooked peas, and serve immediately.

Serves 4

Wild venison in sherry sauce with rice
Venado en salsa con arroz

When I enjoyed this dish seated on the shaded terrace outside the *venta*, I went straight
to heaven. The voluptuous dish fuses lean, tasty wild venison (so much better than the
farmed version), with mellow rice, a splash of wine, and a complexity of spices. It may look
sloppy, but it tastes divine. And like all true comfort food, it is eaten with a spoon.

1 lb 12 oz (800 g) venison cut into bite-size chunks
Salt and black pepper
Extra virgin olive oil
3–4 cloves garlic, finely sliced
2 large onions, peeled and chopped
1 bay leaf
1 teaspoon ground nutmeg
1 teaspoon saffron threads steeped
    in 1 teaspoon hot water
1 cup (250 ml) *fino* sherry
About 2 cups (500 ml) hot beef stock or water
1 ¾ cups (12 oz/350 g) short-grain rice,
    such as Bomba or Arborio
1 large tomato, chopped
2–3 tablespoons cooked peas

Season the venison with salt and pepper. In
a frying pan, heat some olive oil then sear
the venison pieces on all sides. Set aside.

In a deep saucepan, make the *sofrito* (base
sauce): Heat some olive oil and sauté the garlic
and onion until tender, then stir in the bay leaf,
nutmeg, and saffron with its water. Add the
fino and venison, and pour in enough of the
stock to cover the meat. Stir well, then simmer,
covered, until the meat is tender, about 1 hour.

Using a wooden spoon, stir in the rice, adding more
stock if necessary to generously cover it, and simmer
gently, uncovered, until the rice is just tender, 10 to 15
minutes. Add the chopped tomato and peas, season
with salt and pepper, and simmer for 5 minutes more.

Test the rice to check it is done, remove from
the heat, let it rest for 5 minutes, and *ya está*!

Serves 4 to 6

Teresa's apple tart
Tarta de manzana de Teresa

This couldn't be easier, and tastes delicious with dollops of whipped cream.
Choose apples that are not too acidic, such as Braeburn.

Butter, for greasing
1 cup (7 oz/200 g) sugar
1 cup (4½ oz/125 g) all-purpose flour
1 cup (250 ml) milk
2 large eggs
4 apples, peeled, cored, and sliced into thin wedges
3 tablespoons apricot or peach jam
1 cup (250 ml) heavy whipping
   cream, whipped, to serve

Preheat the oven to 350°F (180°C) and grease a 12 inch (30 cm) pie dish or tart pan.

In a bowl, mix together the sugar and flour then stir in the milk and eggs, whisking energetically to make a smooth batter.

Fill the prepared pan with the mixture. Arrange the apple slices on top in a circular pattern, overlapping them slightly. Bake for about 1 hour, keeping an eye on it. When the crust turns golden, prick with a knife to check that it is cooked through. Remove from the oven and allow to cool in the dish.

Meanwhile, in a small saucepan, loosen the jam with 1 to 2 tablespoons water and heat gently until you have a loose glaze, crushing any lumps of fruit. Cool slightly then use a pastry brush to spread this over the tart.

Transfer to a serving dish and serve with whipped cream.

ANGELES "ANANDA" SÁNCHEZ, *home cook and caterer, Jimena de la Frontera*

The last cook in the book revels in the wild, forested sierra on the cusp of Cádiz and Málaga provinces. One of ten siblings, Angeles grew up in and still inhabits the *pueblo blanco* of Jimena, topped by a sprawling Moorish castle and surrounded by a sea of green. Yet her heart lies a half-hour drive away, along a sinuous mountain road that winds down into a fertile valley cradling the village of El Colmenar (also called La Estación de Gaucín). She comes here for spiritual renewal, to be with nature, to swim in the clear water of the Guadiaro river, to forage, and to spend time with two of her sisters.

"For 26 years I worked in restaurants along the coast in Málaga and Marbella, until I discovered a derelict station building in El Colmenar with my husband," she tells me. "After renovating it, we ran it as a restaurant for five years. It was incredibly successful and quite magical. We named it Ananda—which in Sanskrit means 'bliss!'" Sadly, the restaurant closed when her marriage ended but that has not stopped Angeles' culinary trajectory.

Her approach to cooking is intuitive, nourished by what is in season or growing among the cork and holm oaks, and she is guided by a profound sense of *andalusi* techniques and ingredients. There is more though. "My food is all about emotions—of taste and of place, infused with my personality." Bliss, indeed—and the very soul of Andalucía.

Serves 4

Pasta with wild mushrooms
Fideuá con setas silvestres

To cook this, Angeles builds a small fire in her sister's orange grove, with the rushing Guadiaro river and clucking chickens as a soundtrack. "Cooking on wood fires adds so much flavor," she smiles, and in the fading light proceeds to create her edible magic using mushrooms gathered from the forest. Noodles (*fideos*) were popular in the days of Al-Andalus because the dry pasta was perfect for storing, and it is still widely used today, mainly in seafood dishes and soups. Spanish pasta brands number the thicknesses of the noodles from the finest, like vermicelli, to the fattest—like this one. You can make the sauce in advance or cook it fresh for the dish.

9 oz (250 g) Spanish *fideos* no. 4 or thick spaghetti
  (*spaghettoni*) broken into 2 inch (5 cm) pieces
Salt and white pepper
Sprig of sage
Sprig of rosemary

Sauce
2 tablespoons extra virgin olive oil
1 lb (500 g) tomatoes, peeled, cored, and chopped
2 green bell peppers, seeded, deribbed, and chopped
4 cloves garlic, peeled and finely chopped
2 onions, peeled and thinly sliced
9 oz (250 g) meadow or portobello
  mushrooms, cleaned and thickly sliced

First, make the sauce: Warm the olive oil in a large sauté pan, add the tomatoes, peppers, garlic, and onions, cover the pan, and poach over low heat for about 10 minutes. Add the mushrooms, replace the lid, and continue to cook for 10 minutes more.

Stir in the pasta and 2 cups (500 ml) water. Bring to a boil, lower the heat, and simmer gently for about 10 minutes, stirring occasionally, until the sauce reduces and the pasta to absorbs the flavors.

Season with salt, pepper, and the herbs, and set aside to rest for 5 minutes before serving.

Serves 4

Confit pork belly with apricots, prunes, dates, and orange
Panceta confit con orejones, ciruelas, dátiles y naranjas

This succulent, dazzling dish works equally well with duck breast or with pork loin, but Angeles loves the contrast between the fattiness of the pork belly and the acidity of the sour orange, which cleanses the palate. It is a rich dish, hence the portions are not huge, so make sure it follows an abundant starter. Angeles explains that the increasingly popular technique of confit was originally devised to conserve meat. With no moisture or juice, only oil, the meat could keep in an earthenware jar for months.

2 cups (500 ml) sunflower oil
1 lb 5 oz (600 g) pork belly
1 ½ cups (220 g) mixed dried fruit, such as apricots, prunes, raisins, and dates
1 tablespoon clear honey
3 tablespoons extra virgin olive oil
Juice of 3 bitter oranges
Pinch of salt
3 or 4 slivers of bitter orange peel

In a deep saucepan, pour in the sunflower oil and submerge the pork belly completely. Heat to a temperature of just under 100°F (40°C), so that you can dip a finger in without burning, and let it continue to bubble gently, covered, until the meat is tender, about 4 hours.

About 30 minutes before serving, arrange the rack in the top of the oven and preheat the oven to 520°F (270°C).

Meanwhile, in a saucepan, combine the dried fruit with the honey, olive oil, orange juice, and salt. Cook, stirring, over low heat, until it caramelizes, about 5 minutes.

Remove the pork belly from the pan, draining off any excess oil, and transfer to an ovensafe dish. Sprinkle with a little salt and place high up in the oven until the meat has a crisp, golden crust, 6 to 7 minutes.

Transfer to a serving dish, scatter the fruits and their juice over and around the meat, garnish with a few slivers of orange peel, and serve.

Serves 4

Venison fillet with a red berry sauce
Venado con frutos rojos

At last, an Andalusian cook who uses pomegranate seeds! Here Angeles uses wild venison from the hills—she says it's quite tough since it is an older deer; smaller, younger ones are more tender. The slightly tart berries work beautifully with the dark, strong meat.

2–3 tablespoons extra virgin olive oil
14 oz (400 g) venison tenderloin
¼ cup (1 ½ oz/40 g) seedless raisins
3 teaspoons beef gravy granules,
    dissolved in 1 cup (250 ml) water
½ cup (2 ½ oz/70 g) chopped strawberries
¾ cup (2 ½ oz/70 g) fresh cranberries
½ cup (2 ½ oz/70 g) blackberries
2 teaspoons sugar
½ teaspoon sea salt flakes
Seeds of ½ pomegranate
Sage in flower (optional)

Preheat the oven to 250°F (120°C).

In a frying pan, heat the olive oil over high heat and briefly sear the venison on all sides to seal in the juices, then sauté, turning frequently, until cooked to your liking, 5 to 7 minutes. Transfer the meat to an ovensafe dish and keep it warm in the oven.

Add a little more olive oil to the meat juices in the pan, toss in the raisins and gravy and stir until you have a thick sauce, about 5 minutes.

In a separate saucepan, combine the strawberries, cranberries, blackberries, and sugar. Bring to a simmer and cook until the sugar has dissolved and the juice thickens, 3 to 4 minutes.

Remove the venison from the oven, coat with the gravy sauce, sprinkle with salt flakes, and spoon over the berry sauce. Scatter pomegranate seeds on top and garnish with the sage.

Spiced fritters with honey
Pestiños de Navidad

This Andalusian classic comes out to play in any shape or size at Christmas and for numerous Andalusian festivals. In Málaga, *pestiños* go by the name of *borrachuelos*. Their origins are indisputably Moorish, though the pastries are not particularly sweet. Angeles makes them in little twists, infused with orange and spices, and sticky with honey. They could also be dusted with sugar mixed with a little ground cinnamon. Keep the pastries in a sealed container if they are not devoured instantly.

1 cup (250 ml) extra virgin olive oil
1 cup (250 ml) dry white wine
4 cups (1 lb/500 g) all-purpose flour
½ teaspoon yeast
Sunflower oil, for frying
¾ cup (9 oz/250 g) honey
Scant ½ cup (100 ml) water

Spice mixture
½ cup (2½ oz/70 g) raw almonds
3 level tablespoons sesame seeds
1 clove
½ teaspoon ground cinnamon
½ teaspoon anise seeds
Dried zest of 1 orange

In a dry frying pan, toast the spice mixture ingredients, shaking the pan to release the aromas. Tip into a spice grinder or food processor and pulse to a coarse powder.

In a large mixing bowl, combine the oil, wine, flour, yeast, and ground spice mixture and mix well with your hands until it forms a ball. If the dough sticks to your hands, it is too wet; mix in more flour 2 teaspoons at a time. Knead for 10 to 15 minutes until you have an elastic dough, then cover with a cloth and set aside at room temperature for at least 20 minutes.

Using an oiled rolling pin, roll out the dough until it is evenly ⅛ inch (3 mm) thick. Using a sharp knife, slice the dough into small rectangles about 4½ by 1½ inches (11 by 4 cm). With oiled hands, form the rectangles into twists, or roll them diagonally around your finger and seal into tubes, or fold the edges together to make parcels—whatever shape you desire.

In a saucepan, add sunflower oil to a depth of about 2 inches (5 cm). Heat over high heat until it bubbles (about 375°F/190°C). Working in batches, fry the *pestiños*, turning them in the oil, for 2 to 3 minutes or until golden. Transfer to a plate lined with paper towels to absorb the excess oil and set aside to cool.

In a small pan, heat the honey and water; once it simmers, drizzle it over the cooled pastries. Alternatively, you can dunk the cookies in the honey water.

Regional Specialties

BLACK PIGS and JAMÓN IBERICO

From a happy, snorting pig, it is but a short hop in life and death to *jamón iberico de bellota*, the jewel in Spain's piggy crown. Pata negra, Jabugo, Iberian ham…the names multiply for a food product that is a national passion and, increasingly, a worldwide one, even muscling in on Italy's prosciutto di Parma. In Spain, once you have tasted the sweet, velvety slivers of top quality air-cured ham, it is hard to move backwards to ropey *jamón serrano*, the cheaper industrialized product of the white pig.

Only four regions in Spain produce the highly regulated Iberian ham, two of which are in Andalucía: Los Pedroches, in the hills north of Córdoba, and Jabugo, in the Sierra de Aracena of Huelva province (the other two are in Extremadura and in Salamanca). Los Pedroches is a much smaller area of production, more recently classified and winner of prizes in blind tastings, whereas in Huelva some thirty cellar-bodegas cure thousands of legs of *jamón iberico*.

Native to the peninsula, once wild, now domesticated, the chubby, dark gray Iberian pig totters around on slender legs with black hooves (hence *pata negra*, "black hoof"). Its home is the *dehesa*, a unique ecosystem and symbiotic mix of cork oaks, holm oaks, pastures, and grasslands that continues over the border into Portugal. Roaming freely through the *dehesa* these cosseted porcine stars consume grains, grass, roots, insects, wild mushrooms, and acorns. Then, for a period of several months known as the *montanera* (October to February), acorn consumption steps up radically and ultimately gives the ham that much prized nutty flavor.

Watch the labels

The classification system has been recently simplified, though a minefield of fine points can make or break a *jamón iberico*. Broadly speaking, the hams are either *jamones* (hindquarters) or the less coveted, smaller *paletas* (forequarters). Color-coded labels start with top grade black, descending in quality through red, green, and finally white. Premium black labels are from pure breed, free-roaming Iberian pigs fed on acorns during the crucial *montanera* fattening period. Each leg bears a seal showing the vintage year and the ham-maker's name. Bottom of the pile white labels are fifty percent Iberian pigs fed on grain (*cebo*).

By the time of slaughter, the top category pig must have doubled its weight and reached a minimum of 353 pounds (160 kg) to gain the coveted title of *jamón ibérico de bellota*. The minimum age for slaughter is eighteen months (compared to six years for white pigs), after that the hams are kept salted at a low temperature for two weeks (to prevent impurities) then rinsed and hung to cure in naturally ventilated chambers for at least a year, with many cured for up to four years. During this process, as the fat melts, the legs sweat and drip.

The good news

The nutritional benefits of *jamón iberico de bellota* are enormous, since this ham, cured naturally in clean, unpolluted air, contains no preservatives or additives. It is protein-rich and even the delicious, unsaturated fat is good for you, since its oleic acid (incongruously also present in olives, giving rise to the pigs' moniker "olives on legs") is said to help lower cholesterol. High in phosphorus and Vitamin B, low in calories, the benefits soar further if *jamón iberico* is consumed with tomatoes for their anti-oxidant, Vitamin E content, plus a glass of red wine for its high iron content. The perfect diet—and truly *andaluz*!

THE LAND OF TOROS BRAVOS

Whether you like it or not, you cannot miss the bulls in Andalucía—on posters, on TVs, angrily pawing the sandy floor of a bullring, or even their frozen silhouettes by the roadside, incarnating a sherry advertisement. Like the Iberian pig, *toros bravos*, fighting bulls, are also raised in Salamanca and Extremadura, but the most prolific ranches are southeast of Cádiz in La Janda. Here pastures spangled with swaths of pink, yellow, and purple wildflowers blanket the gently undulating *dehesa* in high contrast to the fierce-looking horned creatures that inhabit them.

Grazing in separate fields from their many girlfriends, these *toros bravos* are mostly destined to end their days in the bullrings of Seville, Jerez, Málaga, Córdoba, Granada, Jaen, Almería, and even Madrid. Their tails are bequeathed to that quintessential culinary fate, *rabo de toro*, bull's tail stew, and their meat to market stalls. Although the "art" of the bullfight is highly controversial and has been temporarily banned in Catalunya (a ruling subsequently overturned by Spain's court), it remains a deeply impassioned pastime in Andalucía, whether at the bullring itself during summer *ferias* or in front of TV screens in bars.

In the fields beside them loiters another, more pacific beast, the *retinto*, a native breed of cattle said to have originated in the prehistoric Middle East. Their deep red coats and sturdy horns closely resemble fighting bulls, however the tender, coveted meat disappears without a fight into stews, grills, or roasts.

Early bullfighting

Those dramatic, choreographed confrontations between man and beast represent a sacrificial ritual that, in simplified form, goes back to Roman times, possibly promoted by the Church, with the bull incarnating the devil. Yet it was the Moors who changed it significantly from the brutish spectacle practiced by the Visigoths to a ritualistic event held on feast days. Mounted on highly trained horses (another Arab skill), the Moorish bullfighters confronted and killed the bulls with javelins, aided by men on foot with capes designed to distract the bull. Today of course the *picador* and *matador* roles are reversed, but the sorry end is the same.

Most of the ranches are inside the Los Alcornocales Natural Park where wild olive trees mix with a dense cork oak forest, the largest in Spain. The mild year-round temperatures and high rainfall, accentuated by a summer fog known as *barbas de Levante*, form a subtropical microclimate that nurtures an extraordinary biodiversity as well as lush green meadows for the cattle.

Every bull must die

Over the centuries, selective breeding from native Iberian stock and bulls imported by the Carthaginians has created a naturally belligerent animal that's black, dark brown, or white in color, and with long horns on both males and females. After a year spent close to its mother, the cattle are separated into single-sex groups for a further year, then the males are tested for suitability for *corridas*, breeding, or slaughter.

Aggression, strength, and stamina are key for a fighting bull. After the age of three, the bull becomes a *novillo*, ready for its first bullfight, though by law the top bullrings that stage celebrity matadors only allow beefier four-year-olds. Weighing at least 1000 pounds (460 kg), these are the big boys whose thick, arched necks ripple with muscle and daunting strength.

Their end will come in under twenty minutes with the *faena*, yet the top fighters will segue into an afterlife as idolized trophies hung on bar and restaurant walls, their name, the place and date of the *corrida* engraved on a plaque: a local hero. Bullfighting is unlikely to come to an end in southern Spain for a long, long time.

VENTA DE CARNE
DE TORO DE LA
MAESTRANZA

BLUEFIN TUNA, ATÚN ROJO, and THE ALMADRABA

Frenzied excitement greets the start of the *almadraba* season every May along the Costa de la Luz from Conil to Zahara and Tarifa, and above all Barbate, the tuna "capital." Suddenly the marble slabs of local fish markets heave with huge hunks of glistening red tuna, highly prized for its succulent, buttery body fat; the words *atún rojo* are whispered breathlessly in restaurants, and gourmet *rutas del atún* spring into action. Thanks to freezing techniques, it is now a year-round addiction, too, but altogether this appetite and its industry generate negatives.

Netting technique

For 3,000 years Atlantic Bluefin tuna (*thunnus thynnus*) have been fished using the same Phoenician technique, the *almadraba*, a word referring to the system of capture from Andalusian Arabic meaning "place to fight." Located very close to shore in the exact passage of the migrating fish, a circle of fishing boats and forty or so men corral the tuna into a maze of vertical nets. As they thrash wildly in panic, the tuna are trapped and killed in an ever-tightening circle until, after two hours, comes the *levantá* (raising of the trap) when the extensive nets are lifted and the fish transferred to the boats. The energy, chaos, and violence of this struggle, another visceral Spanish tale of man versus beast, was expressively painted by Salvador Dali in 1967.

Fishermen warn that numbers are dropping drastically, despite the sustainable aspect of this Andalusian practice. Only older, large specimens are selected; the rest are returned to the ocean for a longer life, continuing their journey to the warm waters of the Mediterranean to spawn. These colossal, highly agile fish, dubbed "Ferraris of the ocean" due to their swimming up to 90 miles (150 km) a day, reach over 1100 pounds (500 kg) in weight, but the average captured fish is about 450 pounds (200 kg) and fourteen years old, although some live thirty years.

Tuna fate and transformations

Even if the entire western side of Andalucía is swept up in the spring *atún rojo* frenzy, an overwhelming percentage of the catch is actually shipped to Japan, land of sushi and sashimi, where Bluefin is the most prized fish of all. There, a single fish commands jaw-dropping prices of hundreds of thousands of dollars (in 2017 one Pacific Bluefin was sold for $675,000) because it makes top grade sashimi—even after being deep-frozen. The premium cut is the belly. The shipping process is highly organized, with small, swift ships loaded with the catch shuttling back and forth from Barbate to the Canary Islands to transfer their tuna cargo to a massive mother ship.

The Romans of course reveled in salting fish and greatly expanded the existing tuna industry, notably at their stunningly sited town, Baelo Claudio, right on the beach south of Zahara. Today, Barbate is the Andalusian capital of the Bluefin tuna industry, churning out *mojama*, air-dried and salted red tuna that becomes so densely textured and highly flavored that it needs to be sliced wafer-thin, as well as red tuna preserved in oil, and cured red tuna roe.

Japan also comes to Spain—the many excellent fish and seafood restaurants along this coast have adopted the Japanese *tataki* method of coating fresh tuna loin in sesame seeds, lightly searing it, then slicing it and serving it with a citrus based soy sauce. It is a gastronomic dream to eat, but for how much longer?

Recommended Restaurants

Eating tips: Andalusia's radical eating times mean that quality restaurants rarely open before 1:30–2:00pm for lunch and again at 8:00–8:30pm for dinner. Locals usually stroll in for dinner by 10pm. Any earlier than these times, stall your hunger at a tapas bar.

Also remember that on Sunday afternoons most restaurants are packed with family gatherings, so restaurants are typically closed on Sunday evenings and usually all Monday, too. Tapas bar weekly closures vary—it's a potluck.

The listings below follow the order of the recipe sections of this book, with featured restaurants coming first under each province.

EASTERN ANDALUSIA

In and around Almería

Restaurante El Parque,
Almadraba de Monteleva, 04150 Salinas de Cabo de Gata
+ 34 950 370075, www.restauranteelparque.com
See recipe section.

Nuestra Tierra Taberna,
Calle Jovellanos, 16, Almería + 34 679 897432,
www.facebook.com/TabernaNuestraTierra
See recipe section.

Restaurante Alejandro,
Av. Antonio Machado, 32, El Puerto, Roquetas de Mar
+ 34 950 322408, restaurantealejandro.es
See recipe section.

Taberna Casa Puga,
Calle Jovellanos, 7, Almería + 34 950 231530,
www.barcasapuga.es/
Almería's oldest tapas bar opened in 1870 and is still going strong. Excellent seafood tapas and their own Alpujarran wine, Albuñol.

Tetería Almedina,
Calle Paz, 2, Almería + 34 629 277827
teterialmedina2.wordpress.com
In the web of streets below the Moorish castle, this tearoom specialises in Moroccan tagine, b'stilla, couscous, pastries, and mint lemonade (no alcohol).

Valentín,
Calle Tenor Iribarne, 19, Almería + 34 950 264475
http://www.restaurantevalentin.es/
Extra-fresh seafood and shellfish eaten on a stool outside or seated in comfort inside. Carnivores enjoy steaks and goat meat.

Joseba Añorga Taberna,
Plaza de la Constitucion 4, Almería + 34 950 040694.
http://www.josebaanorgataberna.es/
This sleek Basque gastropub is the opposite of Andalusian tapas style: avant-garde pintxos, plus excellent Spanish wines.

In and around Granada

Restaurante Alcadima,
Lanjarón, Alpujarras + 34 958 770809,
www.alcadima.com/ *See recipe section.*

Restaurante Chikito,
Plaza del Campillo, 9, Granada + 34 958 223364.
www.restaurantechikito.com *See recipe section.*

Parador de Granada,
Calle Real de la Alhambra, Granada + 34 958 221440
http://www.parador.es/en/paradores/parador-de-granada
See recipe section.

Damasqueros,
Calle Damasqueros 3, Granada + 34 958 210550
http://damasqueros.com/
Lola Marin, a fast-rising star of Andalusian cuisine, fuses tradition and avant-garde in weekly tasting menus. Hidden in the Realejo district.

El Claustro,
Hotel Palacio de Santa Paula, Gran Via de Colon 6,
Granada + 34 958 805740
Upscale dining in the Mudéjar setting of a 16th century convent. Creative, modern dishes by Juan Andrés Morilla.

Carmen Mirador de Aixa,
Carril de San Agustín 2, Granada + 34 958 223616.
http://www.miradordeaixa.com
Spectacular views of the Alhambra match elaborate Andalusian dishes. A table on the terrace ensures high romance.

Taberna La Tana,
Placeta del Agua, 3, Granada + 34 958 225248
http://www.labotilleriagranada.es/tana
Cheerful family-owned tapas bar in Realejo serving
excellent wines (400 of them) and delicious bar snacks,
some free.

Casa Piolas,
Calle Ramón Y Cajal, 1, Algarinejo + 34 958 312251
http://www.restaurantepiolas.com/
Unexpectedly offbeat dishes, full of personality,
at this welcoming bar-restaurant in a hill
village west of Granada

In and around Jaén
Restaurante Casa Antonio,
Calle de Fermin Palma 3, Jaén + 34 953 270262
www.casantonio.es/
Contemporary, seasonal dishes by chef Pedro
Beltrán include pickled marinades, stews,
roast meat, and seafood from the coast.

Restaurante Alicún,
Palacio de Úbeda, calla Juan Pasquau 4, Ubeda
+ 34 953 810973, www.facebook.com/restauranteAlicun/
Chef Pedro Hervás creates delicate, unusual Mediterranean
dishes in a formal, Renaissance hotel setting.

Restaurante Zeitum,
Calle San Juan de la Cruz, 10, Úbeda
+ 34 953 755800 www.zeitum.com/
Delicious modern concoctions, full of flavor
and local olive oil (hence the Arabic name
meaning "olive"), reasonably priced

Cantina la Estación,
Cuesta Rodadera, 1, Úbeda + 34 687 777230
www.facebook.com/cantinalaestacion/
Montese de la Torre, chef-owner, regularly renews her
tasting menu in this popular tapas bar and restaurant
styled like a railway carriage. Popular with locals.

Taberna Misa de 12,
Plaza 1 de Mayo, Úbeda + 34 953 828197
www.misade12.com
On a strategic corner of a beautiful square with outside
tables, this tapas bar offers a great selection of small plates
showcasing local produce, plus top wines and olive oils.

CENTRAL ANDALUSIA

In and around Córdoba
Finca las Encinas,
Los Juncares, Iznájar, La Subbética + 34 629 610783
finca-las-encinas.com/   *See recipe section.*

Bodegas Mezquita,
Calle Corregidor Luis de la Cerda, 73, Córdoba
+ 34 957 498117 also at Plaza Cruz del Rastro, 2.
www.bodegasmezquita.com   *See recipe section.*

Casa Mazal,
Calle Tomás Conde, 3, Córdoba
+ 34 957 246304 casamazal.es/en/   *See recipe section.*

Bodegas Campos,
Calle Lineros, 32, Córdoba + 34 957 497500
bodegascampos.com
An elegant, rambling bodega-style restaurant
for upscale dining on Andalusian favorites or
tapas in the buzzing bar. An institution.

La Regadera,
Ronda Isasa 10, Córdoba + 34 957 101400
regadera.es/en
Chef Adrián Caballero devises intriguing small plates
and delicious desserts in this fresh, youthful,
riverside setting.

Garum 2.1,
Calle San Fernando, 122, Córdoba + 34 957 487673
www.facebook.com/Garum2.1/
This pioneering bar has piled up awards for its
avant-garde tapas, notably its salmorejo, and now
has an upstairs restaurant with a roof-top terrace.

Noor,
Calle Pablo Ruiz Picasso, 8, Córdoba
+ 34 957 964055. Noorrestaurant.es
Chef-owner Paco Morales has earned a Michelin star for his
exquisite reinterpretations of Andalucia's Moorish heritage.
Exclusive, aesthetic, pricey—and no ingredients post-1492!

La Fragua,
Calle Tomas Conde - Calleja del Arco 2, Córdoba
+ 34 957 484572, www.facebook.com/LaFraguaCordoba/
Hidden down a side-alley, this lively tapas bar and
restaurant serves appetizing, personalized Cordoban
classics inside or at outside tables to a flamenco soundtrack.

El Churrasco,
Calle Romero 16, Córdoba + 34 957 290819
elchurrasco.com
*Beautiful old restaurant packed with antiques
in the heart of the Judería; Andalusian stalwarts
like oxtail stew are charmingly served.*

Las Camachas,
Avenida de Europa 3, Montilla + 34 957 650004
www.restaurantelascamachas.com
*Regional traditions hold strong at this old-fashioned
roadside inn; local classics like honeyed roast lamb
match Montilla wines from the surrounding hills.*

In and around Málaga
Restaurante Plaza de Toros,
Carretera Del Albergue 1, Antequera
+ 34 951 469333 www.restauranteplazadetoros.es/en/
See recipe section.

Arte de Cozina,
Calle Calzada, 27, Antequera
+ 34 952 840014, artedecozina.com.   *See recipe section.*

La Luz de Candela,
Calle dos Aceras, 18-20, Malaga + 34 951 382251
www.la-luz-de-candela.com/   *See recipe section.*

El Jardín/ The Garden,
Calle Santo Cristo, Frigilana, La Axarquía
+ 34 952 533185 thegardenfrigiliana.com/
See recipe section.

Restaurante José Carlos García,
Muelle Uno, Puerto de Málaga + 34 952 003588
www.restaurantejcg.com
*A slick, sophisticated setting by the marina for refined
cuisine by the city of Málaga's only Michelin-starred chef.*

Uvedoble Taberna,
Calle Cister, 15, Málaga + 34 951 248478
www.uvedobletaberna.com/
*Buzzing tapas bar near the Cathedral transforms
old favorites like ajoblanco—adding melon
and sardines. Lines for tables, so go early.*

El Cabra,
Paseo Maritimo Pedregal 17, Playa de Pedregalejo, Málaga
+ 34 952 291596, www.restauranteelcabra.es/
*They've been grilling and frying fresh Mediterranean
fish by the beach since 1965 and it's still succulent.
Outside tables in the sea air.*

El Refectorium del Campanario,
Paseo de la Sierra 36, + 34 952 203935,
http://www.elrefectorium.net/
*Chic terrace dining with sweeping views over the
bay of Málaga and a changing, seasonal menu,
unexpectedly located in a residential area.*

Bibo Marbella,
Puente Romano Resort, Bulevar Príncipe Alfonso von
Hohenlohe, Marbella + 34 951 607011
www.grupodanigarcia.com.
*This fun brasserie showcases chef Dani Garcia's quirky
creativity without breaking the bank; his two
Michelin stars were earned for the formal,
adjoining Dani Garcia Restaurant.*

In and around Ronda
Restaurante Bardal,
Calle José Aparicio, 1, Ronda + 34 951 489828
restaurantebardal.com/
*Opened in 2016 and awarded a Michelin star in 2017.
Andalucia's latest gastro-star, chef Benito Gómez, offers
inspired, seasonal tasting menus in a designer interior.
His original, more relaxed* Tragatá *is for gourmet tapas.*

Almocábar,
Plaza Ruedo Alameda, 5, Ronda + 34 952 875977
www.facebook.com/Restaurante-Almocábar
*A cozy restaurant beside the old Moorish gateway
serving a variety of reasonably priced, Andalusian
dishes with contemporary twists.*

Mesón Sabor Andaluz,
Calle Huerta 3, Alcala del Valle + 34 956 135510
www.facebook.com/mesonsaborandaluzalcaladelvalle
In a pueblo blanco *in the hills north of Ronda, this family
restaurant blazes an unexpected culinary trail using fresh
local produce, including asparagus, a local speciality.*

WESTERN ANDALUSIA

In and around Seville
Eslava,
Calle Eslava 3, Seville + 34 954 906568
www.espacioeslava.com/   *See recipe section.*

La Salmoreteca,
Mercado Lonja del Barranco
www.lasalmoreteca.com/   *See recipe section.*

Restaurante Abantal,
Calle Alcalde José de la Bandera, 7
+ 34 954 540000, www.abantalrestaurante.es/
Brandishing the only Michelin star in Seville, chef Julio Fernández transforms traditional Al-Andalus ingredients using complex contemporary techniques and presentations.

Tribeca,
Calle Chaves Nogales, 3, Seville + 34 954 426000
http://www.restaurantetribeca.com/
Three brothers run this smart, accomplished, minimalist restaurant, where Mediterranean dishes burst with flavor and complexity.

El Gallinero de Sandra,
Pasaje Esperanza Elena Caro, 2, Seville
+ 34 954 909931, http://www.elgallinerodesandra.es
Young, personalized, and welcoming, near the Alameda. Chef-owner Nacho Dargallo once worked with Ferran Adriá, so expect surprises—the good kind; his Mediterranean cocina is clever and beautifully executed.

Lalola taberna gourmet,
Calle Virgen del Aguila, 8, Seville + 34 955 138359
www.lalolatabernagourmet.com
Cutting edge, delicious small plates by chef Javier Abascal in an airy modern restaurant in Los Remedios, near the fairground.

La Azotea,
Calle Jesús del Gran Poder, 31, Seville
+ 34 955 116 748, http://laazoteasevilla.com/en/
Three branches of this popular Sevillian tapas restaurant juggle fresh Andalusian ingredients in contemporary tapas or larger portions. Hipster alert!

Bodega Santa Cruz,
Calle Rodrigo Caro 1, Seville + 34 954 211694
www.facebook.com/BodegaSantaCruzSevilla
A rare, authentic bar in Santa Cruz, popular with locals and tourists alike for its unpretentious fare and lively atmosphere. Open from breakfast till midnight.

Bar Las Teresas,
Calle Santa Teresa 2, Seville + 34 954 213069
www.facebook.com/BarLasTeresas
An attractive old classic in the heart of Santa Cruz. Jostle with suspended ham legs at the bar and indulge in a great choice of sherry with traditional tapas.

Agustina,
Plaza del Concejo, 5, 41370 Cazalla de la Sierra
+ 34 954 883255
A husband and wife team run this village restaurant in the Sierra Norte de Sevilla, bringing innovative touches to regional classics.

In and around Huelva
Arrieros,
Calle de los Arrieros, 2, Linares de la Sierra (Aracena)
+ 34 959 463717, http://www.arrieros.net/
See recipe section.

Acánthum,
Calle San Salvador, 17, 21003 Huelva,
+ 34 959 245135, http://www.acanthum.com/
Very elaborate dishes at this sharply contemporary restaurant where Michelin-starred chef Xanty Elias (ex-Arzak) remains faithful to his province, only using local produce from land and sea.

In and around Cádiz and Jerez
Alboronía,
Zoco de Artesania, Plaza Peones, Jerez + 34 627 992003,
www.facebook.com/Alboronía-Bar-tapas
See recipe section.

El Faro de Cádiz,
Calle San Félix, 15, Cádiz + 34 956 211068
http://www.elfarodecadiz.com/   *See recipe section.*

El Arriate,
Calle los Moros, 4, 11500 El Puerto de Sta María
+ 34 630 746946,
www.facebook.com/restaurante.e.arriate
See recipe section.

Venta El Soldao,
Los Badalejos, Medina Sidonia + 34 956 417119
See recipe section.

Casa Bigote,
Calle Pórtico Bajo de Guía, 10, Sanlúcar de Barrameda,
+ 34 956 362696, www.restaurantecasabigote.com/
*Starting life in 1951 as a Manzanilla sherry tavern,
Bigote is now Sanlúcar's top seafood restaurant,
hospitable and traditional, overlooking the Guadalquivir
river. The local king shrimp are delicious.*

La Taberna del Chef del Mar,
Calle Puerto Escondido, 6, El Puerto de Sta María
+ 34 956 112093,
www.facebook.com/La-Taberna-del-Chef-del-Mar
The andaluz *chef supremo Angel León,
converted the original Aponiente premises
into this tapas bar after moving his high-end
restaurant to a grander setting nearby.*

Aponiente is Andalucía's most extraordinary
restaurant, now with three Michelin stars so
for deep pockets. www.aponiente.com/en/

Francisco Fontanilla,
Camino de la Fontanilla, Conil de la Frontera
+ 34 956 440802, www.franciscofontanilla.com
*Embracing the Atlantic since 1964, this beach
restaurant specializes in* atun rojo *(Bluefin tuna),
ultra-fresh shellfish, rice, and noodle dishes.
Large, efficient, with consistent high cquality.*

El Campero
Avd. Constitucion, Local 5C, Barbate + 34 650 420792
http://www.restauranteelcampero.es
*Refined seafood dishes with Japanese influences
in the capital of Bluefin tuna. Featuring elaborate
tapas, a tasting menu, and full-scale dining.*

El Refugio,
Calle Cerro Currita, 10, Zahara de los Atunes
+ 34 956 439746, http://www.elrefugiodezahara.com/
*Young, spirited, and friendly, this open-air
restaurant right beside the beach is a relaxed
lunch or sunset spot for fresh seafood and
pork dishes. It fills up fast on weekends.*

BIBLIOGRAPHY

Brenan, Gerald, *South from Granada*,
        Hamish Hamilton, 1957
Carr, Matthew, *Blood and Faith*, The New Press, 2009
Danby, Miles, *Moorish Style*, Phaidon, 1995
Davidson, Alan, *Mediterranean Seafood*,
        Prospect Books, 2012
Drayson, Elizabeth, *The Moors' Last
        Stand*, Interlink Books, 2017
Fernández-Morera, Dario, *The Myth of the
        Andalusian Paradise*, ISI Books, 2016
Fletcher, Richard, *Moorish Spain*, Orion Books, 1994
Franzen, Cola, *Poems of Arab Andalusia*,
        City Lights Books, 1989
Greus, Jesús, *Ziryab y el despertar de Al-
        Andalus*, Entre Libros, 2006
Jacobs, Michael, *Andalucia*, Interlink Books, 2013
Josephs, Allen, *White Wall of Spain*, Iowa
        State University Press, 1983
Lee, Laurie, *As I Walked Out One Midsummer
        Morning*, Penguin, 1969
Lorca, Federico García, *Selected Poems*, OUP, 2009
Luard, Elisabeth, *The Flavours of Andalucia*,
        Collins & Brown, 1991
Luard, Nicholas, *Andalucia: a Portrait of
        Southern Spain*, Century, 1984
Mardam-Bey, Farouk, *La Cocina de Ziryab*,
        Zendrera Zariquiey, 2002
Masía, Concha, *Al-Andalus*, Albor Libros, 2011
Perry, Charles (translator), *A Baghdad Cookery
        Book*, Prospect Books, 2005
Rueda, Fernando, *La cocina popular de Málaga*,
        Diputación de Malaga, 2005
Martinelli, Candida (editor), Perry, Charles
        (translator), *The Anonymous Andalusian
        Cookbook*, CreateSpace, 2013
Pritchett, V.S., *The Spanish Temper*,
        The Hogarth Press, 1984
Richardson, Paul, *A Late Dinner*, Bloomsbury, 2007
Roden, Claudia, *The Food of Spain*,
        Michael Joseph, 2012
Webster, Jason, *Andalus*, Doubleday, 2004

ACKNOWLEDGMENTS

First and foremost, huge thanks to Antonio Molina-Vázquez, friend and colleague, for his generous support and erudite insights from start to finish—copa in hand. To Enrique Ruiz de Lera for helping kick-start the project, to Ana Bermudez at Turespaña for great logistical support, and to Fernando Hernández and the Junta de Andalucía for facilitating my research trips.

Of course my immense gratitude goes to Leyla Moushabeck, my editor, for her thoughtfulness and forensic recipe skills, and to Michel Moushabeck, my publisher, for his vision and making the initial leap of faith. Applause and thanks, too, to the designer, Pam Fontes-May, for capturing the Andaluz spirit so strikingly.

Also, in no special order, gracias to Baldomero Gas of Bodegas Mezquita for igniting my enthusiasm for Ziryab several years ago, to my friend Lorna Scott-Fox for her interest and input, to Maki and Clive at Finca Las Encinas for keeping the table laden, to Sue Scarrott for IT help and tapas, to Maria Marro Perera for sound advice, and to Noirin Azzouni for welcome positivity in the Middle East and Andalucia.

Others I doff my hat to include Manni of Toma & Coe, Manuel Iglesias Fernández in Aracena, Inma Muñoz in Granada, Teresa Silva, and Miguel Ullibarri at A Taste of Spain.

Above all my boundless gratitude goes to all the featured cooks for their wonderful dishes, for their warmth, and for putting up with my pestering so good-naturedly.

Finally, thanks to my late parents, Hilary and Bonar, for providing such a beautiful Spanish retreat all those years ago, belated thanks to JCM for luring me to Andalucía in the first place, and to Richard for joining me on many an Andalusian adventure since—ongoing!

RECIPES BY COURSE

Index

Fish, potato, and
mayonnaise soup, 186
Razor clams in pickled lemon
sauce with potato purée, 262
Slow-roasted lamb jam, 152–53
prunes
Confit pork belly with apricots,
prunes, dates, and orange, 280

Quail in pomegranate sauce, 119
quince
Duck leg with bay leaf
and quince, 119
Foie gras with date and walnut
crumble and quince paste, 212
Iberian pork tenderloin stuffed
with dates in quince and
chocolate sauce, 232
Poached quince scented
with lavender, 125
Quince paste, 135

rabbit
Alpujarran fried rabbit, 77
Country style stewed rabbit, 122
raisins
Marinated Iberian pork with
raisin couscous, 230
Mozarabic monkfish with
a sauce of sweet wine,
raisins, and pine nuts, 252
Ratatouille, Andalusian, 190–91
rice
Black rice with cuttlefish, 263
Braised rice, 124
Chicken and rice, 271
Seafood paella, 54
Soupy seafood rice, 52
Sweet rice pudding, 82
Wild venison in sherry
sauce with rice, 273
Rosemary, stewed partridge
perfumed with, 167
Rose petals, duck fillets with
almond and pistachio sauce,
turmeric couscous, and, 244

saffron
Mozarabic meatballs in almond
and saffron sauce, 142
salads
Arugula and asparagus
salad with orange and
ginger dressing, 115
Carrot salad, 270
Chicken salad with pomegranate,
almonds, and orange, 150
Citrus salad, 194
Cod, olive, and orange salad, 138
Cod, tomato, and red
pepper salad, 37
Cod and orange salad
with shrimp, 101
Enrique's tomato salad, 270
Mezquita salad of eggplant,
tomato, and olives, 140
Nazari salad, 79
Red pepper, onion, and
tuna salad, 269
sauces, dips, and spreads
Aioli, 188
Almond and pistachio sauce, 244
Almond and saffron sauce, 142
Blueberry coulis, 126
Caramel sauce, 44
Chorizo sauce, 198
Foie gras with date and walnut
crumble and quince paste, 212
Garlic sauce, 39, 109
Mozarabic sauce, 42
Pea, mint, and cilantro
purée, 200
Pedro Ximénez sauce, 144
Pickled lemon sauce, 262
Pine nut and cumin sauce, 116
Pomegranate sauce, 119
Quince and chocolate sauce, 232
Red berry sauce, 282
Sherry sauce, 273
Slow-roasted lamb jam, 152–53
Sweet-and-sour sauce, 260
Sweet wine, raisins, and
pine nuts, 252
Tomato sauce, 91
See also hummus; mayonnaise

semolina
Almerian *migas* or "crumbs," 57
Grandmother's migas,
paprika broth, and red
jumbo shrimp, 66–67
soups
Alpujarran chestnut soup, 89
Antequera's chilled
tomato soup, 164
Avocado salmorejo, 224
Beet salmorejo, 222
Butternut squash, almond,
and bacon soup, 74
Cherry and tomato gazpacho, 63
Chickpea and spinach soup, 166
Chikito's oxtail stew, 90
Chilled almond soup with
apple and fig, 99
Chilled orange soup, 174
Chilled tomato and summer
vegetable soup, 100
Chilled white soup, 174
Cod, potato, and garlic soup, 41
El Faro's fish soup with
orange, 250
Fava bean soup, 76
Fish, potato, and
mayonnaise soup, 186
Fish stock, 188
Gazpacho, 100
Marinated sardine lasagna
with ajoblanco, 64
Mushroom salmorejo, 222
Spicy chicken tagine with
ginger and apricots, 243
Spinach soup with
white shrimp, 71
Spareribs baked in honey, 217
Spelt and pickles, skirt steak
macerated in orange with, 264
Spiced fritters with honey, 284
spinach
Chickpea and spinach soup, 166
Clams with spinach
and brandy, 253
Spinach soup with
white shrimp, 71